TWILIGHT ON THE BAY

Corporate seals of steamboat-related companies founded by B. B. Wills.

TWILIGHT ON THE BAY

THE EXCURSION BOAT EMPIRE OF B. B. WILLS

BRIAN J. CUDAHY

Tidewater Publishers
Centreville, Maryland

Copyright © 1998 by Tidewater Publishers

All rights reserved. No part of this book may be used or reproduced in any manner whatsoever without written permission except in the case of brief quotations embodied in critical articles or reviews. For information, address Tidewater Publishers, Centreville, Maryland 21617

Library of Congress Cataloging-in-Publication Data

Cudahy, Brian J.
    Twilight on the bay : the excursion boat empire of B.B. Wills / Brian J. Cudahy — 1st ed.
       p. cm.
    Includes bibliographical references and index.
    ISBN 0-87033-509-X (hc)
    1. Wills, B. B. (Benjamin Bowling), 1897–1986. 2. Excursion boats—United States—History. 3. Businessmen—United States—Biography. I. Title.
HE566.E9C83   1998
387.5'42'092—dc21
[B]   98-16065
                                                                                      CIP

Manufactured in the United States of America
First edition

Contents

	Preface, vii
CHAPTER 1	It All Began at Chapel Point, 3
CHAPTER 2	*Albany* Becomes *Potomac*, 22
CHAPTER 3	*Potomac* Becomes a Legend, 30
CHAPTER 4	Across the Bay to Tolchester, 49
CHAPTER 5	Nanny Boats out of Boston, 72
CHAPTER 6	Meanwhile, in New York . . ., 86
CHAPTER 7	Excursion Boats after the War, 102
CHAPTER 8	Shadows Start to Fall, 131
CHAPTER 9	The Battle of *San Jacinto*, 147
CHAPTER 10	Twilight on the Bay, 158
EPILOGUE	Was It Really the End?, 188
APPENDIX A	Roster of Passenger-carrying Excursion Boats Owned and Operated by B. B. Wills and/or Wills-controlled Companies, 191
APPENDIX B	The Financial Empire of B. B. Wills, 197
APPENDIX C	Chronology: The Life of B. B. Wills, 201
APPENDIX D	*Albany* and the Hudson River Day Line, 205
APPENDIX E	B. B. Wills's Perennial Competition: The Wilson Line, 210
	Notes, 214
	Subject Index, 231
	Vessel Index, 240

Preface

This is a story about excursion boats, a form of transportation—and a form of entertainment—virtually extinct in America today. True enough, in many harbors new kinds of passenger vessels are expanding waterborne options and providing new opportunities for people to travel across the bay, down the river, and out on the sound. But few, if any, of these new vessels are genuine excursion boats in the old-fashioned sense. They are upscale dinner cruisers or gambling vessels equipped with roulette wheels and slot machines. They are new high-speed ferries or perhaps sightseeing yachts.

The true American excursion boat, in its classic manifestation, was a vessel inevitably painted white and more often than not with a buff-colored funnel or two. She steamed away from a downtown pier at nine-thirty or ten o'clock on a summer morning and took mom and pop, all the kids, and a big wicker hamper full of good things to eat on an inexpensive two- or three-hour cruise to a nearby picnic grove, bathing beach, or amusement park. The park might even be owned and operated by the excursion boat company itself. And then, late in the afternoon, when everyone was totally exhausted, she brought them all back again as the sun was slipping behind the water.

Sometimes, too, as mom and pop were headed home with the kids on the local trolley car, the old excursion boat set out on a moonlight cruise from eight-thirty until midnight. Young couples would dance away the night to the strains of Woody Herman, Tommy Dorsey, Gene Krupa, or maybe just three or four young musicians working their way through a local college.

That, in a nutshell, is what an excursion boat was. Like so many other pieces of priceless Americana, the excursion cruise was a tradition that lost its economic viability in rough proportion to the ascendancy of the private automobile as America's primary mode of travel. *Sic transit,* or some such.

This book speaks about more than just excursion boats, however. It is also the story of a man who put together a small empire of excursion boat lines and companies along the East Coast between 1934 and 1967. His name was Benjamin Bowling Wills—"Jack" to family and friends, "the Old Timer" in later years, "Ben" to a few others, and "B. B." to just

The excursion boat *Mayfair* tied up at North River Pier A in New York.

PREFACE   ix

about everyone else. In building his small excursion fleet, Wills helped keep an American tradition alive for a few more years, and for a few more people, than might otherwise have been the case.

The name B. B. Wills is largely unknown today; it was equally unknown in the 1930s and 1940s, the heyday of his excursion boat operations in places like Baltimore, Boston, Washington, and New York. One reason for his name's obscurity is that Wills never named his various lines in a unified fashion. His vessels steamed for companies with diverse names like Potomac River Line, Nantasket Boat Line, Robert E. Lee Steamboat Company, and Tolchester Lines. Not one of the twenty-two separate excursion boats that he owned and operated over the years was ever called, for instance, the SS *Benjamin B. Wills* or had the name "Wills Excursion Lines" emblazoned across its flanks in big, gold-leaf letters.

True enough, there once was a Maryland corporation known as Wills Lines. But Wills Lines was not an operating company; it was little more than a paper corporation established to satisfy the whims of a federal

The coats and jackets suggest it is not midsummer, but otherwise this is a typical excursion boat crowd heading off for a relaxing day on the water. (Photograph by R. Loren Graham, courtesy of the B. B. Wills family.)

The excursion boat *Francis Scott Key*. (Photograph by R. Loren Graham, courtesy of the B. B. Wills family.)

bureaucracy over purely technical matters associated with vessel ownership. B. B. Wills, on the other hand, was singularly uncomfortable with the way the long arm of the federal government kept expanding its regulatory reach during his excursion-boat days.

This book focuses primarily on Wills's excursion boat operations. His other maritime interests and a few nonmaritime ones are also discussed, particularly as they relate to his excursion boat ventures. Topics thus include the ownership of general-purpose shipyards, the buying and selling of war surplus naval tonnage, the brokering and financing of deals for just about anything that floated, the operation of a tanker service to transport fresh drinking water to the U.S. Virgin Islands, and a fleet of Florida-based fishing boats whose specialty was the harvesting of shrimp in the Gulf of Mexico. Wills was also a principal in a sightseeing bus company in Washington, D.C. Later, as his excursion boat days were ending, he went on to become an important force in the rapidly growing field of residential and commercial real estate development.

B. B. Wills's last excursion boat ran in the summer of 1967; he himself passed away in 1986 at the fine old age of eighty-nine. In 1996 his descendants—primarily his grandson, Jeffrey Wills, a professor of classics at the University of Wisconsin in Madison—assembled a quantity of letters, contracts, photographs, invoices, canceled checks, bank statements, newspaper clippings, payroll ledgers, minutes, pilothouse logbooks, and other documents from Wills's excursion boat days that had been gathering dust in the family home on Indian Lane in Washington, D.C. The materials were put in cartons and placed in a storage facility virtually within sight of where B. B. Wills ran his first excursion boat.

The Wills family kindly gave me unrestricted use of these documents and files so that I could tell the story of the excursion boat empire of B. B. Wills. In the pages that follow, I refer to this collection as the Wills Papers, and identify specific documents within that collection. The Wills Paper have since been donated to the Calvert Marine Museum in Solomons, Maryland, where they will be available for further study.

In telling the story of the Wills excursion boat empire, I have endeavored to balance the specialized resources of the Wills Papers with other source materials, such as books, articles, news accounts, and official records. I also feel compelled to point out that while the Wills family has given me access to the private papers of B. B. Wills and made business arrangements associated with the publication of this book, the family neither exercised nor sought to exercise any editorial control whatsoever over the book's content.

Unless otherwise indicated, all the photographs in the book have been supplied by the Wills family and were collected, during his lifetime, by B. B. Wills himself. Many such photographs are the work of the late R. Loren Graham, of Swampscott, Massachusetts. Wills thought very highly of Graham's maritime photography and issued him a lifetime pass to ride any Wills-operated boat in exchange for copies of Graham's photos.

B. B. Wills occupies a small but singular niche in American transportation history. He came to the excursion boat business completely by accident, with no maritime tradition whatsoever in the Wills family to motivate or encourage him. No ancestor stood with Nelson off Cape Trafalgar, no grandfather sailed around Cape Horn, no uncle served with Admiral Dewey during the Spanish-American War. Wills himself

A smartly uniformed excursion boat captain handles the wheel as his vessel heads away from its berth.

never even spent a summer during his own college days (Holy Cross, class of 1922) working as a deckhand on the Martha's Vineyard ferry!

The Wills family today, however, remains proud of the maritime heritage that "the Old Timer" helped create between 1934 and 1967. Wills's son, Eugene Wills, enjoyed a long and distinguished career in the real estate development business in northern Virginia. Just before his untimely death in 1996, Gene Wills was spending his time in retirement supervising the completion of a large oil painting. It is a rendition of the sidewheel steamboat *Potomac*, the very first excursion boat his father owned. Interestingly, she was also a vessel on which Gene himself had spent many summer vacations during his own school years, earning his first dollars.

A number of individuals who assisted me in gathering material about B. B. Wills deserve special mention and thanks. Three grandchildren of B. B. Wills—Jeffrey Wills, Kemp Wills, and Olivia Wills Kane—are in a category apart. Without their help and encouragement this book would not exist.

Another person who was with me the very first time I had an opportunity to review the Wills Papers and who planned to play a more active role in the development of *Twilight on the Bay* is the late Harry Jones. Harry's unfortunate death in 1994 precluded his participation; his contributions remain invaluable.

Others who stepped forward at just the right time to solve a particular problem, suggest a certain source, or provide needed information include John H. Shaum, Jr., Edwin L. Dunbaugh, Henry Bishop, Frank Manwell, the Rev. Edward P. O'Connell, S.J., Edward Ryan, Commander C. C. G. Sharp, of the Royal Navy, Lynn-Marie Richard of the Maritime Museum of the Atlantic in Halifax, Nova Scotia, Jack Corry, and William M. Rau.

TWILIGHT ON THE BAY

CHAPTER ONE

It All Began at Chapel Point

The Potomac River rises in the mountains of Maryland and West Virginia and follows a southeasterly course on its path to the sea. Over its entire length the river passes only one major city, Washington, D.C.

From Washington to Point Lookout and the Chesapeake Bay, a distance of about 100 miles, the Potomac is quite navigable. Tugboats haul barges of sand and gravel from one point to another, and freighters from Canada dock at Alexandria, Virginia, bringing newsprint that will become next week's headlines. Yachts of every shape and size set out from marinas along the river's edge. Even oceangoing cruise ships make their way up the Potomac from time to time, recalling a day when the river was a major thoroughfare for passenger-carrying steamboats.

Cruising down the Potomac from Washington, a person is surrounded by vistas that bring to mind America's heritage. A dozen miles below Washington on the Maryland shore is Fort Washington, a fortification designed by Pierre L'Enfant in the years after the War of 1812 as part of a defensive perimeter around the capital city. Further downriver on the Virginia side is Mount Vernon, the home of George Washington. Not as well known but also a part of history is a Virginia site below Mount Vernon called Freestone Point. Here once stood the summer home of the Lee family: Colonel "Light Horse Harry" Lee, of Revolutionary War fame, and his son, Robert E., whose name is forever associated with a later American war.

About forty miles from Washington, just below Aquia Creek and Wide Water on the Virginia side, the river turns and for several miles flows northeast before turning again and resuming its normal southeasterly course. Here, just above the U.S. Route 301 bridge, a tributary flows into the Potomac from the north. This is the Port Tobacco River, a short stream that begins in the nearby countryside of Charles County, Maryland, and takes its name from the inland town of Port Tobacco.

Even today tobacco is grown commercially in this part of the country, although not nearly so extensively as in years past.

Along the east bank of the Port Tobacco River, just inland from the point where it joins the Potomac, a church sits on a promontory slightly back from the river. Appropriately, the area is called Chapel Point. The church is Saint Ignatius, which a roadside marker identifies as the oldest continuous Roman Catholic parish in North America.[1] The red brick church and other parish buildings are located mostly inside a copse of trees.

Just below the top of the hillside down toward the river is a small graveyard, partially surrounded by an old wrought-iron fence. Various family names, including Bowling and Mudd, grace the tombstones. The Mudd names are from the same family line that produced Samuel Mudd, M.D., the physician who treated John Wilkes Booth's broken leg in the early morning hours of April 15, 1865, after Booth had fatally shot President Abraham Lincoln.

The unfortunate Doctor Mudd is not interred at Saint Ignatius. His resting place is adjacent to Saint Mary's Church, a few miles inland in the Charles County community of Bryantown. Many other members of Doctor Mudd's family, though, are buried at Saint Ignatius.

From the little graveyard of Saint Ignatius, one can see the Port Tobacco River flowing gently into the larger Potomac. Ironically, at this very place on the river, John Wilkes Booth and a man named David Herold rowed across the river on April 21, 1865, in an effort to reach Virginia. Booth had presumed that in Southern territory, his assassination of President Lincoln would be regarded as an act of high patriotism and that his escape would be abetted.

Another family name on many gravestones in the Saint Ignatius churchyard is that of Wills. The Wills family traces its roots in Charles County to pre-Revolutionary days. While not an extraordinarily wealthy family, the Willses grew enough tobacco to send a young man by the name of Francis Reed Wills off to medical school at the University of Maryland, from which he graduated in the late 1820s.

Wills was a physician, a contemporary and a colleague of Doctor Mudd. Doctor Wills lived in nearby LaPlata, Maryland, in a fine and stately home called "Preference," which he built early in his career, a decade or more before the Civil War. Crops and livestock raised in the fields surrounding "Preference" earned Doctor Wills many ribbons and prizes over the years at the annual Charles County Agricultural Fair. In 1853, for instance, he was awarded first-place honors for the "best slaughtered mutton" and the "best quarter-acre of Irish potatoes."[2]

St. Ignatius Church, Chapel Point, Maryland. (Photograph by the author.)

"Preference" was still standing in 1998 and could be seen to the west of Route 301, three miles south of LaPlata and slightly back from the road.

Slavery was practiced in antebellum Charles County, and the tobacco-growing members of the Wills family—including Doctor Wills—were slaveholders. While the state of Maryland itself remained loyal to the Union throughout the Civil War, sentiments in a place like Charles County, which shares a border with Virginia, were both mixed and strained. Some Charles County residents felt that Union troops encamped on their soil during the war were more an army of occupation than one of defense. Many sons of Charles County crossed the Potomac during the war and fought under the Confederate flag.

After the Civil War, Doctor Wills accepted an appointment as assessor for Charles County, thus adding a range of public service duties to days already busy with both medical and agricultural responsibilities. Upon his death in 1872, Doctor Wills left twelve children by two marriages. One of his sons, born in 1857, was Philip Reed Wills.

In June 1892, Philip Reed Wills married Mary Louise Bowling at Saint Mary's Church in Bryantown. Philip Wills, generally known as "Mister P. R.," led an active life as a businessman and public figure in Charles County. He first worked as a farmer and in 1883 became a hotel manager in LaPlata. In 1904 he was appointed a state tobacco inspector, and he served as federal food administrator for Charles County during World War I. His principal business affiliation, however, was a lengthy tenure as president of the Southern Maryland National Bank in LaPlata. The town was founded and eventually supplanted Port Tobacco as the Charles County seat, after the building of the Baltimore and Potomac Railroad in 1872. The railroad line became part of the Pennsylvania Railroad and was known as the Popes Creek Branch, or the Popes Creek Secondary.

Benjamin Bowling Wills

Philip Reed Wills and Mary Louise Bowling bore eight children between 1895 and 1901; one child died within days of her birth, but the other seven grew to adulthood. Of these, one was Benjamin Bowling Wills, born with a twin sister—Catherine Lee "Polly" Wills—on September 16, 1897. The twins were baptized at Saint Ignatius Church on September 23, 1897.[3]

Benjamin Bowling Wills grew up in his father's home in Bel Alton, Maryland, a short distance south of LaPlata and inland from Chapel

Philip Reed Wills and Mary Louise Bowling Wills, parents of B. B. Wills.

Point. As a youngster he worked in tobacco fields in the Charles County countryside. He attended two different colleges. For two years, he studied at Washington College in Chestertown, Maryland. Then, at the urging of the local Jesuit Fathers who administered Saint Ignatius Parish at Chapel Point, young Wills was sent off to the College of the Holy Cross in Worcester, Massachusetts.

Benjamin Bowling Wills in 1922, the year he graduated from the College of the Holy Cross.

Among his classmates at Holy Cross in the early 1920s, B. B. Wills was thought to be the only student who hailed from below the Mason-Dixon line. In fact, his Charles County dialect proved to be such a liability when he went away to school that he wrote home to his father asking for extra money to pay for special speech tutoring that a professor was offering.[4] Wills and 115 other graduates were awarded their bachelor of art degrees from Holy Cross in the spring of 1922.

During his college years, young B. B. Wills began to dabble in the field that would become his first full-time occupation. While still an undergraduate, he established a part-time business selling school-related memorabilia. Pillows, banners, sweaters and other merchandise—all emblazoned in appropriate collegiate colors—represented the product line that Wills sold, first to his own schoolmates and later to students at colleges and universities all along the East Coast. He would take orders from his classmates during the weeks before Christmas, but because students were generally an impecunious lot, he would agree to ship the merchandise home COD. The packages arrived just before the holidays, and while the students would be in no better financial position than they were back in Worcester, they now had access to additional resources, namely, good old dad.[5]

After graduation, Wills attempted to make a career out of his collegiate sideline. He drove to campuses up and down the East Coast and enjoyed some success in booking orders for his line of merchandise. After about a year on the road, Wills decided that the life of a traveling salesman left much to be desired. He was no Willy Loman, the inveterate salesman in Arthur Miller's *Death of a Salesman*. He closed out his business and headed south. It was 1924, and Wills decided to try his hand in the then-booming Florida real estate market.

Wills began working for the Bancroft Sales Agency in Miami, a firm whose letterhead identified its practice as "general real estate." Heavily involved in trying to secure northern investors for a 605-acre parcel near Miami that the Bancroft Agency was developing and promoting, Wills wrote to many friends and relatives back home, soliciting their financial participation. Apparently he found many willing investors and was on the verge of earning some serious commissions for his efforts.[6]

In 1926, however, the Florida real estate market collapsed miserably. Some have suggested that the collapse was a harbinger of future economic difficulties for the country at large, but for a newcomer in the Florida real estate game like Wills, it proved fatal. Lacking the resources to ride out the bad times, Wills folded his tent and headed home to Bel Alton.

Some evidence suggests that Wills's health was not good in the years immediately before and after his graduation from Holy Cross and while he was working in Florida. In 1920, for example, he was hospitalized in Worcester from March 18 until May 23. From late December 1925 through mid-January 1926 he was hospitalized in Baltimore. Whatever the specifics of these early hospitalizations—they apparently involved some kind of digestive problems, and he also had a touch of tuberculosis—Wills's life was otherwise free of serious illness and he would live to the age of eighty-nine.

The Florida real estate market may have collapsed, but the decade was still the Roaring Twenties and business enthusiasm was running high. When he returned home to Maryland, Wills immediately went to work on another venture, one that would set his professional course for the next four decades.

"The Pride of the Potomac"

The motivation for what Wills did next remains unknown. But in 1926, he signed a contract with the Jesuit Fathers at Saint Ignatius Church to purchase 851 acres of land that extended from the church down to the Port Tobacco River. The price was two hundred thousand dollars, a truly substantial sum. It was to be paid in installments over a period of twelve years, with 6 percent interest accruing on all unpaid balances.[7] On this site Wills proceeded to build an amusement park, which he called Chapel Point Park, "The Pride of the Potomac."

Check drawn by B. B. Wills in 1928 to the Corporation of Roman Catholic Clergymen for a mortgage payment on the Chapel Point property. In later years, Wills made such payments directly to a bank.

IT ALL BEGAN AT CHAPEL POINT 11

Chapel Point was not a traditional commercial amusement park, with roller coasters, thrill rides, and the like. From the outset and for all of its days, Chapel Point was primarily a relaxing picnic grounds and bathing beach. "A resort of beauty and refinement. Nature with its creative hand paused and turned out a masterpiece on the picturesque banks of the Potomac," boasted a brochure promoting Chapel Point during its early years.[8]

There were some rides at Chapel Point, however. A miniature railway, a merry-go-round, and a Ferris wheel were added over the years; there was also a shooting gallery.[9] Although Chapel Point was an amusement park in that it provided amusement, it was never a mirror image of Luna Park, much less Disneyland, and was primarily a beach and picnic grounds. In its earliest years, Chapel Point Park even lacked such conveniences as electricity and telephone service.

The park welcomed its first paying customers during the summer of 1926. One can easily imagine visitors to Chapel Point sitting down under a tree in the afternoon after finishing off the fried chicken and potato

The miniature railway at Chapel Point Park, once owned by an amusement park outside Bridgeport, Connecticut.

salad from the picnic hamper and reading a few chapters in that year's Pulitzer Prize–winning novel *Arrowsmith*, by Sinclair Lewis.

In 1926, the year that Chapel Point Park opened, Charles Lindbergh's conquest of the North Atlantic by air was still a year away, and Calvin Coolidge was president. The United States was enjoying a period of unusual prosperity, before the stock market crash of 1929 and the Great Depression would whisk it all away.

During its first four seasons, 1926 through 1929, Chapel Point served customers who arrived primarily by automobile, with some others traveling by bus. The park's accessibility primarily by car restricted the market to a small percentage of the people who lived in Washington, the city Wills always saw as his principal source of customers. Automobile registrations in the mid-1920s were a small fraction of what they are today. In 1925, for example, there were 20 million automobiles in the United States and ownership stood at 0.16 cars per capita. In 1990 the figure had jumped to 150 million and 0.60 per capita.

In an effort to improve patronage, Wills made arrangements for direct motor coach service between Washington and Chapel Point on weekends. Buses left the Washington, Virginia and Maryland Coach Company's terminal at Pennsylvania Avenue and Twelfth Street, N.W., between 12:30 and 1:30 P.M. on Saturday, and between 8:30 and 10:00

Postcard view of Chapel Point with the steamboat dock in the foreground.

A.M. on Sunday. Before and during World War II, the ordinary workweek in America was not Monday through Friday, as it is today; it was that plus a half-day's work on Saturday. The early afternoon bus departures from Washington on Saturday were thus geared to the end of the workday—and the workweek—at noontime. Round-trip fare was $2.10, and the buses left Chapel Point for the return to Washington between 5:00 and 7:00 P.M. on both Saturday and Sunday.

Chapel Point was passably successful, and Wills continued to expand the range of activities available at the park. On July 4, 1928, as he was fond of boasting for many years afterward, over five thousand customers visited Chapel Point. But Wills also realized that the remove of Chapel Point from Washington was a shortcoming that required further attention.

During the early years of Chapel Point Park, B. B. Wills married for the first and only time. On April 11, 1928, he and Gertrude Clementine Gosnell, a schoolteacher from Granite, Maryland, in western Baltimore County, exchanged vows in Sacred Heart Church in Washington, D.C. Their first home was on the grounds of Chapel Point Park. Over the years, the couple had three sons: Benjamin B. Wills, Jr. ("Ben"); J. Eugene Wills ("Gene"); and P. Reed Wills II ("Reed").

Enter the Wilson Line

In seeking to expand the customer base for Chapel Point, B. B. Wills looked to the Potomac River. A convenient excursion boat steaming down the river from Washington could deliver thousands of additional customers to the park each day.

A passenger steamboat running between Chapel Point and Washington was not a new idea. In the mid-1880s, the Jesuits had formed a joint venture with two brothers—J. C. and W. M. Howard—to build a resort at Chapel Point called the Hotel Belleview. Patrons of the resort arrived from Washington by steamboats such as *George Law, Harry Randall,* and *Samuel. J. Pentz*.[10] This waterborne service was little more than a distant memory, though, when Wills opened his Chapel Point Park on the same picturesque site four decades later.

Up on the Delaware River, an old and venerable steamboat company was evolving into something new and different. The Wilson Line had its beginnings in the nineteenth century as the Philadelphia and Wilmington Steamboat Company. Under the leadership of Capt. J. Shields Wilson, a premiere marine engineer in America, the line became a stable company specializing in freight and passenger transportation between Philadelphia, Chester, and Wilmington.[11]

New ownership took over J. Shields Wilson's company in 1930, however, and realized that there was little future for an old-fashioned steamboat line engaged in basic point-to-point transportation for people and goods over a route already served by several railroads plus an expanding network of highways. On the other hand, the wholesale grocer in Philadelphia, say, who was once a steady Wilson Line customer by virtue of the cases of canned peas and carrots that he regularly shipped to stores in Wilmington aboard Wilson Line boats—but that he now sent by truck—might become a new kind of customer. He might be persuaded to use the line if the company offered him an opportunity to take his family on a pleasant summer's day outing to a picnic grove or an amusement park downriver from Philadelphia. The new owners thus began to reorient the company into a leisure-oriented excursion boat operation, a change clearly evident in the new name they selected for the enterprise, Wilson Excursion Line.

One implication of this new corporate policy was a willingness to expand operations to waterways beyond the Delaware Valley. In early 1930, the new Wilson Line management signed a contract with B. B. Wills "to operate a first class steamboat or steamboats from Washington, D.C., to said Chapel Point and return, said steamboat to have a capacity and facilities for at least two thousand passengers."[12] The boat was to run six days a week, with no Tuesday service, and Wilson Line was free to continue beyond Chapel Point to a place such as Colonial Beach, Virginia. The only stipulation was that Chapel Point be the first stop after the boat left Washington and also that the passengers be given at least 2½ hours to enjoy themselves at Chapel Point. Wilson Line was to be charged no landing fee for stopping at Chapel Point, but the company did have to give Wills five cents for each fare-paying passenger who got off at Chapel Point on Wednesday, Thursday, and Saturday, and ten cents on Sunday. The charges would stay in effect until Wills paid off the expense for dredging and marking a channel from the Potomac up to a new wharf at Chapel Point, which the operating contract with Wilson Line required him to construct.

On March 22, 1930, Wills signed an agreement with the Lukens Dredging and Contracting Corporation of Baltimore to dredge such a channel and turning basin. The cost was established as twenty cents per cubic yard, with a minimum of seventy thousand cubic yards to be removed and shifted by hydraulic dredge to a point in the Port Tobacco River 1,200 feet to the west of the new channel. The final cost was an esti-

IT ALL BEGAN AT CHAPEL POINT   15

mated fifteen thousand dollars. Wills gave Lukens several promissory notes bearing interest at 6 percent, with payment for the full job extending through July 1931.[13]

And it all worked out, more or less. Wilson Line's 1888-built propeller steamboat *City of Chester* was renamed *City of Washington* to reflect her new assignment. She made the first revenue trip down the Potomac to Chapel Point on May 30, 1930, and successfully returned to Washington the same day.

It was a day that saw President Herbert Hoover leave Washington by motor car early in the morning and travel north to Gettysburg, Pennsylvania, to deliver a Memorial Day address from the very podium Abraham Lincoln had used on the Fourth of July sixty-seven years earlier. Unlike Lincoln's, Hoover's speech was broadcast to large portions of the nation using the recently developed technology of interconnected "networks" of previously independent radio stations.

At noon on that Decoration Day, as *City of Washington* approached the Port Tobacco River near Chapel Point for the first time, a friendly horseshoe-pitching contest was held at Washington's Griffith Stadium between a group of U.S. senators and members of the House of Representatives. Griffith Stadium was available for such purposes whenever the Washington Senators—the city's baseball team—were out of town.

Wilson Line's *City of Washington*, the excursion boat that inaugurated service between Washington and Chapel Point in 1930.

As passengers were boarding the Wilson Line steamboat for the return trip from Chapel Point to Washington that Friday afternoon, a drama was unfolding in the Atlantic Ocean off Cape Fear, North Carolina. The two-year-old German airship *Graf Zeppelin*, Dr. Hugo Eckener in command, was completing its first intercontinental flight of the season, a lengthy 13,400-mile, trans-Atlantic journey from its home base in Friedrichshafen to Rio de Janeiro, and then north to Lakehurst, New Jersey. Fuel was reportedly running low aboard the giant airship, so a scheduled diversion for a flyover of Havana, Cuba, was canceled. Then, gale-force winds off the North Carolina coast began to raise further concerns.

Everything turned out well on that Memorial Day though. *City of Washington* made a successful return trip up the Potomac to the nation's capital; *Graf Zeppelin* landed safely in Lakehurst the following morning; and President Hoover, after his appearance in Gettysburg, headed into the woods of northern Pennsylvania for a weekend of serious trout fishing.

By Labor Day of 1930, seventy-five thousand people had visited Chapel Point, a new single-season record. Wilson Line took advantage of the permissive language in its contract with Wills and arranged for *City of Washington* to continue beyond Chapel Point to Colonial Beach, about fifteen miles further down the Potomac from the mouth of the Port Tobacco River. At the end of the 1930 season, Wilson Line informed its stockholders that "SS *City of Washington* produced revenues of substantial proportions which largely offset declines in passenger revenues in the Philadelphia District."[14] On the strength of this success, the company continued to expand its operations into new markets in subsequent years.

In 1931, the second season of Wilson Line operation to Chapel Point, a disaster almost derailed the service. In early April, *City of Washington* caught fire at the company's maintenance base on the Christiana River in Wilmington, and her wooden decks and cabin work were totally destroyed. But Wilson Line pulled off a near miracle that spring, and two months later *City of Washington* had been totally rebuilt and was ready to carry passengers on the Potomac. The achievement was remarkable, considering that the fire required the rebuilding of everything above the main deck.

In 1932, its third year on the Potomac, Wilson Line adjusted its sailing schedule a bit, presumably with Wills's concurrence. *City of Washington* steamed away from the Seventh Street Wharf in Washington to Chapel Point on Monday, Wednesday, and Friday; on Thursday and

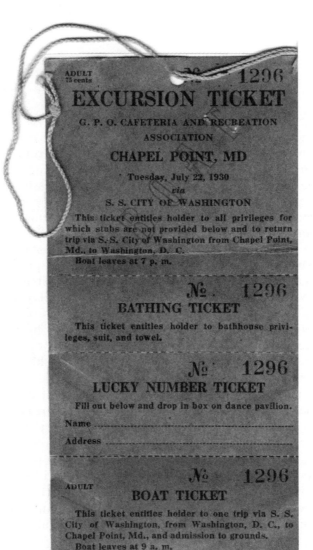

Admission ticket for Chapel Point Park.

Saturday she made trips to Colonial Beach, but with no stop at Chapel Point en route. On Sunday, though, she performed a hat trick: a day cruise out of Washington to both Chapel Point and Colonial Beach, plus a moonlight dance cruise out of Washington later in the evening.[15]

Exit the Wilson Line

Wilson Excursion Line may have been pleased with *City of Washington*'s performance on the Potomac in 1930, but they were less pleased in 1931 and downright discouraged in 1932. The reason, of course, was the Great Depression, which saw attendance at Chapel Point Park plummet during the third year of Wilson Line service by a massive 67 percent over figures from 1930, the first year. [16]

The contract between Wilson and Wills was up for renewal after the 1932 season, but Wilson Line elected not to continue the relationship. An opportunity to take over the popular Washington–Mount Vernon excursion boat service had arisen after the demise of the previous operator on that route. Wilson Line consequently decided that the shorter run to Mount Vernon would be a better Potomac River deployment for *City of Washington* than the lengthy trip to Chapel Point and Colonial Beach.

In addition, Wilson Line had secured an interest in the Marshall Hall amusement park on the Maryland side of the river opposite Mount Vernon, thus providing dual destinations out of Washington along a considerably shorter route. One steamboat could thus make multiple trips during a single day's time. Tourists and others interested in America's history and heritage could sail to Mount Vernon, whereas local Washingtonians out for a day of relaxation and fun might find Marshall Hall more to their liking. Unlike Chapel Point, which had only a few modest rides, Marshall Hall was a classic amusement park, complete with roller coaster. As a result, when *City of Washington* returned to the Potomac from her winter quarters in Wilmington to begin the 1933 season, she confined herself to the Marshall Hall/Mount Vernon run. Chapel Point, meanwhile, found itself in the same position it was prior to 1930: all its customers had to arrive by automobile or bus.

Chapel Point itself had not been doing well either. Wills fell behind on his mortgage payments to the Corporation of Roman Catholic Clergymen, the legal entity under which the Jesuit Fathers conducted secular business. Although the mortgage was formally held by the Jesuits, Wills made his payments to a local bank. Once, the Jesuits actually advanced Wills money to meet a specific payment and to avoid default.[17]

Wills also had to ask for leniency in the redemption of the promissory notes he had given the Lukens Corporation for dredging the new channel from the Potomac River up to his wharf on the Port Tobacco River.[18]

Business at Chapel Point continued to deteriorate. "Here it is the first of September and with the summer practically over all of my hopes are gone to collect any appreciative [sic] amount to satisfy my mortgage and other obligations," Wills claimed.[19] That was 1931. A year later it was the same theme: "So far, in this neck of Maryland, we have had practically no summer resort weather. We opened with a cold Decoration Day and the last two Sundays have been almost a complete blank on account of the rainy and cold weather."[20] The picture looked no better a few weeks later: "It is now July 12 and we have enjoyed only one fair Sunday of business which was yesterday. Our June receipts were approximately one-half of last year's June and only one-third of June two years ago. Practically all of my big picnics have been canceled on account of the depression."[21]

Chapel Point Park was clearly Wills's primary business venture on the land he had purchased from the Jesuits. Some tenant farmers continued to grow tobacco on the property, however, and Wills received modest royalty payments from them each year. Wills also had vague plans for some kind of commercial development. Chapel Point was accessible by water, of course, and the Popes Creek Branch of the Pennsylvania Railroad, the old Baltimore and Potomac of 1872, was only two miles away in Bel Alton. Wills felt that once the railroad saw the commercial possibilities that Chapel Point represented, "they would soon connect these two miles."[22] Should such a railroad spur be built, Wills, ever the optimist, envisioned excursion passenger trains coming down from Baltimore to bring summer visitors to his park from an urban market he had yet to tap. Wills considered the kinds of commercial development possible at Chapel Point: "A big lumber and supply yard for one thing would pay well there, and at the same time fit in with Chapel Point's own building program."[23] No such commercial development ever materialized at Chapel Point, however.

Wills contacted other steamboat operators to ask if they had any interest in picking up where Wilson Line left off, but he had no luck. In an effort to diversify his investments, in June 1931, Wills had entered a joint venture with the Peninsula Transit Corporation, an early operator of over-the-road motor coaches between Norfolk and Baltimore, to build a bus transfer station on land that he owned in the town of T.B., Maryland, just across the line in Prince George's County.[24] In addition to allowing Baltimore–Norfolk passengers to get out, stretch their legs for a

How better to remember an organization's pleasant summer outing at Chapel Point Park than with a formal phtograph? Here a group poses in the picnic grove down near the river circa 1929. Steamboats would later land directly behind the pavilion in the background. Rides, ballfields, and other attractions are off to the left and somewhat behind the photographer's position. Panoramic effect was achieved by the use of a special camera that rotated to take in the full scene.

few moments, and use the restrooms, the station was also a place where passengers from Norfolk could change to a connecting bus to Washington. The bus terminal opened for business in October 1932.

Wills had an apartment built for him and his wife over the bus depot. One cold night during the winter of 1933–34—or so goes the story—B. B. Wills was sitting in his apartment. He asked himself, "If the Wilson Line can go into the amusement park business, why can't I go into the excursion boat business?"[25]

Various versions of this account of how Wills's excursion boat idea was born have appeared in print.[26] Other evidence, however, suggests that before the start of the 1933 excursion season, Wills was actively trying to obtain an excursion boat that he might operate between Washington and Chapel Point. In a letter dated May 30, 1933, Wills wrote to Alfred V. S. Olcott of the Hudson River Day Line in New York, releasing Olcott and the Day Line from an option that Wills had earlier been given to purchase their steamboat *Albany*.[27] The boat had been out of service for a season or two because of a general downturn in Day Line business brought on by the Great Depression, and Wills had hoped to develop a partnership with interests in Colonial Beach to bring *Albany* to the Potomac. He could not put such a deal together, though, in time for the 1933 season. An earlier letter dated May 2, 1933, indicates that Wills had given some thought to purchasing a vessel called *Steel Pier* for Potomac River service.

Steel Pier, originally named *Miami*, had previously run between Florida and Cuba, but by 1933 she was operating short, seasonal ocean cruises out of Atlantic City, New Jersey. The Atlantic City Steamship Company offered Wills a chance to inspect the vessel at winter layup in Camden, New Jersey, and specified that the asking price was seventy-five thousand dollars.[28] *Steel Pier*'s draft of 21.8 feet would have rendered her extremely questionable for Chapel Point service, however, since Wills's newly dredged channel was only ten feet deep.

In concluding his letter to Olcott in May 1933 surrendering his option to purchase the Day Line's *Albany* for Chapel Point service, B. B. Wills kept his prospects open: "You may see me in New York early this fall and we will talk the proposition over further."[29] It proved to be a telling prediction.

CHAPTER TWO

Albany Becomes *Potomac*

Over the winter of 1933–34, Wills came to terms with the Hudson River Day Line in purchasing their sidewheel steamboat *Albany*. He did so entirely on his own, without any financial support from partners in Colonial Beach.

Buying a Steamboat

The Hudson River Day Line had gone into receivership on January 11, 1933.[1] Therefore, when Wills purchased *Albany* in early March 1934, the sale was technically in the form of a court-supervised auction. But it was a fully prearranged auction, Wills was the only bidder, and the price he offered for the fifty-four-year-old steamboat, twenty-five thousand dollars, had been negotiated and agreed upon beforehand. Wills had put down a thousand dollars in earnest money to secure the deal on February 13, 1934.

The transaction was not a cash sale. On March 6, 1934, the day of the prearranged auction, Wills handed the Day Line a certified check for four thousand dollars which, coupled with his earlier deposit, represented a down payment of five-thousand dollars. He also signed over to the same company a preferred mortgage of twenty thousand dollars on the vessel. A payment schedule stipulated that the mortgage be paid off by 1936, with 6 percent annual interest on any unpaid balance.[2]

Having bought himself an excursion boat, Wills next faced the challenge of getting it from the Hudson to the Potomac and then putting it in shape to run between Washington and Chapel Point. This was indeed a daunting prospect.

Wills was suddenly faced with all the responsibilities of steamboat ownership, which entailed tasks that he had never done before, but that he would do countless times over the next three decades. For example,

The Hudson River Day Line's *Albany*, shown in 1895.

he had to arrange proper insurance coverage on his newly acquired vessel. Wills contacted the New York insurance broker Frank B. Hall and Company and quickly learned that marine underwriters quoted different rates depending on key factors. Underwriters considered whether an excursion boat was inactive during the long months of fall, winter, and spring layup, or whether it carried revenue passengers in scheduled steamboat service. The former category, in insurance lingo, was "port risk" and was written at a relatively low premium. Full insurance coverage—"navigation insurance," it was sometimes called—for whatever period a boat was expected to be engaged in revenue passenger service, understandably involved a much higher premium.[3] Wills continued to do business with Frank B. Hall and Company for many years.

Wills had determined that *Albany* would proceed to Chapel Point under her own power; federal inspectors would thus have to declare her seaworthy. On March 26, 1934, officials from the Albany, New York, office of what had long been called the U.S. Steamboat Inspection Service—but which by 1934 was officially called the Bureau of Navigation and Steamboat Inspection of the U.S. Department of Commerce—boarded *Albany* at her layup berth at the Knickerbocker Ice Company pier in Athens, New York. Three days later, the inspectors forwarded a list to Wills identifying thirty items of repair that had to be attended to before the vessel could be declared ready to go. Most were relatively minor, specific matters: "All sluice gates in bulkheads to be put in operating condition." One item was potentially open-ended, though: "Vessel to be dry docked to ascertain condition of hull and all hull openings below and above water line."[4]

Albany was given provisional authority to proceed under power to New York for such a dry docking, and on April 12, 1934, she was towed from her layup berth in Athens to Hudson, New York, for coaling. The next day—Friday the thirteenth—with her boilers fired up for the first time in 3½ years, *Albany* moved out under her own power and headed downriver for New York City. It proved to be her final trip through the beautiful and historic Hudson Valley, where she had carried passengers so faithfully for over five decades.

On Saturday, April 14, *Albany* was handed over to the Tietjen and Lang Dry Dock Company in Hoboken, New Jersey. An estimate prepared by the company prior to the vessel's arrival quoted a price of $719.70 for a routine dry docking and hull cleaning, plus $235.50 extra if the work involved an additional "lay day."[5] But this was before anyone had gotten a look at what kind of deterioration, if any, had befallen the iron-hulled vessel below the waterline during almost four years of inac-

Steel Pier, an excursion boat that Wills considered for Chapel Point service before he purchased *Albany* from the Hudson River Day Line.

tivity. The final bill from the shipyard was modest enough. An additional $283.95 in work had to be performed over and above the original estimate, but the "lay day" was avoided and the total bill came to $1,003.45.[6]

With the work at Tietjen and Lang finished, *Albany*'s inspection was completed and she was given clearance by the federal inspectors and her own insurance underwriters to head for Chapel Point. The steamboat left New York early in the morning on April 20, 1934. She had actually cast off from the Day Line's North River Pier 81 late in the afternoon on the previous day, but when she reached Upper New York Bay, the weather was not auspicious for a coastwise passage in the open sea. As a result, *Albany* lay over near the Statue of Liberty until the following morning. Unaware of this development, B. B. Wills had departed from New York by automobile on April 19 and drove south to Lewes, Delaware, where *Albany* was scheduled to make her first stop. Wills grew concerned when the vessel failed to materialize at Lewes the next morning, and he contacted the Coast Guard. They dispatched a cutter to investigate, and, according to Wills, "I got a report back saying they had sighted SS *Albany*, but it was going so fast they couldn't catch it."[7]

Albany steamed into Delaware Bay that afternoon and tied up for the night at Lewes. She incurred two charges while there: $13.42 for 5,368 gallons of city water she took on, and $5.00 for overnight wharfage.[8] The

Check drawn by B. B. Wills to the Hudson River Day Line in April 1934.

next morning, *Albany* left Lewes and headed up the Delaware River to the eastern end of the Chesapeake and Delaware (C&D) Canal. Her insurance underwriters required that she be towed through the waterway, rather than transit the canal under her own power. In 1934 the C&D Canal had yet to be enlarged to its current dimensions, hence the precaution. By early evening *Albany* was in Baltimore for another night's layover.

Finally, on Sunday, April 22, *Albany* departed Baltimore and steamed south in the Chesapeake Bay to Point Lookout, Maryland, and the mouth of the Potomac River. Coming around and taking a course to the northeast, she reached Chapel Point shortly after lunchtime.

The trip south from New York had required an extraordinary amount of fuel. Because *Albany* was a coal burner, coal was stored in all sorts of nooks and crannies throughout the vessel. Whether it was the impact of seeing all this dirty stuff aboard his newly acquired steamboat or, more probably, the fact that Wills had done some homework beforehand on the relative cost of oil versus coal, as soon as the boat reached Chapel Point, he decided to have her converted to oil fuel.

He asked the same Tietjen and Lang shipyard back in Hoboken, where *Albany* had earlier been dry-docked, to quote a price for such a conversion. In a letter dated April 30, 1934—eight days after *Albany* reached Chapel Point—the company told Wills that based on specifications furnished by Wills, the base price for an oil conversion would be $19,518 plus an additional $2,026 if a carbon dioxide fire extinguishing system were also included.[9]

This estimate was, of course, quite hefty; it would have added, in effect, an 80 percent surcharge to the $25,000 that Wills had already paid for the boat itself. Apparently, however, the Tietjen and Lang estimate assumed the shipyard would send its own workers south to Chapel Point and perform all aspects of the conversion. In other words, the estimate from Tietjen and Lang was for "parts and labor." What Wills did instead was purchase the "parts" from Tietjen and Lang, but hire his own people to take care of the "labor," or at least most of it.

Around May 3, 1934, an oil burner and its associated equipment were shipped from Hoboken to Bel Alton aboard a Pennsylvania Railroad boxcar. Tietjen and Lang billed Wills a total of $5,600 for the equipment.[10] Wills satisfied Tietjen and Lang not by drawing a check for the full amount owed, but by sending the company seven separate promissory notes, in varying amounts, that added up to $5,600. The notes would come due on various dates during the summers of 1934 and 1935, when Wills expected to have adequate cash to handle such expenses. This meant that in addition to outyear payments on the mortgage for the Chapel Point property and the dredging of a channel in the Port Tobacco River, Wills had now obligated himself to pay off the cost of the vessel itself and her conversion to oil fuel out of future earnings.

Being new to the steamboat business, Wills himself did not know the difference between an oil pump and a monkey wrench, but in the spring of 1934 he hired a cadre of skilled people who did. A handwritten payroll record identifies no fewer than seventy-three separate individuals who were involved in various aspects of preparing the vessel for revenue service, including the conversion to oil fuel.[11] Some of these were local day laborers and even clerical personnel from Charles County, but most of the skilled people are noted on the payroll as being Hudson River watermen from Athens, New York. These include Alexander Hickey, who served as captain on the trip down and during the conversion period, and most importantly, Charles Requa, the chief engineer. The payroll record shows that at $689.36, Requa's compensation exceeded that of any other individual between early March and mid-July 1934. Not included on Wills's payroll, but critical to the success of the conversion, were technical people whom Tietjen and Lang sent to Chapel Point to provide advice and assistance.

While the coal-to-oil fuel conversion was the most expensive improvement on his newly acquired vessel, *Albany*'s almost three years of inactivity had taken a toll on her wooden superstructure. Considerable carpentry and joinery work was required to get her ready for her new assignment on the Potomac. These repairs were also done at Chapel Point between mid-April and late May.

Beginning with the purchase of *Albany* in 1934 and for the remainder of his excursion-boat-owning days, B. B. Wills believed that a dance floor was an absolute necessity aboard a day passenger vessel. And not just any old dance floor, he thought. It had to be a *large* dance floor! A major change in *Albany* from her Hudson River days was the installation of not one, but eventually two, dance floors. One floor was laid on the main deck, and another on the saloon deck. A bandstand was positioned midway between the two decks so couples on either dance floor could trip away the light fantastic to music from a single orchestra.

In preparing *Albany* for her new assignment, Wills was able to take advantage of something else. Namely, on December 5, 1933, the twenty-first amendment to the Constitution was ratified, rendering legal again the manufacture and sale of alcoholic beverages throughout the land. Wills converted a one-time cloak and package room forward on *Albany*'s main deck into a bar, and he installed a second bar in the dining room on the main deck aft to take advantage of the repeal of Prohibition.

When Albany *Became* Potomac

Finally, by early June 1934, all the work was finished and *Albany* was ready to begin her new assignment. Renamed *Potomac*, she was given a final inspection by the U.S. Coast Guard on June 7, and the next day she made her first trip upriver to Washington, D.C.[12]

On the day that *Potomac* steamed into Washington harbor for the very first time, President Franklin D. Roosevelt, then in his second year in office, sent a message to the Seventy-third Congress as it was about to adjourn. He told them of his plan to submit new social legislation in the next session that would help insure the security of older and disabled Americans. Also that day, a wireless report out of Geneva, Switzerland, predicted that Premier Mussolini of Italy and Chancellor Adolph Hitler of Germany would soon meet in Venice to discuss disarmament, as well as the possible creation of a new Mediterranean alliance; it would be the first meeting of the two European fascist leaders. In Moscow, meanwhile, the newspaper *Pravda* published the results of a lengthy analysis that concluded that the economy of the empire of Japan was insufficient to permit that country's ever waging a modern war. And on the lighter side of current events, in Boston's Fenway Park on June 8, the Red Sox defeated the visiting Washington Senators, three to two, in twelve innings. Boston's rookie left-hander Fritz Ostermueller not only pitched all twelve innings, but singled with two out in the bottom of the twelfth to drive in the winning run.[13]

As the sun set over the nation's capital that June evening, these and other developments both great and small were pondered and discussed by people of high office, low office, and no office at all. Down on the city's waterfront, a paddlewheel steamboat that had operated on the Hudson River for over fifty years was secured for the night at her new berth.

Regular public service to Chapel Point did not begin until June 27, but *Potomac* probably made a few special trips there between June 9 and June 26. She began to offer moonlight dance cruises out of Washington in early June and also ran several onetime excursions. On Saturday, June 16, for example, she sailed out of Washington at the unusual hour of 7:30 A.M. on a day-long cruise down the Potomac to Saint Mary's City as part of the state of Maryland's Tercentennial Celebration.[14] Eight days later, she left Washington shortly before noon for a five-hour nonstop public cruise.

The weather in Washington on June 27, 1934, was hardly auspicious for an outdoor activity like the start of a new excursion boat service; it was overcast and rainy. A scheduled baseball game at Griffith Stadium that day between the Washington Senators and the Saint Louis Browns had to be postponed.

Wet and rainy weather would have been appreciated elsewhere in the country in June 1934. As *Potomac* was beginning to acclimate herself to her new home waters, a terrible drought continued to plague the nation's midsection, which helped bring about the disaster known as the dust bowl.

CHAPTER THREE
Potomac Becomes a Legend

In the years after B. B. Wills put *Potomac* into excursion service between Washington and Chapel Point, he went on to become the owner and operator of almost two dozen day excursion boats in cities up and down the East Coast. Of them all, *Potomac* would always remain his favorite.[1]

The Potomac River Line

An early order of business after Wills purchased *Albany* from the Hudson River Day Line on March 6, 1934, was that a new company had to be formed to operate the vessel. On March 21, 1934, two weeks after Wills had bought the vessel, which was still moored on the Hudson River in Athens, New York, a certificate of incorporation was executed in Washington. It established the Potomac River Line as a Maryland corporation, with A. Gwynn Bowie of Upper Marlboro, Maryland, and Ernest C. Guy of Washington, D.C., joining Wills as the three founders of the new firm. The same document also named Bowie, Guy, and Wills as the sole members of the organization's board of directors. The firm's principal office was located "at T.B. Bus Terminal, Brandywine, Prince George's County, Maryland," which was also Wills's home at the time.[2]

Albany was still in Athens two weeks later when the new board of directors held its first formal meeting at the bus terminal on the evening of April 4, 1934. During this meeting Wills was elected president and treasurer of the Potomac River Line, Guy was named vice president, and Wills's wife, Gertrude, was designated secretary of the new company. At the same meeting, the board also voted to award Wills the entirety of the corporation's common stock in exchange for his "delivering to the Corporation title to the S.S. *Albany*, free and clear of all encumbrances, liens, claims and demands whatsoever, with the exception of a purchase-money mortgage of twenty thousand dollars ($20,000.00), and

The one-time Hudson River Day Line steamboat *Albany* worked for *Wills* as *Potomac* from 1934 through 1948. (Photograph by R. Loren Graham, courtesy of the Mariners' Museum, Newport News, Va.)

in further consideration of and payment for services rendered by the said Benjamin B. Wills in connection with the acquisition of the said S.S. *Albany* and the promotion and organization of the corporation."[3]

The par value of the stock awarded to Wills at this meeting was ten thousand dollars. *Albany* was subsequently conveyed from the personal ownership of B. B. Wills to that of the new corporation, and her name was changed to *Potomac*.

Service and schedules that first season of 1934 called for three round-trips each week between Washington and Chapel Point, plus moonlight dance cruises out of Washington almost every night of the week. *Potomac* was also available for private charter parties on days when she did not steam downriver to Chapel Point. Soon enough, Potomac River Line adopted a service feature that Wilson Line had utilized: sending *Potomac* beyond Chapel Point to Colonial Beach, Virginia, for those desiring an even longer river cruise.

Wharf space in Washington's pint-size harbor was not easy to come by for the 1934 season. The only pier that Wills could lease for *Potomac* was at Water and O Streets, near Fort McNair and across the street from the trolley carbarn. There was virtually no parking at this location; furthermore, not only was the Wilson Line's pier at Seventh Street easier for passengers to reach than the Water Street pier, Seventh Street was the first excursion boat landing families saw when heading for the waterfront by streetcar. It is not difficult to imagine people who intended to take a day trip to Chapel Point aboard *Potomac* quickly getting off the trolley when they saw *City of Washington* tied up to her pier with steam up and ready to cast off, and after buying a ticket to Marshall Hall by mistake, deciding that they might just as well go there anyway.

Having purchased a steamboat, rented a wharf, and organized a corporation to own and operate the vessel, Wills next had to make sure potential customers were aware of the new service he was about to offer. A mass mailing was sent out in the spring of 1934 to organizations known to have booked group sailings aboard *City of Washington* in earlier years. The letter was upbeat: "This is to let you know that we have just completed the purchase of a fine boat for Potomac River trips. This steamer is the largest and fastest excursion vessel ever operated on the Potomac. . . . Within the very near future we will have our circular and full information available. For the present, until we get our Washington office settled, address all communications to B. B. Wills, Brandywine, Maryland, or Phone Brandywine 21."[4] Subsequently, Wills followed up with a sustained campaign of newspaper advertisements for his new service. The profit and loss statement in table 3-1 shows that advertising was a significant expense for Potomac River Line's first season of operation in 1934.

TABLE 3-1
Profit and Loss Statement, Potomac River Line, 1934*

Total income (tickets)	$42,785.01
Administrative and operating expenses:	
Advertising	$4,252.03
Boat repairs	$1,709.39
Boat salaries	$5,656.26
Boat supplies	$626.51
Depreciation, boat	$874.94
Fuel	$7,195.97
Insurance	$1,448.97
Legal and audit	$914.50
Music	$3,620.00
Officers' salaries	$2,513.40
Office salaries	$1,332.66
Other and misc.	$3,611.69
Total expenses (boat)	$33,752.32
Net profit (boat)	$9,032.69
Total income (concessions)	$24,329.33
Total expenses (concessions)	$18,590.04
Net profit (concessions)	$5,739.29
Total net profit	$14,771.98

*From Potomac River Line, Profit and Loss Statement, October 4, 1934, prepared by P. B. Howell (accountant), Wills Papers, collected by Professor Jeffrey Wills of the University of Wisconsin.

In 1935, before *Potomac* embarked on her second season, Wills was able to secure a better Washington dock, one that passengers could see from the trolley car *before* they reached the Wilson Line's Seventh Street Wharf. It included a large parking lot, and as Wills himself later said, particularly with respect to moonlight cruises: "the streetcars were running, and we had the dock yard and boat all lit up and our barkers on the street and when the streetcar stopped a lot of the people coming down for a moonlight ride got off the streetcar and went on our boat."[5]

The trip from Washington to Chapel Point was lengthy, approximately 52 statute miles. *Potomac* was a fast vessel that could manage

Complimentary season pass issued by the Potomac River Line.

Potomac docked at Chapel Point Park.

approximately 18 miles per hour, although adverse wind and tide conditions might slow her from time to time. In any event, considering the time it took to get under way at one end of the trip and to dock at the other end—plus an occasional stop at Alexandria, Virginia, to board additional passengers—a trip between Washington and Chapel Point was roughly a three-hour proposition. A day's outing that departed from Washington at 9:30 A.M. and returned at 6:30 P.M. would involve three hours at Chapel Point Park and around six hours aboard *Potomac*. This was not a good ratio; five or six hours ashore and three or four hours aboard the steamboat would have been better. Such a lengthy steamboat trip helps explain why the Wilson Line was willing to drop Chapel Point service entirely in favor of shorter trips to Marshall Hall after the 1932 season. It also helps explain the future policy direction taken by B. B. Wills and the Potomac River Line.

The Years after 1934

The irony is that while *Potomac* was purchased for the avowed purpose of supplying Chapel Point with customers, it was *Potomac*'s overall success, as much as anything else, that soon led to the demise of Chapel Point Park. Trips to and from the Pride of the Potomac quickly became a minor part of the boat's routine operations; soon enough they became no part of it at all.

In that first year, 1934, *Potomac* steamed downriver to Chapel Point three times a week. The next year, she ran to Chapel Point on Tuesday, to Chapel Point and Colonial Beach on Saturday, and to Colonial Beach—but *not* Chapel Point—on Sunday.

The real money to be made with *Potomac*, Wills soon realized, was not in all-day, round-trip excursions to Chapel Point or anyplace else, but in the two- and three-hour evening dance cruises out of Washington. On such trips virtually all tickets were sold at the adult rate, and refreshments tended to be rounds of drinks from the newly installed bar, not popcorn, candy, and soda for the kids.

Chapel Point itself continued to be a financial disappointment. In 1935, for example, Wills incurred a net loss of almost three thousand dollars on the operation, which even included a payment of ten cents per head from the Potomac River Line for each passenger brought to the park aboard *Potomac*.[6] Wills soon realized that he could never turn the Pride of the Potomac into a profitable enterprise. With his attention now turned more and more to the day-to-day business of running the

Potomac River Line, and with the possibility of his venturing into other East Coast excursion boat operations, in 1936 Wills reached an accommodation with the Corporation of Roman Catholic Clergymen. He would, in effect, "default" on his mortgage and return the property to the Jesuit Fathers from whom he had purchased Chapel Point ten years earlier in 1926.

It was an amicable settlement, although as a purely technical matter the Corporation of Roman Catholic Clergymen had to bring suit against Wills and his wife in Circuit Court for Charles County so that their agreement would have the force of law.[7] The Jesuits had been most helpful—and patient—over the years in allowing Wills the flexibility to tailor annual mortgage payments to suit the actual cash flow at Chapel Point Park.[8] The formal document releasing Wills from his mortgage responsibilities was filed in the Land Records of Charles County on September 29, 1936.[9] Between 1926 and 1936, Wills made payments to the Jesuits of $90,567.03 against the $200,000.00 mortgage they held on the Chapel Point property. Wills noted that "all monies paid on account of this property is a complete lost [sic] to this taxpayer."[10]

The property reverted back to the Corporation of Roman Catholic Clergymen, and *Potomac* made her final call at Chapel Point on Sunday, September 12, 1937. By then Wills no longer owned the property and the place was little more than a quiet picnic grounds, the various rides and

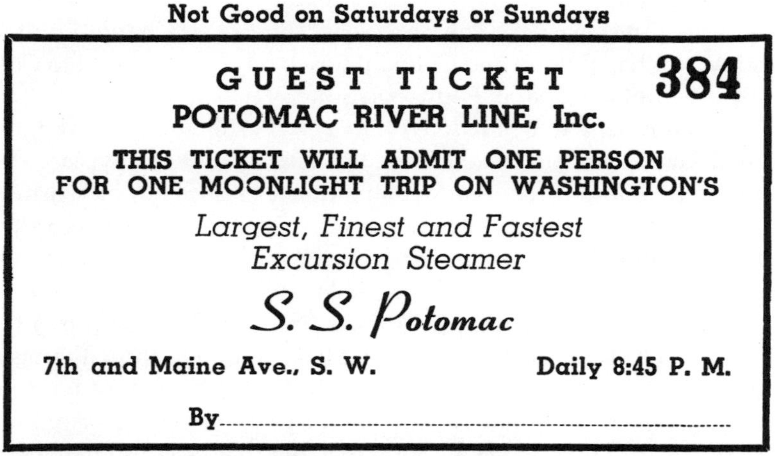

Not Good on Saturdays or Sundays

GUEST TICKET 384
POTOMAC RIVER LINE, Inc.

THIS TICKET WILL ADMIT ONE PERSON FOR ONE MOONLIGHT TRIP ON WASHINGTON'S

Largest, Finest and Fastest Excursion Steamer

S. S. *Potomac*

7th and Maine Ave., S. W.   Daily 8:45 P. M.

By_____

Guest ticket for a weekday trip aboard *Potomac*.

other amusements having long since been sold off and trucked away. No excursion boat has ever since ventured into the Port Tobacco River.

In March 1990, over a half-century after *Potomac* left Chapel Point for the last time, B. B. Wills's daughter-in-law Kathleen Wills—the wife of his son Ben, Jr.—wrote a letter to Gene Wills, another of the Old Timer's sons, talking about the days of Chapel Point Park: "They spoke of many things. Kitty especially remembered when the *Potomac* would come in. Her brother would take you, Marcella, Ben and herself—all holding hands—down to the boardwalk to see the boat come in. What a sight that would have been."[11]

Now, over sixty years after B. B. Wills turned his back on the Pride of the Potomac, the area around Chapel Point remains rural, rustic, and unspoiled. The spot where the park once stood is one or two small riverfront farms, while just to the north along the Port Tobacco River the state of Maryland has established a public preserve also called, ironically, Chapel Point Park. Duck blinds dot the water's edge, and, in season, people launch small boats, go fishing, hike along the river, and maybe enjoy a quiet picnic lunch. Visitors to today's Chapel Point Park never arrive in any great numbers, however, nothing remotely like the five thousand people and 1,252 automobiles that visited the original Chapel Point Park on July 4, 1928. At today's Chapel Point Park, a dozen or two automobiles would quickly overwhelm the small parking lot near the river.

Contemporary navigational charts for the lower Potomac River reveal no evidence whatsoever of the channel that B. B. Wills once had the Lukens Dredging and Contracting Corporation dredge so that steamboats could draw up to his pier at Chapel Point. One can see evidence of the pier itself, though, in the form of deteriorated pilings rising out of the water away from the shore. Up on the hillside and back from the river, the spire of Saint Ignatius Church continues to point skyward.

Liverpool Point

In 1935, even before the demise of Chapel Point, Wills leased another piece of property on the Maryland side of the Potomac, but much closer to Washington, called Liverpool Point. Wills was still of a mind to establish his own destination for day excursionists traveling aboard *Potomac*, but on a much lesser scale, with a much lower investment, than Chapel Point. A Potomac River Line brochure from the period characterized Liverpool Point as "a new and attractive little picnic grove on the

Maryland shore 36 miles from Washington, just across the river from Quantico."[12]

A five-year lease on a parcel of 17-plus acres at Liverpool was executed in the name of Wills's wife, Gertrude G. Wills, on May 17, 1935.[13] Liverpool Point had few of the amenities of Chapel Point; it was a picnic grove by the side of the river with a small bathing beach, and that was about it.

The lay of the land made it much easier for *Potomac* to stop at Liverpool Point, where the main river channel is close to the Maryland shore. With a short and simple dock extending out into the river, there was no need for expensive dredging of a completely new channel, as was required at Chapel Point. *Potomac* made her first call at Liverpool Point during the 1935 excursion season.

Liverpool never developed into a serious and long-term venture, though. *Potomac* only stopped there sporadically after 1935, with her last call being in 1939. Like those at Chapel Point, pilings from the old dock at Liverpool Point are still visible today extending out from the Maryland shoreline.

What made *Potomac* a roaring success, however, were the evening dance cruises. On most Saturday nights, as well as the evenings before Memorial Day, the Fourth of July, and Labor Day, the steamboat was usually scheduled to make *two* after-dark trips. One was the usual "moonlight" cruise that departed Washington shortly after 8:00 P.M. and returned about 11:30. The second was called a "midnight" cruise; it departed between 12:00 and 12:30 A.M. and sailed the river for about two hours. In later years Wills spoke about these dual moonlight and midnight cruises, especially on evenings when Potomac River Lines had paid premium dollars for a big-name band: "We figured that it would take the receipts of one cruise to pay for the band and the advertising and the second cruise would be profitable," Wills said.[14]

Wills, incidentally, often had some of the major dance bands of the era performing during *Potomac*'s moonlight and midnight cruises. Performers included names like Gene Krupa, Dizzy Gillespie, Duke Ellington, and Billy Butterfield.[15] As the nation's capital, Washington was a popular city for touring musicians, and the Old Timer was quick to take advantage of any band that might be in town and to book them for a night or two aboard his steamship.

Every *Potomac* trip did not feature big-name bands, of course. On most cruises, music was provided by local musicians. One orchestra leader who enjoyed a long association with B. B. Wills was Jack Corry. After playing aboard *Potomac* for many years, Corry moved his musicians ashore and became a fixture for many seasons at a Washington amusement park called Glen Echo. Like his onetime employer B. B. Wills, Jack Corry eventually turned his back on excursion boats and amusement parks and made a career for himself in the world of Washington real estate.

With the success of the dance cruises, *Potomac* ultimately shifted from offering round-trip day excursions between Washington and Chapel Point, Colonial Beach, or Liverpool to specializing in evening cruise service. Table 3-2 shows how the style of cruises changed over five years of service, 1935 through 1939.

By 1937, the only destination that *Potomac* continued to serve with any kind of regular round-trip excursions was Colonial Beach, although into the 1940s an occasional charter would steam to Quantico, Virginia, as well. Neither destination, however, was owned or managed by B. B. Wills. He had become an excursion boat operator only; his days as an amusement park owner—at least on the banks of the Potomac River—were over.

TABLE 3-2
Potomac's Changing Service Patterns, 1935-1939*

	1935	1936	1937	1938	1939
Nonstop day cruises	0	6	8	6	9
Moonlight cruises	68	115	112	105	120
Midnight cruises	2	3	4	11	17
Round-trips to					
Liverpool	11	4	1	0	1
Chapel Point	11	19	1	0	0
Colonial Beach	11	13	19	16	14
Chapel Point and					
Colonial Beach	3	0	0	0	0
Total trips per season	106	160	145	138	161

*Numbers represent trips per seasonal year. Single sheets reporting every trip made by *Potomac* between 1935 and 1939 are bound together into a large volume. The 1935 data begins on July 1, although the vessel most certainly began her season several weeks earlier that year. Statistics shown for 1935, therefore, represent less than a full season's operations. From Purser's Report, Potomac River Line, 1935–1939, Wills Papers, collected by Professor Jeffrey Wills of the University of Wisconsin.

Potomac kept right on running throughout World War II. The heavy Bunker C fuel she burned was a precious commodity during the war—although not nearly as difficult to obtain as gasoline or diesel fuel. The Potomac River Line was able to secure allocations from federal authorities, in all likelihood because her service out of Washington was felt to provide needed recreation for both military and civilian personnel engaged in the war effort. Wills also did not hesitate to claim in his petitions to the Office of Defense Transportation in Washington for Bunker C allocations that his vessel provided the only direct passenger service between Washington and Colonial Beach and thus could be regarded as an element of the nation's essential transportation network.[16] Such claims bordered on the preposterous, however, since *Potomac* only sailed to Colonial Beach once a week and never visited there again after the 1942 excursion season.

The vessel did consume a significant amount of fuel. She normally required 1,500 gallons for a typical three-hour moonlight cruise, 5,200 gallons for an all-day trip to Colonial Beach plus a moonlight. A full season's work by *Potomac*—mid-May to mid-September— required 275,600 gallons of Bunker C fuel.[17]

Published reports claim that *Potomac* was reconverted from oil to coal fuel for a single wartime season, most likely 1943.[18] There is no evidence to support such a contention among the Wills Papers, although some documents in the collection indicate that Wills at least petitioned for a Bunker C allocation for both the 1943 and 1944 seasons.[19]

Wartime brought a few other unusual wrinkles to routine service patterns of the Potomac River Line. For example, there were periodic blackouts staged to acclimate the nation's capital to the regimen that would be expected should enemy aircraft appear overhead. On the evening of June 17, 1942, such an exercise was conducted and most institutions in the District of Columbia were cooperative to a fault. In the middle of the blackout, however, *Potomac* was making her way back to her pier in southwest Washington after a cruise, every light aboard blazing brightly. Although B. B. Wills claimed that he had been misinformed about what was required of him, civilian defense officials suggested that Wills was downright uncooperative, even surly, when confronted on the night of the blackout.[20] As a result, *Potomac* was prohibited from operating on evenings when future blackouts were conducted.[21]

Another change that the vessel had to observe during the war years was the need to slow down and navigate under a temporary railroad bridge built across the river between Alexandria, Virginia, and the District of Columbia. The span was ordered by federal officials as a precautionary measure in case the Long Bridge, the area's sole Potomac River crossing for freight and passenger trains operating between the northeast and the south, became incapacitated, accidentally or otherwise. After the war the temporary bridge was dismantled and Long Bridge regained its previous status of exclusivity.

Throughout the World War II years, the Potomac River Line was kept busy running excursions out of Washington. A colleague of Wills in the excursion boat business, John A. Meseck, of New York, dropped him a note during the summer of 1942: "We hear that you have been doing a good moonlight business, and that Washington is growing by leaps and bounds. Glad to know that the boats keep busy."[22] After V-J Day and a return to normalcy, Wills would characterize his wartime operations on the Potomac as a time of "gravy."[23]

The Columbia Steamship Company

Benjamin Bowling Wills's personal satisfaction with the operation of excursion boats is evidenced by the way the Potomac River Line quickly shifted its corporate focus. From a mere supplier of customers for Wills's Chapel Point Park, the steamboat line became an operation managed for its own purposes. Interestingly, the year after he put *Potomac* into service out of Washington, Wills formed another Washington-based excursion boat company that also operated Potomac River cruises. Despite the similarity of the two operations, Wills's Columbia Steamship Company never directly competed with his Potomac River Line, for reasons discussed below.

The Columbia Steamship Company was a venture that Wills formed in partnership with a man named Edward Maier. Together, Wills and Maier purchased *Southport,* a wooden-hulled, former Maine coast propeller steamboat, and brought her to Washington. Columbia Steamship set up shop for the excursion season of 1935 from the same pier near O Street that *Potomac* had used in 1934. *Southport* was much smaller than *Potomac*: 245 gross tons versus 1,415; 125.6 feet long versus 314.

What was truly different about *Southport* and Columbia Steamship, however—and why the venture was not competitive with the Potomac River Line—was that it sought customers solely among Washington's African American community. In the language of the times, B. B. Wills explained that *Southport* was assigned to "the colored trade."[24] Running exclusively in charter service, the markets she served were social, civic, and religious organizations among Washington's black community anxious for a day's outing on the Potomac River. From time to time—early in an excursion season, for instance—*Southport* might substitute for *Potomac* as Potomac River Line's basic vessel, but primarily she made charter and other special trips for black passengers, and black passengers only.

The larger question this raises, of course, is this: If *Southport* and Columbia Steamship were exclusively carrying black passengers, were African Americans excluded from traveling aboard *Potomac*? The answer appears to be yes. Among the Wills Papers are charter contracts executed by the Potomac River Line over the years. As late as 1950 and 1951, the standard contract contained a lot of boilerplate language, with blanks that would be filled in to specify all the variables such as date, time, price, destination, chartering organization, whether an orchestra would be supplied, and so forth. One of the standard provisions in Potomac River Line's excursion contract read as follows: "All reputable

Southport, an excursion boat Wills used to inaugurate service out of Washington in 1935 exclusively for African Americans.

persons in good standing up to ____ capacity shall be admitted," and a number was typed into the blank. The number could vary, depending on whether a particular charter involved exclusive use of the entire vessel, or if the chartering party was one of several expected aboard a particular cruise.

In some contracts—but not all—an additional phrase was typed above this preprinted sentence, with an arrow indicating that it belonged between the words "persons" and "in." The added phrase was "of the Caucasian Race."

Many charter contracts in the Wills Papers contain this added phrase. An interesting example is a contract between the Potomac River Line and the Twenty-fifth Infantry Association of Arlington, Virginia, for an afternoon cruise on the Potomac River on Saturday, July 7, 1951.[25] The signatures of two officers in the U.S. Army appear on this contract. Ironically, this military-affiliated organization felt it proper to accept such exclusionary contract terms at the very time that President Harry S Truman was striving to desegregate the nation's armed forces.

The Robert E. Lee Steamboat Company

Columbia Steamship proved to be a short-lived venture and operated for only two excursion seasons, 1935 and 1936. It was succeeded, however, by yet another enterprise whose Washington operations were also marketed exclusively among black church and social organizations. The successor organization to Columbia Steamship did not begin on the Potomac River out of Washington, though; it had its beginnings in the tidewater country of Virginia.

In 1936, Wills formed a venture with a man named Fabian P. Noel to establish the Robert E. Lee Steamboat Company. While the two men were equal partners, Noel, more so than Wills, was the head man of the organization. The honor was fitting: Noel was an old-line steamboat man who was entitled to be called "Captain Noel."

The Wills–Noel corporation had taken title to a former Chesapeake Bay overnight steamboat called *Dorchester*, which had been owned and operated by a subsidiary of the Pennsylvania Railroad. When built in 1912, *Dorchester* flew the house flag of the Baltimore, Chesapeake and Atlantic Railway, a PRR subsidiary that served the Chesapeake Bay area.

In July 1923, the Baltimore and Virginia Steamboat Company, also a PRR subsidiary, was organized, and in November 1928 it acquired the steamboat properties of the Baltimore, Chesapeake and Atlantic in exchange for common stock in the new company.[26] In 1936 Wills and Noel purchased *Dorchester* from the Baltimore and Virginia Steamboat Company, converted her into a day excursion boat, and renamed her *Robert E. Lee*. She was a sidewheeler powered by an inclined engine and had been built by the Maryland Steel Company at Sparrows Point. The steamboat got her original name from Dorchester County on the Chesapeake Bay in Maryland.

Dorchester's final assignment before being sold to Wills and Noel was an unhurried, delightful trip that would be difficult to re-create today. She slipped out of Baltimore late in the afternoon and steamed southward down Chesapeake Bay, but poked her way into inlets and rivers here and there during the night to stop at various way landings. *Dorchester* was not a swift and direct overnight packet boat; she was more of a tramp steamer, Chesapeake Bay style. The next morning found *Dorchester* working her way up the lower Potomac, again making frequent stops throughout the day to drop off and pick up both freight and passengers. The steamboat did not reach Washington, her destination, until the next morning. Then, after laying over for the day, in late afternoon she repeated the whole process en route back to Baltimore. Two nights, one full day, and 320 or more circuitous and often overlapping miles of travel to reach a destination a mere 40 miles away as the crow flies, and 200 miles by water over the most direct course. The fare for such a leisurely cruise? Including transportation charges, stateroom, *five* meals, a fast return trip by train, plus taxi connections between dock and depot was, as late as 1931, $12.12.

Why did Wills and Noel rechristen their newly acquired vessel *Robert E. Lee*? Their reasoning was simple enough. The company was based in Richmond, Virginia, and their initial plan was to run the vessel in general charter and moonlight service out of such Virginia cities as Richmond, Hopewell, Newport News, and Norfolk. Not only was Robert E. Lee a name with some degree of honor in most of Virginia, but an earlier steamboat called *Robert E. Lee* had achieved legendary status in America's popular culture by virtue of an 1870 race with a rival vessel, *Natchez*.

Through the 1936 and 1937 seasons, Wills and Noel ran *Robert E. Lee* out of various cities in the Old Dominion, and this was her exclusive service. This style of excursion boat operation was sometimes called "barnstorming." A vessel would not stay in any single port for an entire summer season; it would book as many charter cruises as possible in a particular place, and once having run them, would move on to a new city and repeat the cycle.

Robert E. Lee, another Wills vessel that served the African American market in Washington. (Photograph by R. Loren Graham, courtesy of B. B. Wills family.)

With the demise of Columbia Steamship in 1937, however, the African American market in Washington was not being served, and *Robert E. Lee* was brought to the Potomac to take *Southport*'s place. Thus came to pass the strange anomaly of Wills and Noel's marketing a product to the black community of Washington that was named in honor of a general who led Confederate forces during the Civil War.

By the early 1940s, Wills and Noel had had a rather nasty falling out. The formal minutes of annual meetings of the board of directors of the Robert E. Lee Steamboat Company are replete with instances of Wills's blocking, in his capacity as corporate secretary, votes on such routine matters as approving the minutes of previous meetings because such meetings had apparently approved a pay increase for Captain Noel.[27] Eventually Wills bought out Noel's interest in the company. An attorney whom Wills retained to help settle his differences with Noel wrote to Wills, saying: "If you don't either take over the whole thing or get out, I will think it is because you enjoy fighting with Noel."[28]

The Robert E. Lee Steamboat Company continued to serve Washington's African American community for many years and provided a parallel service to that offered by Potomac River Line. The company, however, never completely abandoned its barnstorming heritage in Virginia's tidewater region. In 1948, for example, *Robert E. Lee* concluded its Washington work in early August and then headed south on August 12 to handle charter cruises along the James River. She ran charters out of Norfolk, Richmond, and Hopewell for the next month before heading back to Washington in mid-September for her winter layup there.

The next spring, *Robert E. Lee* returned to the James River in late May and ran another month's worth of cruises in tidewater country before returning to Washington and her normal assignments in late June. The following year, 1950, *Robert E. Lee* began the season by heading from Washington to Baltimore for dry-docking in late May, and then running cruises out of Baltimore for almost two months before returning to Washington on July 27.[29]

In the excursion boat empire of B. B. Wills, *Robert E. Lee* was, effectively, two different vessels. First, like a traveling circus, she was a barnstormer that came to town, ran some cruises, and then moved along. Second, she picked up the mantle of *Southport* and the Columbia Steamship Company and operated cruises out of Washington, D.C., that were marketed exclusively to the African American community. *Robert E. Lee* continued to steam out of Washington until 1952.

The Potomac River Line, the Robert E. Lee Steamboat Company and the Columbia Steamship Company reflected the social mores of the larger society they served, and they reflected it all too accurately. In 1934, when B. B. Wills inaugurated excursion boat service out of Washington, segregation of the races was a matter of social practice and custom around the nation's capital and the fact that African American customers were unwelcome at the ticket windows of the Potomac River Line was simply not exceptional. Wills himself felt no compunction to assume a leadership role in reforming society's views on matters of racial justice, nor was his company ever targeted as a case in point by those who did. As a result Wills's Washington-based excursion boats experienced none of the racial unrest that was beginning to permeate the nation. There were no court orders, no protests, no lawyers, no writs, no picket lines, no stories in the newspapers pertaining to segregation aboard his vessels.

One recorded incident in Washington, however, did involve racial segregation on excursion boats of the Wilson Line. On September 15, 1950, the company refused to let four African Americans purchase tickets for the Marshall Hall/Mount Vernon boat, claiming that it was simply observing "the community's custom of segregation." While hardly a onetime or isolated incident, it was the necessary case in point that led to a formal review by the Interstate Commerce Commission (ICC). On November 2, 1951, the ICC ruled that Wilson Line's action represented "unreasonable prejudice and disadvantage" and that the company must "cease and desist" from the practice in the future. In responding to the ICC, Wilson Line said that since the time of the incident, it had changed its policy, and the ICC refused to grant the petitioners' request for monetary damages, asserting that "the evidence is inadequate to support a finding of damages."[30]

The ICC's decision became effective for the 1952 excursion season. By that time Wills's Potomac River Line would be a mere shadow of its former self and the Robert E. Lee Steamboat Company about to fade into history. Nevertheless, even after World War II, racial segregation was an accepted fact of life in the way the two companies carried out their day-to-day operations.

The Robert E. Lee Steamboat Company eventually took on another face. In later years, when Wills was devoting the bulk of his time to the real estate development business, and *Robert E. Lee* herself had been reduced to scrap, the Robert E. Lee Steamboat Company remained a

A rising tide raises all boats . . . but not all trucks. Spring floods have come to Washington, and the Potomac River Line's headquarters are awash. The vessel whose stern is visible is *Robert E. Lee.*

corporation whose original Virginia charter was still valid. Attorneys were consulted, meetings were held, and it was determined that the charter of the old steamboat company could be amended to include new and different purposes more useful in the business of developing tracts of suburban land into new ranch houses.

On August 15, 1955, the board of directors of the Robert E. Lee Steamboat Corporation gathered in formal session. A quorum being present, it was moved, duly seconded, and unanimously voted that henceforth "The name of the said corporation shall be Potomac Excavating Corporation. . . ."[31]

But all of this is to get substantially ahead of our story. B. B. Wills's excursion boat operations began in the summer of 1934 with the Potomac River Line, expanded a year later with the formation of the Columbia Steamship Company, and expanded again in 1936 with the organization of the Robert E. Lee Steamboat Company. The next expansion, in 1937, took Wills north to the port of Baltimore.

A family portrait: B. B. Wills; his wife, Gertrude Gosnell Wills; and their three sons (left to right) Benjamin, Reed, and J. Eugene.

CHAPTER FOUR

Across the Bay to Tolchester

When B. B. Wills began operating the Potomac River Line in 1934, he was establishing a brand new steamboat company, which he would continue to run for all of its days. When he expanded his steamboat holdings beyond the Potomac in subsequent years, he usually did so by taking over older and established excursion boat companies.

Tolchester Beach

The first of such operations to come under Wills's control linked downtown Baltimore with a 54-plus acre resort and amusement park complex 27 miles across the Chesapeake Bay in Kent County, Maryland, called Tolchester Beach. The original Tolchester steamboat company was formed in 1878 and once operated vessels out of Baltimore to various destinations up and down the Chesapeake Bay. By the mid-1930s, however, the company had discontinued all of its routes and services except the key link between Baltimore and Tolchester Beach.[1]

In 1936, when Wills put together a group of financiers to buy out the assets of the bankrupt Tolchester Beach Improvement Company—the formal name of the older steamboat operator—there were no bridges across the Chesapeake Bay. To get from Baltimore or Washington to any point on the Delmarva Peninsula required one to travel aboard a ferry or a steamboat. The alternative was a long journey north to the head of the Bay by train, bus, or automobile, and then south again on the other side.

B. B. Wills saw his takeover of the line primarily as another excursion boat and amusement park venture, with people traveling from Baltimore and its environs for a day of relaxation and fun at Tolchester Beach itself. Moonlight cruises out of Baltimore would, of course, turn a few extra dollars. But Wills also believed that once he established himself on

49

the Chesapeake Bay with the seasonal Baltimore–Tolchester excursion route, he might expand the service into a more general-purpose year-round trans-Chesapeake ferry operation for both passengers and automobiles. A year-round ferry had also been a corporate goal of the previous Tolchester company, although Chesapeake Bay historian David Holly suggests that this goal was one factor that led to the financial demise of the Tolchester Beach Improvement Company.[2]

In late 1936, Wills and his associates purchased certificates of deposit that represented the bonds of the Tolchester Beach Improvement Company of Kent County. The older company had declared bankruptcy in February 1935 under Section 77B of the National Bankruptcy Act but continued to operate during the 1935 excursion season under the supervision of a federal court in an effort to regain solvency. The 1936 season saw a court-appointed receiver in charge of the company, but by the fall of that year any effort to reorganize was seen as hopeless and a first mortgage was foreclosed by the trustee in bankruptcy. That was when Wills and his associates, acting as a bondholders' protective committee, "bought in" the property for sixty thousand dollars.

Their intention was to acquire the assets of the older company and to resume operations of the park at Tolchester Beach and the steamboat that linked it to Baltimore, both of which were owned by the Tolchester Beach Improvement Company. The move was promptly challenged in court, however, by a rival group who had in mind the swift liquidation of the company's holdings. The rival had offers in hand: twenty-five thousand dollars from the Chesapeake Steamship Company to acquire docks and wharves in Baltimore, and sixty-five thousand from the Wilson Line for the resort and amusement park at Tolchester Beach, plus the company's steamboats.[3]

Not until April 1937, when the litigation had run its course and the position of the bondholders' protective committee was sustained by the courts, did Wills and company take title to the Tolchester property. Wills himself put up 50 percent of the capital needed to launch the new venture. His principal investing partner was Baltimore businessman Beverly Ober; other participants invested relatively minor sums of money.

In May 1937, a Maryland corporation, Tolchester Lines, was established, and on June 7 of that year the new company began operations. Wills was pleased that the court had finally settled the matter, and settled it in his favor. He was displeased, though, that his new company was getting a late start during its initial season and "had not been in a position to start booking in March, as is customary."[4] Despite the late

Tolchester, the first Wills excursion boat to operate in Baltimore.

start, the new Tolchester Lines posted a modest profit at the end of its first season of operation—$6,331.60.[5]

In the deal that Wills structured, he and his backers would take over the amusement park, the picnic grounds, and a thirty-three-room hotel at Tolchester Beach, plus an old vertical beam sidewheeler that bore the name *Tolchester*. Wills also took title to a former New York ferryboat that the older company had purchased in 1925 and renamed *Express*. *Express* was a candidate for little more than the scrap heap by 1937, though, and was carried on the books as an asset with a value of only thirty-five hundred dollars; Wills soon disposed of her.[6]

Tolchester was one of the oldest passenger boats that Wills ever owned and operated. Originally named *St. Johns* for a river in Florida that gives the port of Jacksonville access to the sea, she first worked an ocean route between Jacksonville and Charleston, South Carolina. In later years, the vessel moved north and became a fixture between Manhattan, Coney Island, and Rockaway Beach in New York for many seasons. Still later she ran on the Potomac River out of Washington to Colonial Beach.[7] The Tolchester Beach Improvement Company purchased her in 1933 to supplement and eventually replace such older and venerable vessels as *Louise* and *Emma Giles*.[8]

The Tolchester Beach Improvement Company had also begun to feel competitive pressure from another excursion boat operator that had instituted a new service out of Baltimore in 1931. That was when the Wilson Line pulled their *State of Delaware* off her usual Delaware River route out of Philadelphia and sent her south to begin a new excursion service on the Chesapeake Bay. It was the second straight season that saw Wilson Line open a new route outside the Delaware Valley where the company had long confined itself. In the previous season, 1930, the Wilson Line had begun running *City of Washington* on the Potomac in conjunction with B. B. Wills and Chapel Point Park (see chapter 1).

Because the original Tolchester company owned the amusement complex at Tolchester Beach, there was no possibility of Wilson's making Tolchester the destination for its new Baltimore excursion service. Instead, Wilson Line ran *State of Delaware* to a place on the western shore of the Bay known as Seaside Park, a community today called Chesapeake Beach. There had been no excursion boat service between Baltimore and Seaside Park since a sidewheeler called *Dreamland* stopped running there after the 1925 season.

Seaside Park/Chesapeake Beach is about 50 miles south of Baltimore, so an all-day excursion required passengers to spend considerably more time aboard the steamboat than they did on the much shorter

27-mile cruise to Tolchester. For those who appreciated relaxing hours steaming up and down the Chesapeake Bay on a large and modern excursion boat, the Wilson Line's new Baltimore service with the eight-year-old *State of Delaware* was made to order. For families with restless youngsters, however, the shorter cruise to Tolchester meant more hours ashore to enjoy such less confining amusements as the bathing beach, playground, rides, and concessions.

State of Delaware inaugurated Wilson Line service out of Baltimore on May 27, 1931. In 1936, Wilson Line replaced *State of Delaware* on the Seaside Park run with an older steamboat that had recently been thoroughly rebuilt. This was *Dixie*, formerly called *Brandywine*, a Wilson Line veteran built in 1885. *State of Delaware* was sent north to New York as Wilson Line continued to expand into new markets. In 1941, Wilson put yet another rebuilt steamboat into Baltimore–Seaside Park service, a vessel called *Bay Belle*. The rebuilt vessel would remain a fixture along the Baltimore waterfront for the next two decades.

The hotel and pavilion at Tolchester Beach. (Photograph courtesy of John H. Shaum, Jr.)

When B. B. Wills took over the Baltimore–Tolchester route, he never particularly liked *Tolchester*, especially after seeing her in action during the new company's first season of operation, 1937. She was too expensive to operate, in part because she had to carry 100 tons of ballast to meet stability requirements, her dance floor was far too small in Wills's view, and she was simply old and outmoded. In a business plan written in January 1938 in preparation for the new company's second season operating out of Baltimore, Wills called her "the antiquated S/S *Tolchester*" and "not a second-rate boat, but perhaps a third-rate one."[9]

As a result, shortly after Wills acquired the old steamboat, he began to look for a replacement. The first vessel he identified as a possible new excursion boat for Tolchester service was *Chester W. Chapin*, an 1899-built overnight passenger steamer that worked out of New York for the New England Steamship Company but which was on the market when that company abandoned its Long Island Sound services in 1937.

Active negotiations were proceeding. Wills's partner in the Robert E. Lee Steamboat Company, Capt. Fabian P. Noel, traveled north and inspected the *Chapin* on November 8, 1937; he found her to be sound in all respects. Wills himself predicted that the *Chapin*, "when acquired, will outclass all excursion boats which have ever been at this port, and will in fact be one of the finest excursion steamers afloat."[10]

But the deal that would have brought *Chester W. Chapin* to the Chesapeake Bay and Tolchester Lines never materialized. Instead, she was purchased by another Long Island Sound operator, the Colonial Line, and continued in service out of New York for several years as *Meteor*; then during World War II she was acquired by the federal government. Although the steamboat that began life as *Chester W. Chapin* eventually saw service on the Chesapeake Bay, it was as an overnight boat running between Baltimore and Norfolk, and Washington and Norfolk, not as a day excursion boat on the Baltimore–Tolchester route.[11]

Wills's failure to acquire the vessel might have been a blessing in disguise, according to steamboat historian Edwin L. Dunbaugh of New York. In the fall of 1937, as a boy of ten, Dunbaugh traveled with his father, who was then vice president of Colonial Line, the company that eventually acquired *Chester W. Chapin*, to look over the vessel in Newport, Rhode Island. "Wills may also have discovered after further inspection that *Chester W. Chapin* would not have converted easily to excursion service," Dunbaugh commented. "I would also suspect that she might have had too much draft for Tolchester Beach."[12]

While the new company continued to keep an eye out for a suitable replacement, *Tolchester* soldiered on out of Baltimore, despite what the

Old Timer believed to be her many liabilities. An interesting assortment of vessels were given some consideration as replacements over the ensuing years; they are identified in table 4-1.

TABLE 4-1
Vessels Considered as Replacements
for *Tolchester*, 1937–42

Off. No.	Name(s)*	Owner	Gross Tons	Year Built
127379	*Chester W. Chapin*	New England Steamship Co.	2,688	1899
92830	(2) *Steel Pier* (1) *Miami*	Cape Cod Steamship Co.	1,775	1897
116712	(3) *Town of Hull* (1) *Shinnecock* (2) *Empire State*	Nantasket-Boston Steamboat Co.	1,402	1896
206501	*Rensselaer*	Trojan Steamship Corp.	2,690	1909
92294	(4) *Montauk* (1) *Montauk* (2) *King Edward* (3) *Forest City*	Clow & Nicholson Transportation Co.	418	1891
127281	(3) *Naugatuck* (1) *Cape Charles* (2) *Allan Joy*	Sound Steamship Lines	1,308	1898
206077	*Wauketa*	Sutton Line	543	1908

*The numbers preceding the vessel names signify the order in which the names progressed: at the top of the column is the name of the vessel during its ownership by B. B. Wills.

Whether negotiations were equally serious for all the vessels in table 4-1 is uncertain, but each was given consideration, however cursory. Wills himself traveled to Minnesota to inspect Clow and Nicholson's *Montauk* in late 1942, for instance. Earlier that year he had contacted the Cape Cod Steamship Company in Boston, by then the owner of *Steel Pier* (originally *Miami*), a vessel Wills had considered for Chapel Point service back in 1933, inquiring about her availability. Cape Cod Steamship quickly wired Wills an encouraging reply: "RE. STEEL PIER OUR DIRECTORS WILLING TO ENTERTAIN ANY REASONABLE OFFER."[13] But once again, nothing substantive developed, despite the urgency of replacing *Tolchester*.

Sutton Line's *Wauketa* had previously been owned in New York by Meseck Line and, before that, had worked on the Great Lakes for the

Detroit–Port Huron Steamship Company. The vessel actually steamed south to Baltimore and briefly operated for Tolchester Lines in 1942 under a charter arrangement of some sort. Wills never purchased her, though, and she soon moved to Newport News, Virginia, and to her final owner, the Chesapeake and Ohio Railway.

Ferryboats

Although Wills was unable to replace *Tolchester*, he was able to supplement her service. He accomplished this at first not with additional excursion-type vessels, but with an automobile-carrying ferryboat that Wills saw as the beginning of a year-round service across the Chesapeake. In June 1937, the same month the new company began running *Tolchester* in Baltimore–Tolchester excursion service, the Public Service Commission (PSC) of Maryland authorized Tolchester Lines to inaugurate a year-round ferryboat service over the same route.

Wills chartered the 1923-built double-ender *Chelsea* from the Reading Company and put her in service in November 1937. The state of Maryland agreed to help underwrite the new service with a fourteen-thousand-dollar annual subsidy. The Reading had used the 1,028-ton *Chelsea* between Philadelphia and a rail passenger terminal across the Delaware River in Camden, New Jersey.

Instead of running *Chelsea* over the full 27-mile route between Baltimore and Tolchester, Wills envisioned the ferryboat line as terminating at Bay Shore instead of downtown Baltimore. Bay Shore was 14 miles from downtown Baltimore at the entrance to Baltimore Harbor. Thus, instead of a two-hour, 27-mile cruise between Baltimore and Tolchester, the shorter ferry crossing would be 8 miles long and take only 45 minutes. Wills had identified three pieces of property in the Bay Shore area, any of which, he claimed, would make a fine terminal for his new ferryboat operation.

Excursion service between Baltimore and Tolchester Beach aboard *Tolchester*, on the other hand, was primarily geared to a clientele who reached the company's Light Street pier by trolley car; thus a downtown departure point was important, and the two-hour ride across the Bay regarded, simply, as part of a day's outing. The new ferry crossing, in contrast, was designed to serve the year-round needs of people driving their own automobiles to and from a variety of destinations. The remove of Bay Shore from downtown was as much an advantage to such travelers as proximity to the trolley cars was for excursionists heading for a day at the beach.

While awaiting approval from the state PSC to operate Tolchester–Bay Shore, Wills ran *Chelsea* over the longer Baltimore–Tolchester route, on which she could only make two daily round trips. Five would become the rule, however, once the new Bay Shore terminal was in service. Eventually, Wills planned to buy more ferryboats and operate even more service over the new route.[14]

The problem was, Wills never received authority to inaugurate Tolchester–Bay Shore service. His petition was denied by the Maryland PSC shortly after it was filed; the only cross-bay ferryboat service he was allowed to operate was over the full 27-mile Baltimore–Tolchester route.

Wills had originally planned to purchase *Chelsea* from the Reading Company and substantially upgrade the vessel. Passenger cabins on the main deck would be removed to expand the vehicle carrying capacity, and the vessel would be converted from coal fuel to oil with equipment liberated from the otherwise unusable ferryboat *Express*. Once the possibility of operating to and from Bay Shore was ruled out by the action of the PSC, though, Wills canceled his charter and returned *Chelsea* to the Reading. Nevertheless, he looked forward to an improved political climate in Annapolis some day in the future and the possibility of resurrecting the Bay Shore–Tolchester idea. With this in mind, Wills continued to operate a modified service for automobiles on the 27-mile Baltimore–Tolchester route, even after terminating his lease of *Chelsea*.

In late 1937, Wills took *Southport* out of Potomac River service for the Columbia Steamship Company, cut down her second deck forward of the pilothouse to give automobiles access to the main deck, installed a ramplike device at her bow, and made her the automobile-carrying component of his Baltimore–Tolchester service. As an automobile-carrying ferry, the diminutive *Southport* carried a mere *twelve* cars. Many felt that the structural alterations needed to permit the carrying of automobiles ruined the lines of what had been a classic-looking coastal steamboat.

Twelve cars per trip, and two round trips per day, meant that Wills had the capacity to carry just two dozen automobiles across the Chesapeake Bay in each direction over a day's time. So while Wills saw the potential that a cross-bay ferry service represented—and perhaps even foresaw the kind of traffic volumes later generated on summer weekends after the Chesapeake Bay Bridge was built—a ferry service that moved two dozen cars per day was little more than a token gesture, even given the limited number of registered automobiles around Baltimore in the late 1930s. Today, a single traffic lane on the Chesapeake Bay Bridge can handle twenty-four vehicles traveling at posted speed in less than two minutes.

A few years after *Chelsea* had been returned to the Reading Company and *Southport* reconfigured to handle automotive traffic over the full Baltimore–Tolchester route, the Maryland legislature took action that appeared to breathe new life into the Bay Shore terminal proposal. In April 1939 a onetime ten-thousand-dollar state subsidy was authorized to help get the venture under way, and B. B. Wills found himself in the market for a bona fide double-ended ferryboat.[15]

When the city of Baltimore had discontinued a cross-harbor ferry line between the foot of Broadway in Fells Point and Locust Point in January 1939, the municipal ferryboat *Howard W. Jackson* was declared surplus and put up for sale. In 1940 Wills purchased her for thirteen thousand dollar to have a proper vessel for the shorter cross-bay run out of Bay Shore. Schedules were even prepared showing the *Jackson* beginning her day's work each morning from the Tolchester pier in downtown Baltimore and making her first cross-bay trip from there, then

Southport, as converted into an automobile-carrying ferry for service between Baltimore and Tolchester Beach. Compare with photo of the same vessel on page 42. (Photograph by R. Loren Graham, courtesy of B. B. Wills family.)

ferrying over and back to Bay Shore four times during the day before making a final sail in the evening out of Tolchester and back to Baltimore.

But a Bay Shore–Tolchester ferryboat line would never be realized. *Howard W. Jackson* represents the first of many vessels that Wills would buy and then attempt to sell without ever operating in revenue service.

After World War II, Wills indulged in such "ship-brokering" activities deliberately and frequently. He even established a separate company called Boat Sales, Inc. to handle such transactions. When he purchased the *Howard W. Jackson* in 1940, though, Wills did so assuming that he would soon put the vessel into operation. He never did, however. In the end, he simply tried to get a good price for her from another ferryboat operator. At one time, the Norfolk County, Virginia, ferry people had an option to buy the *Jackson*, but when they learned how slow she was, they let the option expire. The steamboat twice caught fire in Baltimore while she was owned by Wills, and by the late 1940s, she had deteriorated so much that her only value was as scrap.[16]

Returning to the early days of Baltimore–Tolchester service under the house flag of Wills's new Tolchester Lines, a company goal continued to be the replacement of the aging *Tolchester*. While *Southport*'s advent on the route provided only minimal capacity for automotive traffic, it did serve to supplement *Tolchester* with additional passenger-carrying capacity and additional daily departures from each terminal. *Southport*, although still owned by Columbia Steamship and merely leased to Tolchester Lines, continued to work the service until 1941, when she was taken over by the federal government for war-related assignments. After the 1940 excursion season, however, Wills did finally obtain a bona fide excursion boat for Tolchester service, one that would turn out to be the most valuable—and versatile—a boat he ever owned.

Susquehanna *Becomes* Francis Scott Key

Built in Baltimore by C. Reeders and Sons in 1898 for Chesapeake Bay service, *Susquehanna* was a three-deck propeller boat with an iron hull driven by a two-cylinder compound engine. Originally owned by a predecessor company of the Tolchester Beach Improvement Company, the boat mainly worked the route between Baltimore and Port Deposit, Maryland, at the mouth of her namesake, the Susquehanna River.

By 1940, *Susquehanna* had migrated to New York, where she was doing general-purpose excursion work for Sound Steamship Lines.[17]

That year, Wills purchased the *Susquehanna* through the New York brokerage house of Cambell and Gardner. Notarizing the bill of sale was a young man named Francis J. Barry.[18] The young entrepreneur later played an important role in the demise of Wills's excursion empire in New York City (see chapter 6).

Wills hoped that *Susquehanna* would fill a variety of assignments in his expanding excursion boat empire. While she clearly was not *the* vessel he had long been seeking as a permanent replacement for *Tolchester,* the name he gave his latest acquisition, *Francis Scott Key,* clearly suggests that her primary assignments would be out of the port of Baltimore. Sailing between Baltimore and Tolchester, a vessel steams past the very spot where Francis Scott Key, the man, was imprisoned aboard a British ship during the War of 1812. From this point, "by the dawn's early light," Key had looked out and seen the "broad stripes and bright stars," of his country's flag flying from nearby Fort McHenry and later wrote a memorable poem describing the experience. Most of *Francis Scott Key*'s early work for Wills turned out to be on the Potomac, though, where she was frequently used for military-related charter trips between Washington and points south of the city.

Loss of Tolchester

Before the 1941 season got under way in Baltimore, Wills experienced a major setback, the first of several that would befall him over the years. On May 15, 1941, as *Tolchester* was being made ready for another summer of work, she caught fire at Light Street Pier 16 in Baltimore and suffered substantial damage. It was an especially nasty fire that destroyed not merely *Tolchester,* but also several nearby Light Street piers, plus a barge. Eight alarms were sounded and 150 firefighters were needed to bring the blaze under control. But for their swift action, the entire Baltimore Inner Harbor might well have gone up in flames. Ten firemen sustained injuries.

The day before the fire, *Tolchester* had been brought back to her Light Street pier after an annual inspection at Maryland Drydock. She was scheduled to open the season on May 30. *Southport,* her automobile-carrying running mate on the Baltimore–Tolchester run, was moored close by *Tolchester* when the fire broke out, but was pulled to safety with little or no damage.

At first there was talk of rebuilding, but Wills soon realized that the fire had inflicted far too much damage on the fifty-three-year-old steamboat to make that practical. Although her iron hull was salvaged and sold off for additional years of work as an unpowered barge, the veteran excursion boat was finished. The matter of finding a replacement excursion boat for *Tolchester* now escalated from a mere corporate desire, as it had been since Wills took over the operation in 1937, into an operational necessity.

Tolchester Lines quickly obtained a veteran Chesapeake Bay propeller steamboat called *Mohawk*. Earlier, as *Anne Arundel*, she had worked out of Baltimore, first for the Weems Line, then for other companies. Some researchers suggested that Wills first leased *Mohawk* and shortly thereafter purchased her.[19] Other sources, in particular a letter from Charles Efford, the president and general manager of the Rock Creek Development Company—*Mohawk*'s owner—suggest that there was no lease transaction, but simply a direct sale.[20] In any event, *Mohawk* went to work for Wills after *Tolchester* was lost, and Wills also dispatched *Francis Scott Key* north from Washington to Baltimore. Between them,

Mohawk, formerly *Anne Arundel*, one of the vessels that Wills purchased as a replacement for *Tolchester*. (Photograph by R. Loren Graham, courtesy of B. B. Wills family.)

the two steamboats exceeded the carrying-capacity of *Tolchester* during the 1941 excursion season.

In the fall of 1941, after the regular season was over, Wills sent *Francis Scott Key* south to generate additional income during the otherwise inactive winter months. The service he had in mind involved afternoon excursions out of Miami. Promoted as trips to the Florida Keys, the boat rides were in fact little more than tours of Biscayne Bay with a return in ample time for a moonlight dance cruise in the evening. Wills contracted with a local Miami electrical company to prepare a double-sided, four-by-eleven-foot neon sign to promote the service. The dark blue sign with white painted letters featured neon tubing illuminated in green, rose, and white. Neon, of course, would one day become a genuine form of artistic expression, especially in the art deco world of Miami and Miami Beach. In 1941, though, it was just another sign.

Francis Scott Key was in Miami on December 7, 1941, when the United States was plunged into World War II. She finished up her winter assignment there, but when it came time to return north in late March, the threat of enemy submarines made a normal coastal journey outside Cape Hatteras a risky proposition. As a result, the vessel steamed north that spring via the Intracoastal Waterway, with published accounts at the time claiming that she was the largest vessel ever to travel any appreciable length of that protected passage. Wills himself was sufficiently impressed by the trip that he spoke to the press about it—something he almost never did. He even went so far as to suggest that the Intracoastal Waterway was a rare national resource that could be used to transport all kinds of bulk commodities if only the country would design and build a fleet of pocket-sized cargo vessels that could navigate through the waterway's restricted confines.[21] Although he did not say so, Wills undoubtedly had himself in mind as a potential operator of such cargo vessels. In any event, in the spring of 1942, when *Francis Scott Key* steamed north from Florida, Nazi submarines were beginning to extract an awful toll on Allied merchant shipping off the East Coast.

Tolchester Lines continued to operate throughout the war years. *Mohawk* was requisitioned by the federal government for military service in the Hampton Roads area early in the war, but *Francis Scott Key* was not and consequently was available for Chesapeake Bay service during the 1942 and 1943 seasons. In addition, as noted earlier, Wills chartered *Wauketa* from the Sutton Line in New York, and she too worked Baltimore–Tolchester in 1942.

As he had done with *Potomac* and the Washington–Colonial Beach route, Wills put forth a plausible enough case to federal officials that the cross-bay route between Baltimore and Tolchester provided needed transportation service, in this instance for shipyard workers who lived on the Eastern Shore. He was thus allocated quantities of Bunker C fuel oil to keep the service in operation. In practice, however, the fuel rations were used almost entirely to make regular excursion-style trips between Baltimore and Tolchester Beach, not any kind of specialized trips to local shipyards. Apparently, though, *Francis Scott Key* did run an expanded Baltimore season in 1942 and 1943. If any significant number of shipyard workers used these crossings for commuter purposes, they did so very unobtrusively and would have had to ride the trolley car between the Light Street pier where the Tolchester boats docked and the shipyards where they worked.

By contrast, Wilson Line received no wartime fuel allocations for its Baltimore–Seaside Park service, so it was suspended for the duration. This excursion route would never again be resumed, as matters subsequently turned out. Wilson's *Dixie* and *Bay Belle* were nevertheless both deployed in genuine commuter service directly to various shipyards in and around Baltimore, but under the terms of charter contracts. Fuel for such purposes was readily available.

Because *Francis Scott Key* was permitted to steam outside Baltimore Harbor during the war, she was issued recognition codes by the U.S. Coast Guard since she was subject to challenge by armed vessels patrolling the Chesapeake Bay. The codes were delivered by hand to the steamboat's master in an envelope marked "DO NOT OPEN UNTIL CLEAR OF THE DOCK." The identification codes were to be communicated either by signal flag or by flashing light, but *never* by radio. As an example, one set of codes instructed that if *Francis Scott Key* were challenged between 0000 hours on April 13 and 2350 hours on April 15, 1943, the steamboat should show "top flag" *x-ray*, "middle pennant" *nine*, "bottom flag" *roger*, and "reply letter" *charlie*. At the bottom of the document specifying these codes were these words: "THIS PAPER MUST NOT FALL INTO ENEMY HANDS; CONFIDENTIAL."[22]

Although these identification instructions were to be either returned to the federal government or destroyed upon their expiration, a single set has been retained among the Wills Papers. The same form that was issued to *Francis Scott Key* for wartime trips on the Chesapeake Bay was also issued to merchant ships making ocean voyages to distant countries. One of the options for returning the instructions at journey's end specifies delivering them to the nearest British or American consulate upon reaching a foreign port. Perhaps *Francis Scott Key*'s master was unable to find any such consulates in Tolchester Beach.

Francis Scott Key shuttled back and forth between Washington and Baltimore during the early war years. In August 1942, for instance, she was operating on the Potomac under charter to the Adjutant General's School of the U.S. Army, ferrying military personnel between downtown Washington and Fort Washington, Maryland, approximately 12 miles apart on the Potomac River. During *Francis Scott Key*'s absence from Baltimore, *Wauketa* worked the Tolchester route alone.

It was in the midst of World War II, though, when Wills finally obtained a permanent and reasonably adequate replacement vessel for *Tolchester*. By this time he had developed a number of business contacts among the various operators of excursion boats in New York Harbor, and it was out of New York that he purchased a sidewheel steamboat named *Bear Mountain* from the Mandalay Line.

Bear Mountain had been built at Harlan and Hollingsworth in Wilmington, Delaware, in 1902 as *William G. Payne*. Eventually she became *Highlander* and was running in excursion service out of New York for the McAllister Steamboat Company. The McAllister operation was dealt a cruel blow in April 1924, however, when its fleet of three excursion boats and one passenger-carrying barge was destroyed by fire in winter quarters at West 155th Street and the Hudson River in upper Manhattan. Of the quartet, only *Highlander* was deemed worthy of rebuilding. She emerged from a shipyard in Kearney, New Jersey, in early 1925 with an all-new superstructure and a brand new name, *Bear Mountain*.

The rebuilt *Bear Mountain* became a modest favorite in New York excursion service, primarily running up the Hudson to a popular picnic grounds and her namesake park, Bear Mountain. On June 13, 1927, when New York Harbor staged a mighty welcome for aviator Charles Lindbergh after his valiant conquest of the North Atlantic, *Bear Mountain* was among the vessels that escorted Lindbergh to the tip of lower Manhattan and the start of a ticker-tape parade up lower Broadway.[23]

Bear Mountain continued to operate for the McAllisters or the Mandalay Line, a McAllister subsidiary, on into the early years of World War II. Wartime fuel restrictions impacted Mandalay's operation, though, and the company welcomed the opportunity to sell the vessel to Wills at the start of the 1943 excursion season. The sidewheeler made an undoubtedly risky coastal passage from Sandy Hook to Cape May. She then headed up the Delaware and on to Baltimore via the Chesapeake and Delaware Canal, where she was quickly put to work on the Baltimore–Tolchester route. While *Bear Mountain* was operated by Tolchester Lines, she was technically owned by Wills's Potomac River Line and leased to Tolchester under the terms of a "bareboat" charter.

Under a bareboat charter, the chartering entity supplies the crew and operates the vessel as if it were its own. In a more general charter arrangement, the owner supplies both vessel and crew and retains control of routine operations. Bareboat chartering and other arrangements between companies fully controlled by B. B. Wills became even more common as his excursion boat empire expanded.

Wills purportedly intended to rename *Bear Mountain* to reflect better her new service, with *Tolchester* being the most likely designation. But he never did rename the boat, and for all her years on the Baltimore–Tolchester run plus a few afterward on the Potomac, *Bear Mountain* carried the name of a destination as distinctively "New York" in the world of excursion boats as would be Times Square or the Statue of Liberty in a larger context.

Wills was pleased with *Bear Mountain*, although he did not welcome her arrival on the Tolchester route as enthusiastically as he had *Chester W. Chapin* a few years earlier. *Bear Mountain* remained Tolchester Lines' mainstay for six excursion seasons, 1943 through 1948, and enjoyed a relatively unremarkable tenure. One exception was a untoward incident during a late Sunday return trip to Baltimore in June 1946.

Capt. William T. Elliott was in command of *Bear Mountain* that evening. After leaving Tolchester Beach a little after 9:30 P.M. with 983 passengers aboard, the vessel's right paddlewheel became tangled in a piece of floating debris in the middle of the Chesapeake Bay. The big steamboat was instantly and completely disabled.

The boat lacked any kind of ship-to-shore radio equipment. Captain Elliott first tried to signal a passing yacht to request help, but to no avail. Finally the doughty Baltimore–Love Point ferryboat *Philadelphia* ("Smoky Joe" of the Pennsylvania Railroad) happened past. Once she came alongside, Elliott asked her skipper to contact the Coast Guard once he returned to Baltimore.

Meanwhile, the clock kept ticking, *Bear Mountain* kept drifting, and it was after midnight by the time "Smoky Joe" reached port. The ferryboat captain telephoned G. G. Huppmann, the longtime general manager of Tolchester Lines, who first tried to dispatch a commercial towboat to rescue his stranded steamer. When towboat companies were unable to assemble crews at that hour of the morning, he called the Coast Guard. They sent patrol boat No. CG-85009 to the spot where the ferry captain had reported *Bear Mountain* disabled, but search as they might, the Coast Guardsmen could find no excursion boat.

Bear Mountain, of course, continued to drift from where she had earlier encountered "Smoky Joe." Captain Elliott eventually dropped anchor off Swan Point to await help. Wisely, Purser Robert Francis discontinued the sale of beer aboard the vessel immediately after the accident. The sale of soft drinks, sandwiches, and hot dogs nonetheless continued until about two o'clock in the morning. Then, with all supplies exhausted, ice water became the only available form of refreshment. The passengers approached the whole business with more than a little good humor, particularly once it became apparent that *Bear Mountain* was in no danger. The band kept playing until six o'clock in the morning—one is left to wonder if "Nearer My God to Thee" was in the repertoire—and many people supposedly warded off the chill of the night by dancing until dawn. Some passengers tried to sleep, but few succeeded.

Morning saw a Coast Guard air-sea rescue plane dispatched on a search mission, and when it located *Bear Mountain* riding at anchor it radioed the steamer's position to CG-85009. At 11:05 on Monday morning, the diesel-powered tugboats *Hustler* and *Blanche T. Rogers* of the Harbor Towing Company maneuvered *Bear Mountain* into her berth at Light Street Pier 16. The long voyage home was finally over.

Repairs to the steamboat *Bear Mountain* were minimal and easily made in a few hours; the big sidewheeler headed out on a moonlight cruise that very evening after she was declared seaworthy by the Coast Guard. Many disembarking passengers that morning voiced concern that a vessel such as *Bear Mountain* was not equipped with some kind of radio-telephone. They were not at all assuaged when Comdr. Alfred W. Kabernagel of the U.S. Coast Guard in Baltimore told them that "it is not required by law that vessels like the *Bear Mountain* carry either telephones or wireless. Where such equipment is provided it is because the owner so elects and not to meet any regulation that has been imposed."[24] The owner of *Bear Mountain*, obviously, did not so elect.

At the end of the 1948 season, Tolchester Lines scheduled a season finale for *Bear Mountain,* an all-day, 200-mile cruise from Baltimore to Washington with passengers whisked back to their point of origin by motor coach after a full day on the Chesapeake Bay and the Potomac River. Fare for the twelve-hour trip was $6.00, including the return bus ride back to Baltimore, $2.50 additional if a passenger wished to indulge in a Maryland half-chicken dinner en route.

When *Bear Mountain* set out from Light Street Pier 16 in Baltimore for Washington on Sunday, September 19, 1948, though, it was not just a routine post-season trip. It was more an example of what the oceangoing cruise industry today calls a "repositioning" cruise. *Bear Mountain* spent the 1948–49 winter in Washington. The following spring, 1949, would see her replacing Wills's beloved *Potomac* in service out of the nation's capital, with yet a different vessel taking *Bear Mountain*'s place on the Baltimore–Tolchester run.

The Management Style of B. B. Wills

B. B. Wills did not practice a management style that one might find in a college textbook for Management 101. His was not an exemplary practice of delegating authority, empowering subordinates, distinguishing between long-term policy and day-to-day operations, setting a strategic vision, or attending to other similarly lofty matters. To understand Wills's style, one must view him as the principal of a small industrial enterprise with satellite operations in various locations. Wills, working out of his Washington headquarters, emerges as a man with an insatiable appetite for involving himself in the most minute of details.

A good example of Wills's micromanagement style is the correspondence between Wills and Edward Mitchell, his resident manager in Boston, in 1945. By then, Wills had expanded his excursion enterprise to Boston Harbor (see chapter 5). The men were discussing a differential of a few dollars in a monthly statement rendered by a Massachusetts soft drink supplier. "I think I have the Coke man over a barrel," Mitchell felt compelled to report in writing to his boss 450 miles away at one point in the protracted saga.[25]

For Wills, such concern with detail was no exception to the rule—it *was* the rule. Wills's addiction, of course, was a feverish desire to control costs, something critical in an industry whose growth potential was, at best, severely limited. Although the correspondence between Mitchell and Wills can be seen as Wills's obsession with minor detail, it could also be viewed in a more positive light. By focusing attention on a specific detail like the Coca-Cola purchases, Wills the executive was issuing a general policy directive to his field officer in Boston. The directive was that the survival of the Boston operation demanded careful attention to every item of expense.

Did Wills indulge in excessive and pointless meddling in minute details that a chief executive would be better advised to ignore? Or was this his way of making the point that cost control is a very important corporate priority? The truth probably lies somewhere between these extreme interpretations. The fact remains, though, that B. B. Wills kept his hand firmly on the corporate tiller.

One area of business that was always retained in Washington was insurance coverage for the fleet. As mentioned in chapter 2, insurance premiums varied depending on whether an excursion boat was in actual revenue service, or laid up awaiting the return of another season of work. The insurance term for a policy to cover an out-of-service vessel was "port risk," and Wills was scrupulous in the extreme in saving every possible penny by converting policies from active operation to port risk immediately upon the end of an excursion season. Although he was perfectly honest in reporting when a vessel had concluded its active season or when it was expected to resume operations the next spring, he was just as precise in firing off letters to his insurance agent seeking refunds or credits if a given vessel was delayed by even a few days in shifting from inactive to active status.

Loan repayment was another area that helps paint a picture of Wills's management style. In his various agreements to pay a vendor or supplier over time and under some particular set of terms, Wills was continually seeking to renegotiate such agreements. He was often successful, generally citing unusual or unexpected business conditions as contributing to his supposed inability to meet the schedule originally agreed to. As noted previously, he managed to back away from his original plan for paying off the mortgage held by the Jesuits on the Chapel Point property. His original agreement with the Lukens Dredging and Contracting Corporation for clearing a channel and a turning basin in the Port Tobacco River called for the bill to be paid in full by July 1, 1931. Two years later, in July 1933, a promissory note for $4,803.40 remained unpaid and had to be extended even further.[26] The same thing happened with respect to paying off the mortgage on *Potomac*, which was held by the Hudson River Day Line.[27] The loan was eventually paid off, but not according to the schedule Wills originally specified.

None of this is to suggest that B. B. Wills failed to meet his obligations or was deceptive when he entered into business agreements. He simply took advantage of every opportunity that came his way to negotiate better arrangements with his creditors during the term of an obligation. The only outright default documented in the Wills Papers involved a purely technical matter having to do with certain taxes and fees due to the District of Columbia and the state of Maryland by the Potomac River Line in 1944. By failing to pay in a timely manner, the corporation's charter was actually in default, and the Potomac River Line "ceased to exist" for a period in the middle of an otherwise continuous period of operation. The charter was quickly restored to good status on May 5, 1945, when the back taxes were paid.[28]

Another aspect of Wills's management style is not that he formed so many different maritime companies over the years, but how he arranged to lease and purchase vessels from one company to another. For example, in the official minutes of the annual meeting of the board of directors of one Wills-owned company, a formal motion authorized the president of the company (Benjamin B. Wills) to negotiate and arrange for the bareboat charter of a particular excursion vessel from another company, under whatever terms and conditions the other company's president set forth. This arrangement seems straightforward until one realizes that the president of the *other* company is also Benjamin B. Wills. A similar pattern emerged with respect to one Wills-owned company selling an excursion boat to another, with the selling company holding a mortgage— often a very large one—on the vessel.

These sales transactions may have been part of a strategy to "add value" to the overall worth of B. B. Wills's various holdings. On at least one occasion, a Wills-controlled company tried to discount (i.e., sell) a mortgage that it held on a vessel owned by another Wills-controlled company to a conventional lending institution. The bank in question quickly declined, pointing out that the sale price of the vessel, and the outstanding balance of the mortgage, bore no relationship to the true market value of the asset in question.[29]

Another unusual business practice of this entrepreneur was a penchant for selling vessels to bona fide second parties (companies that he neither owned nor controlled) without truly "letting go" of the boats. Several times, Wills negotiated the sale of an excursion boat to another party, but held a large first mortgage on the vessel, a mortgage of such detailed specification with respect to rights retained by the seller that it would be difficult to characterize the transaction as a true sale in any normal sense. In some agreements, for example, the new owners could not make any structural or mechanical alterations to the vessel. In another agreement, the new "owner" could not even change the vessel's name. Wills was acting, of course, to protect his own interest and to ensure that should a buyer default in meeting scheduled mortgage payments, a repossessed vessel would not be changed or altered. Business considerations aside, Wills loved to hang onto things, even after he had supposedly let them go.

A final aspect of how Wills managed his excursion enterprise involves the role of elected public officials. His cultivation of politicians appears to have been more irregular than systematic over the years.

After World War II, a presidential reorganization proposed allowing the U.S. Coast Guard to retain certain regulatory control over merchant shipping that it had assumed from civilian agencies during the war. Wills fired off a number of letters to members of Congress in opposition to this proposal.[30] His overtures were in vain, though, and the Coast Guard assumed permanent responsibility for functions that in earlier years had been assigned to the U.S. Steamboat Inspection Service and successor agencies.

Wills also contributed campaign funds to various political candidates, although his donations were evidently neither frequent nor generous.[31] Perhaps the most amusing correspondence between B. B. Wills and an elected public official dates to 1942, when the state's attorney for Prince George's County in Maryland wrote him with an unusual request:

> Dear Jack [Wills's nickname]:
> You will probably recall that several years ago you were good enough to get me a mattress and spring from the Simmons people in Baltimore at a substantial discount.
> Now that my family has increased I find myself in the market for several more. As I remember the last transaction, I believe the discount was 50%, which means a considerable saving, and I am wondering whether you would be good enough to repeat the favor. If so, do you happen to have a catalog showing the different sizes, colors, etc.? I remember that you had one last time.
> Trusting things are going well, and with best regards, I am... [32]

Wills quickly replied that he contacted the mattress people and learned that wartime shortages had reduced their production to virtually nothing, but that he would keep his eye out for something appropriate and be back in contact shortly.[33]

The writer of this letter was A. Gwynn Bowie, a personal friend of B. B. Wills and one of the incorporators of the Potomac River Line back in 1934. The idea that an elected official would make such a request on the formal letterhead of his public office helps characterize the mores of the time and shows the kind of relationships a businessman like Wills comfortably maintained with public officials.[34]

From the evidence available, B. B. Wills was likely neither a polished nor a skilled political operative. He probably enjoyed his greatest success in enlisting elected officials to support his activities during the early days of the Tolchester operation, when the Maryland legislature twice voted subsidies to help support his trans-bay ferryboat services. On the other hand, his lobbying efforts for favorable business legislation in Massachusetts after World War II would be totally ineffective. Wills also realized much frustration in his dealings with the Interstate Commerce Commission.

Finally, a 1964 letter typifies Wills's bold, take-charge style and deserves at least honorable mention in any all-time chutzpah competition. It was written by the Old Timer to the National Car Rental System. One of Wills's employees apparently had hired a car "a number of months ago." Not only was the car involved in a minor traffic accident, it also remained parked on Tolchester Lines' pier in Baltimore for all those months, totally forgotten and never returned to National Car Rental. Once he discovered the car parked on the pier, Wills fired off a letter to the company explaining all of this and concluding, "Normally, you would pay one dollar a day storage. Now, in view of the accident we are waiving any storage charges."[35] Furthermore, if National would please send a man over to the pier, Tolchester Lines would be happy to give him the keys to the car. Whether National Car Rental was equally generous in waiving criminal prosecution against Wills and his company for grand theft/auto remains unknown.

From his office in Washington, B. B. Wills was an executive with an appetite for getting into the most minute details of his various excursion boat operations. Whether such a trait is seen as desirable or otherwise in the abstract, in the real world of excursion boat operations circa 1930 and 1940, it may have been the only kind of management style that enabled the Wills empire to survive and reach the dimensions that it eventually did.

CHAPTER FIVE

Nanny Boats out of Boston

The Nantasket–Boston Steamboat Company was an old and venerable Massachusetts institution that could trace its beginnings to 1818, a mere eleven years after Robert Fulton's historic voyage up the Hudson River in 1807 made steam navigation a practical reality. In 1942, when the company was a robust 124 years old, B. B. Wills made an effort to add it to his expanding excursion boat empire.

Early History

Nantasket–Boston Steamboat began as a provider of basic point-to-point transportation between Boston and a number of communities primarily to the south of the city during the nineteenth century. By the twentieth, the company had evolved into a seasonal excursion boat line whose principal destination was an amusement park in the town of Hull at a place called Nantasket Beach. A small percentage of the line's later-day clientele were commuters, bound from seaside homes in Hull to offices in downtown Boston and back, but by the late 1930s the vast majority of the line's customers were seasonal day excursionists heading for relaxing hours of surf and sand at Nantasket Beach, the thrills and excitement on the rides at Paragon Park, or sometimes both.[1]

Compared to other excursion boat services in America, a ride between Boston and Nantasket was relatively short in distance (12 miles) and short in duration (a little more than an hour under normal conditions). As a result, the pattern that developed on the Boston-Nantasket route called for frequent departures from early morning on into the evening hours, with a fleet of three or four steamboats normally assigned to the service. If passengers missed the boat they had planned to catch, they did not need to worry: there would be another an hour or so later. Except, of course, if they missed the last trip out of Nantasket back to Boston in the evening. Then they were in a bit of trouble!

Like so many other waterborne transportation enterprises, in the years leading up to World War II the Nantasket–Boston Steamboat Company found itself sailing troubled financial waters. Annual patronage levels of almost a million passengers as recently as 1937 had fallen to a mere six hundred thousand by 1940. Bostonians, of course, were starting to use automobiles more, and steamboats less, for their summer trips to Nantasket. Furthermore, the growing popularity of the automobile not only changed the way people traveled to and from Nantasket, but also made destinations that were farther from Boston, such as Cape Cod, accessible for even a short one-day summer outing.[2] As the Great Depression deepened in the late 1930s, prospects grew even gloomier for the Nantasket–Boston Steamboat Company.

The excursion season of 1941 saw an important change for the financially troubled company. After the passage of permissive state legislation in early 1941, residents of Hull voted at a town meeting to purchase the wharf at Nantasket from the company, thereby providing Nantasket–Boston Steamboat with a badly needed cash infusion to settle a few outstanding bills. The action also freed the company of any responsibility for, and expense of, repairing and maintaining the wharf. The state legislation authorized Hull to borrow up to $130,000 to finance the acquisition of the property; following this action, Federal Judge Elisha H. Brewster approved a reorganization plan for the troubled company so that it could take advantage of the newly available resources.[3]

While well-intentioned, the steps taken by the town of Hull in 1941 were totally insufficient to restore the company to a sound financial condition. More fundamental change would be needed before the steamboats could emerge from winter quarters for the next excursion season, 1942.

Unfortunately, the year 1942 would also see the imposition of stringent control measures on any passenger boat operations in and around Boston Harbor by the U.S. Coast Guard as part of the overall war effort. Under these port rules, so-called, excursion boats could continue to sail between Boston and Nantasket, but only during specified daylight hours and subject to any short-term suspension of service that the Coast Guard might choose to impose. In addition, passengers were prohibited from taking photographs or even using binoculars aboard the company's excursion boats. Soon enough, the most popular and direct route between Boston and Nantasket, which navigated through a passage called Hull Gut, was closed off entirely by the Coast Guard because of its proximity to newly installed submarine nets. Nantasket-bound excursion boats had to sail a slightly longer and roundabout course. Fuel rationing would have represented yet another barrier to normal operations during the war, except that the Nantasket–Boston company's vessels were coal burners. Fortunately, coal was not subject to the same wartime restrictions as oil for such purposes as excursion boat operations.

Enter B. B. Wills, Round One

It was precisely at this moment of uncertainty between the 1941 and 1942 excursion seasons that B. B. Wills first appeared on the Boston Harbor scene offering to purchase the assets of the troubled Nantasket–Boston Steamboat Company for thirty-five thousand dollars, in cash. Wills, however, was not thinking of preserving and continuing the existing level of Boston-Nantasket service. Of the four steamboats the company owned, Wills wanted to transfer two, and possibly as many as three, to his other operations, primarily Baltimore-Tolchester. He planned to leave but a single vessel working the Boston-Nantasket run, at least for the duration. Given Coast Guard restrictions, Wills argued, it would be impossible to run a full and typical schedule between Boston and Nantasket no matter who owned the boats, so why not accept his offer, take the money, and let him move a few of the vessels south? Wills's Boston attorney, Philip White, assured everyone who had an interest in the Boston-Nantasket service that more normal service would be resumed once the war was over.[4]

The older company was in no position to dictate the terms of its own liquidation. When trustees of the bankrupt company voted to accept Wills's offer, the sale appeared to be going forward. Wills made a down payment of five thousand dollars to secure the deal, and in early 1942 in federal court in Springfield, Massachusetts, Judge Brewster acted favorably on a petition filed by the trustees to sell the property to Wills. Wills then forwarded a thirty-thousand-dollar certified check to White to complete the transaction.[5]

New Englanders, though, have a reputation for being a protective lot who dislike seeing their hallowed traditions disrupted, especially by *outsiders*. So when an alternative offer suddenly materialized that would mean the fleet could stay in New England waters, another federal judge, George C. Sweeney, overruled Judge Brewster's earlier action and put his seal of approval on the new proposal. In doing so, he was also saying "no" to the Wills transaction, which Wills had every reason to believe was signed, sealed and delivered. Except that it was not.

The competing offer—also for thirty-five thousand dollars—had come from Joseph Stone, whose father, David Stone, was the owner of Paragon Park. Some creditors then argued that it would be better to put the whole company on the auction block and realize whatever cash the assets would yield, but Judge Sweeney doubted that such a sale would bring in any more than the thirty-five thousand dollars that Stone was prepared to pay. Wills's offer for the same amount also buttressed the judge's position, and the Stone proposal included a reasonable enough assurance that steamboat service between Boston and Nantasket would be maintained. The sale to Stone went through, Wills got his money back, and under Stone's ownership the line continued to call itself the Nantasket–Boston Steamboat Company.[6]

In his bid for the steamboat company, Stone had promised to maintain service over the old route to whatever extent the Coast Guard's wartime restrictions permitted. The promise was fortuitous; when gasoline and tire rationing soon became a way of life, the old steamboats would become essential for the survival of the Stone family's Paragon Park. War-related construction work adjacent to the shipyards in nearby Quincy also promised even further disruptions for automobile travel to and from Nantasket.

Stone would quickly discover that the Coast Guard–imposed port rules in Boston were very real. For the 1942 excursion season, only two of the company's four steamboats, *Allerton* and *Nantasket*, were put in service. Both were propeller-driven overnight boats that had formerly steamed on the Hudson River. The Nantasket company had purchased the boats after a tragic fire on Thanksgiving Day in 1929 destroyed all but one of its own fleet. The company's other two vessels—sidewheelers *Mayflower* and *Town of Hull*—remained tied up for the 1942 season. The wooden-hulled *Mayflower* was the sole Nantasket vessel to survive the 1929 fire.

Another wartime change involved where vessels were permitted to dock in Boston. Nantasket boats had long departed from Rowes Wharf on Atlantic Avenue, a short walk from South Station. Because Rowes Wharf had been taken over by the U.S. Army for the duration, the Nantasket–Boston Steamboat Company had to shift its operations to nearby India Wharf, a few blocks further north.

Wartime affairs sometimes caused mysterious interruptions in the excursion service. During the summer of 1943, Capt. Jack Watson was forced by the Coast Guard to halt the steamer *Nantasket* in the middle of an otherwise routine trip from Boston to Nantasket. All 350 passengers aboard were ordered below deck and had to remain there for over five hours until the Coast Guard allowed the steamer to get under way again. Since it was too late to continue on to the beach Captain Watson headed back to Boston and everyone had his or her fare refunded.

The Steamboat Town of Hull

Although rebuffed in his effort to acquire the entire Nantasket–Boston fleet and take over the operation in 1942, Wills pressed forward with an effort to purchase one of the company's four steamboats, the 1898-built sidewheeler *Town of Hull*. He saw *Town of Hull* as a potential replacement for *Tolchester*, especially after the latter caught fire before the start of the 1941 season. On September 7, 1942, for instance, Wills wrote to Moran Towing and Transport in New York asking if they could tow

Empire State in New York in 1933. The vessel later became the Boston–Nantasket Steamboat Company's *Town of Hull*. (Photograph from author's collection from Steeplechase Amusement Company.)

Town of Hull from her winter quarters in Nantasket to Baltimore.[7] Joseph H. Moran II, secretary of the towing firm, wrote back to Wills on September 10 quoting a price of six hundred dollars a day for what would likely be a four-day tow, but advising, "Our tug will not be able to get into Nantasket Beach, and the services of an assisting tug to tow the steamer to deep water in Boston Harbor will be for your account."[8] Earlier in 1942 Wills had contacted the Combustion Engineering Company of New York about that firm's conducting a survey of *Town of Hull's* boilers and other equipment relative to "getting the S.S. *Town of Hull* in commission by June 15."[9]

Town of Hull was an interesting vessel that might have made an excellent replacement for *Tolchester* assuming that Wills's perennial requirement for an oversized dance floor aboard his excursion boats could be realized. Built as *Shinnecock* for the Long Island Railroad in 1898, she worked an overnight route between New York and Shelter Island for many years before becoming a Manhattan–Coney Island day excursion boat in 1932 under the name *Empire State*.[10] Sidewheel-propelled and driven by a two-cylinder inclined engine, she was brought to New England by the Nantasket–Boston company in 1936 and christened *Town of Hull* after the residents of that community conducted a subscription drive to purchase stock in the steamboat company and to help underwrite the acquisition. The later 1941 wharf purchase apparently was not the first time that citizens of Hull initiated civic action to help stabilize steamboat service between their community and Boston.

Some ambiguity exists concerning the precise ownership status of *Town of Hull* during this period. *Merchant Vessels of the United States* shows her as owned by the Nantasket–Boston Steamboat Company from 1936 onward. In several letters written in 1942, however, B. B. Wills speaks of her as being owned by the David Feinburg Company of Medford, Massachusetts.[11] One possibility is that during the time that Stone owned the company, various vessels might have been pledged as collateral to raise working capital for the overall operation. If it were such a mortgage holder, the David Feinburg Company could have been regarded as *Town of Hull's* de facto owner. This, however, is merely speculation.

Whatever the situation, *Town of Hull* never sailed for Tolchester Lines or for anyone else, for that matter. In the fall of 1944, a vicious Atlantic hurricane made its way up the coast, tore the vessel from her moorings in Pemberton, and sent her crashing onto the rocks of Peddocks Island. The fleet of the Nantasket–Boston Steamboat Company was thus reduced to three boats, *Allerton*, *Nantasket*, and *Mayflower*.[12]

Enter B. B. Wills, Round Two

Toward the end of World War II, B. B. Wills made another effort to add Nantasket–Boston service to his growing excursion boat empire. This time he was successful.

The Stone family, while recognizing the absolute importance of continued steamboat service for the economic survival of Paragon Park, decided that they did not want to continue the actual operation of a steamboat company. In late 1944, after three seasons of ownership and operation, the Stones sold the company and its boats to B. B. Wills. Through a subsidiary company he had earlier established in Baltimore called Maryland Boat, Wills took title to the three vessels, *Allerton*, *Nantasket*, and *Mayflower*.[13] In early 1945 Wills formed a new entity, the Nantasket Boat Line, and when seasonal excursion boat service resumed that summer between Boston and Nantasket, it was under the auspices of Wills's new company.

Certificate for one share of stock issued by Nantasket Boat Line in 1945 to Gerald E. Bruen.

The first meeting of the incorporators of the Nantasket Boat Line was held in Boston on June 9, 1945. The three incorporators—Gerald E. Bruen, Victor H. Petersen, and Wills—quickly nominated themselves as the new corporation's board of directors and elected Wills its president. An early action of the board was to authorize the issuance of one hundred shares of capital stock, with one share allocated to Bruen, one to Petersen, and the remaining ninety-eight to Wills. The board also elected Wills's wife, Gertrude, as vice president of Nantasket Boat Line.[14]

Gerald Bruen was a Boston attorney who would handle legal matters for Nantasket Boat. He had been counsel to the selectmen of the town of Hull in 1942 when Wills's earlier effort to purchase the company was rebuffed. Not at that first meeting but shortly thereafter, Edward F. Mitchell of Boston was hired to manage the Nantasket Boat Line. Mitchell remained associated with Wills and his various excursion boat operations for the next two decades.

Because it took Wills some months to set up routine business procedures for the newly formed Nantasket Boat Line, on into the first excursion season of 1945, the company was actually run as if it were part of Maryland Boat. Payroll and other disbursements were made with Maryland Boat checks drawn on Baltimore banks, for instance. In early 1945, Wills contracted with the Boston office of Peat, Marwick and Mitchell to set up books and other business procedures for Nantasket Boat, but he soon grew unhappy with their progress and even more unhappy with their fees. He terminated the contract in late July and sent his own man up from Washington to finish the job. All of this irregularity caused the Internal Revenue Service to raise some questions about Nantasket Boat's 1945 tax return, but Wills satisfied the IRS, and the return was eventually accepted as filed.

Also in July of that year, the Nantasket Boat Line's board of directors voted to purchase the steamer *Nantasket* from Maryland Boat for thirty thousand dollars, payable over five years with 4 percent interest on the unpaid balance. *Allerton* and *Mayflower* remained under Maryland Boat ownership and were leased to Nantasket Boat for service. Of the three boats, the wooden-hulled *Mayflower*, built in 1881, was by far the oldest. Wills felt that she was decidedly past her prime. Although she was fired up and used in revenue service during Wills's first summer running of the route, in 1945, she never steamed again thereafter and remained tied up at the town pier in Nantasket. Wills made several efforts to dispose of her on the second-hand market; he once thought he had located a willing buyer for *Mayflower* in Savannah,

Georgia.¹⁵ Unfortunately, no one was especially interested in laying out the money to put an 1881-built wooden-hulled sidewheeler back into revenue service. In 1948 she was sold to local interests who converted her into a landlocked nightclub just a short walk from the pier in Nantasket.¹⁶

Allerton and *Nantasket*, the two former Hudson River boats, thus became the backbone of the fleet during the Wills years. Although the Old Timer saw the Nantasket boats as a source of vessels for his other operations when he first attempted to purchase the company in 1941, matters had quite reversed themselves by 1945, and *Mohawk, Francis Scott Key*, and others were shifted north to fill in on the Nantasket run in various years. With the lifting of many wartime restrictions before the 1945 excursion season—and with *Allerton* out of service for conversion to oil fuel—*Mohawk* was dispatched to Boston that summer to ensure that the new Nantasket Boat Line would have adequate capacity during 1945, its first season of operation.

Wills's Nantasket Boat Line was anxious to emphasize its continuity with the older company, not to position itself as something new and

Wooden-hulled *Mayflower*, a veteran on the Nantasket–Boston run. (Photograph by R. Loren Graham, courtesy of B. B. Wills family.)

different. From the outset, the firm's stationery had this notation printed at the bottom: "Oldest Excursion Line in United States—Established 1818." The *service* was correctly regarded as old. The operating *company*, on the other hand, was brand, spanking new!

Nantasket Boat took in $173,808.38 in gross receipts that first summer under Wills's ownership. The cost of running the company—fuel, salaries, advertising, depreciation, and so forth—came to $163,017.84, leaving a profit of $10,790.54.[17]

Under Wills's management, Nantasket Boat Line typically scheduled ten or twelve weekday round-trips between Boston and Nantasket each summer, and more on Sundays and holidays. Some trips would also stop at Pemberton, a largely residential community within the town of Hull, on their way to and from Nantasket. While precise schedules varied from year to year, on weekdays the first trip usually left Boston for Nantasket a little before eight o'clock in the morning, the last trip of the day around nine o'clock in the evening. The first sailing from Nantasket, geared to the needs of commuters, left at seven in the morning, whereas the all-important final trip of the day cast off from Nantasket sometime around eleven o'clock at night. To maintain schedules, boats would occasionally be dispatched from one terminal to the other without passengers. In many transportation sectors, such non-revenue moves are called dead-head trips. On the Nantasket Boat Line a trip that was run without revenue passengers was designated a "wild" trip.

TABLE 5-1
Mohawk Schedule, June 30, 1946

lv. Nantasket	7:15 a.m.	11:30 a.m.	2:37 p.m.	5:54 p.m.	8:54 p.m.
lv. Pemberton	7:50	11:56	—	—	—
ar. Boston	8:43	12:45 p.m.	3:53	7:07	10:08
no. passengers	9	53	96	1,250(*)	683
lv. Boston	10:15 a.m.	1:15 p.m.	4:07 p.m.	7:22 p.m.	10:15 p.m.
ar. Pemberton	—	—	—	—	—
ar. Nantasket	11:07	2:23	5:18	8:32	11:25
no. passengers	1,250*	1,250*	629	80	"wild"

From SS *Mohawk*, Daily Report of Passengers Carried and Miles Run, Wills Papers.
*The vessel's capacity was 1,250 passengers

June 30, 1946, was an exceptionally busy day for *Mohawk* (table 5-1). It was the Sunday before the first Fourth of July that the country would celebrate since the end of World War II. *Mohawk* was in service from 7:15 A.M. until 11:25 P.M. and made five round-trips. A more typical summer weekday for any of the Nantasket–Boston boats would involve three, or at most four, round-trips. Interestingly, on three of her ten trips that day, *Mohawk*'s passenger count was exactly 1,250, which also just happened to be her licensed capacity. In a series of short articles on B. B. Wills in *Steamboat Bill*, Frank Manwell, who worked for Nantasket Boat in the late 1940s, remarked that as a vessel's passenger count began to approach its licensed capacity in Boston, the count clock would sometimes "malfunction" and vessels would leave port with a few more cash-paying customers aboard than federal regulations permitted.[18] Whether that was the case aboard *Mohawk* on June 30, 1946, will likely never be known. In any case, her purser's report for that very busy June day in 1946 shows that on three trips, she carried exactly as many passengers as her licensing permitted.

The Nantasket Boat Line would remain a seasonal fixture in Boston Harbor for the next seven years. Service was steady and dependable, although there were unusual incidents from time to time.

On July 28, 1947, *Nantasket* departed Rowes Wharf for an afternoon trip to the beach with two hundred passengers aboard when she experienced engine troubles. This would have been only an incidental bother, except that a severe storm passed through Boston while the vessel was drifting without power. Although there were no injuries and *Nantasket* eventually got under way on her own, it was touch and go for the better part of an hour and the incident was prominently featured on the front page of the next day's newspapers.[19]

A year before the *Nantasket* episode, a twenty-four-hour strike in late June 1946 disrupted service for a day until Wills and the union settled their differences. Three years later, another labor dispute threatened the start of the 1949 season, this time between the company and the National Organization of Masters, Mates and Pilots, Local 11. The dispute resulted in a work stoppage from May 28 through June 3. A board of conciliation and arbitration appointed by the Massachusetts Department of Labor and Industries was impaneled and presented a detailed set of recommendations for settling the strike.[20]

On July 14, 1949, the steamer *Nantasket*, Carlton E. Day, Master, went aground on Peddocks Island on her third trip of the day from Boston to Nantasket. Her 693 passengers were evacuated by tugboats and Coast Guard launches and *Nantasket* was refloated at 2:27 A.M. the next

Allerton, a former Hudson River steamboat working the Nantasket–Boston run. (Photograph by R. Loren Graham, courtesy of B. B. Wills family.)

morning. Although there were no injuries, dry-docking revealed minor damage to the hull and rudder, and Wills received an insurance settlement of $5,107.23.[21]

On August 17, 1949, as Capt. Harry Lewis was easing *Francis Scott Key* up to the wharf at Nantasket, a thirty-three-year-old man did a swan dive into the water from the vessel's top deck. First Mate David King and a passenger promptly went in after him, and with Captain Lewis giving deft engine commands, the man was safely rescued. The jump was a stunt, apparently, not a suicide, but only the courage and skill of Lewis and King kept it from becoming an outright tragedy.[22]

Two years later, on August 12, *Nantasket* went aground in dense fog during a midday trip from Boston to Nantasket with 827 passengers aboard. Again the site was Peddocks Island, and fortunately, no one was injured. Capt. Elmer Purdy blamed the mishap on cross tides, which, he said, "can be very dangerous in heavy fog."[23]

Wills adopted many of the same sales techniques at Nantasket Boat that he had earlier perfected on the Potomac River Line and in Baltimore. He quoted substantial discounts for advance group purchases, which began at 20 percent off regular ticket prices for parties of 25 to

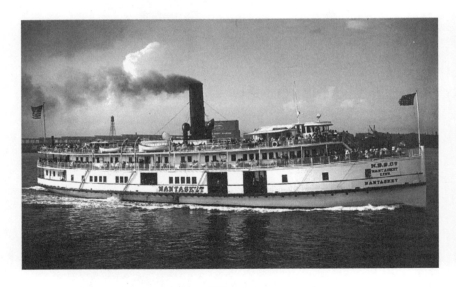

Nantasket, the other former Hudson River propeller boat used in Nantasket–Boston service. (Photograph by R. Loren Graham, courtesy of B. B. Wills family.)

100, up to 40 percent off for parties over 500. He also promoted all-day exclusive charters—a whole boat reserved for one group—with prices ranging from $500 for the 1,250-passenger-capacity *Mohawk* on a Monday, to $700 for the 1,500-passenger-capacity *Nantasket* on a Thursday or Friday. Exclusive charters included a five-piece orchestra and a quantity of posters that a sponsoring church or civic organization could arrange to have displayed in neighborhood store windows to promote the upcoming boat ride.

Wills followed *Allerton's* conversion from coal to oil in 1945 by doing the same thing to *Nantasket* the following year, and in 1947 he complemented his Boston service to and from Nantasket Beach with excursion service across Massachusetts Bay between Boston and Provincetown at the eastern tip of Cape Cod (see chapter 7).

Meanwhile, the "Nanny Boats" continued to steam back and forth between downtown Boston and Nantasket Beach in the town of Hull. A steamboat tradition that began in 1818 and had looked directly into the face of complete abandonment during the Great Depression had earned itself a reprieve, thanks to B. B. Wills.

CHAPTER SIX

Meanwhile, in New York . . .

Between the time Benjamin Bowling Wills attempted to take over the Nantasket–Boston Steamboat Company in 1941 and the day in late 1944 when he actually did, he added yet another passenger boat service to his growing empire. It happened in New York in the wartime year of 1943.

To Bedloe's Island

Few harbor attractions anywhere in the world are in the same league as New York's Statue of Liberty. Crafted in copper by the French sculptor Frédéric-Auguste Bartholdi in 1884, it featured an internal support structure of steel that was the work of a young engineer whose most prominent achievement was still in the future. His name was Alexandre-Gustave Eiffel. After the 151-foot tall statue was completed in France, it was broken down into 350 separate pieces, packed in 214 crates, and shipped to America aboard the French frigate *Isere*. Its journey completed, the Statue of Liberty was presented to the United States as a gift from the people of France to commemorate the French role in the American Revolutionary War and the bond of friendship between the two nations.

Next came a public subscription spearheaded by newspaperman Joseph Pulitzer to raise money in the United States for a proper stone pedestal for the new statue. The Statue of Liberty—now 305 feet tall from the base of the pedestal to the tip of its torch—was dedicated on Bedloe's Island in Upper New York Bay on October 28, 1886, by President Grover Cleveland, accompanied by a legion of dignitaries. It was a site that Bartholdi himself had selected for the statue before he began work on the project.

Over the years, the Statue of Liberty has celebrated two important anniversaries. President Franklin D. Roosevelt visited Bedloe's Island in the fall of 1936 in the middle of his first reelection campaign for a low-key ceremony marking the Statue of Liberty's fiftieth anniversary. A gala hundreth anniversary was staged on July 4, 1986 with President Ronald Reagan presiding. The pageant featured a parade of tall ships, plus an international naval review led by the battleship USS *Iowa* (BB-61). By then, Bedloe's Island had become Liberty Island, the name it bears today.

Tourists have long enjoyed taking a short boat ride from the lower tip of Manhattan out to Liberty Island to visit this marvelous attraction. To transport visitors to the island and back, the U.S. National Park Service today contracts with a private boat operator.

In early years, before the park service assumed responsibility for Liberty Island, the Statue of Liberty was administered by the War Department since Bedloe's Island had earlier been the site of a harbor fortification, Fort Wood. In fact, the Statue of Liberty's pedestal sits atop the stone walls of Fort Wood. Typically, the War Department executed ten-year agreements with private vessel operators to provide ferry service for both visitors and workers. When such contracts reached their term, the department solicited new bids.[1]

An Unusual Operation

Unlike more typical excursion boat operations, which were seasonal, the ferry service to the Statue of Liberty was a year-round operation. Summer months, however, normally saw heavier passenger traffic than in winter. Instead of a cruise of two or three hours between a city and a picnic grove or an amusement park some distance away, a vessel took only ten to fifteen minutes to steam its way from the southern tip of Manhattan Island to the dock on Bedloe's Island. On the Statue of Liberty run, more time is usually spent loading and unloading passengers at each end of the line than steaming back and forth from one landing to the other.

The Statue of Liberty ferry, nevertheless, was a steady money maker. More important, the service was totally immune to troublesome trends—like increasing automobile ownership—that were generating serious uncertainties for the conventional excursion boat industry in the United States. Over one-half million passengers typically rode the boats in a year's time in those days. Furthermore, the service required little or no advertising or marketing efforts to be successful. The Statue of Liberty promoted itself, and since boats were the only way people could get there, an operator only needed to sit back, sell tickets, and count the receipts at the end of the day. In more recent years, a New York maritime executive had this to say about the statue ferry: "The only marketing expense they've got is taking out an ad in the Yellow Pages."

Enter the Sutton Line

In 1939, a routine call for bids by the War Department resulted in a slight surprise. Daniel McAllister's McAllister Navigation Company, successor to the older McAllister Steamboat Company, was expected by most harbor observers to emerge successful and secure a ten-year renewal of its franchise to operate the state ferry route. Instead, a rival firm unexpectedly submitted a better proposal and won the lucrative contract. Thus did the Sutton Line, owned by Charles Sutton of New York, displace McAllister as the contract provider of passenger service to the Statue of Liberty.

As matters subsequently developed, however, the year 1939 was not an auspicious time to undertake such a new maritime responsibility. Once war was declared in December 1941, the excursion boat industry was subjected to all kinds of economic uncertainties; Sutton Line soon found itself hard pressed to meet its contract requirements on the Statue of Liberty run.

Despite wartime constraints, fuel was not the issue. Given the need to emphasize the patriotic dimension of the overall war effort, service to the Statue of Liberty was never really threatened by fuel shortages. Passengers riding out to Bedloe's Island and back, however, were given a strict warning not to take any photographs of harbor activity en route. Similar strictures prevailed on almost every passenger vessel plying the waters of any U.S. port during wartime, although the degree to which such rules were enforced supposedly varied from city to city.

Late in the summer of 1942, Charles Sutton sold his entire steamboat company, the Sutton Line, to George Sanders, a New Yorker from the Jackson Heights section of Queens. The sale included Sutton's ten-year contract with the federal government to operate the Statue of Liberty ferry, a contract whose term was scheduled to run through 1949.

At the time, B. B. Wills was working with Charles Sutton and George Sanders in connection with his bareboat charter of Sutton's *Wauketa* for Tolchester service that season. When the three men met in New York in

Sutton Line transferred *Deepwater* to Wills when he took over the Statue of Liberty ferry service in 1943. (Photograph by R. Loren Graham, courtesy of B. B. Wills family.)

late August 1942, Wills told Sanders that he would be interested in purchasing the statue ferry operation from him, if Sutton Line's heavily mortgaged sidewheeler *Claremont* could be kept out of the deal.[2]

Sanders, for reasons of his own, was willing to sell off the statue ferry. After several months of reasonably intense negotiations, Wills bought out the remaining term of the ten-year contract with the War Department to operate the statue ferry. Included in the overall transaction was a thirty-six-year-old steamboat named *Deepwater*, which Sutton Line had been using on the run. She was named for Deepwater, New Jersey, where she had once worked for a Wilson Line subsidiary. (Everywhere Wills turned, he ran into some trace, however faint, of the Wilson Line.) Excluded from the 1943 transaction was *Claremont*, which the Sanders-controlled Sutton Line would continue to operate on an excursion route up the Hudson River. Two other vessels once used by the Sutton Line on the Statue of Liberty ferry had not been conveyed to Sanders in 1942. *Mayfair* and *Madisonville* eventually did wind up in Wills's fleet and see service on the statue ferry, but not until after World War II.

Madisonville was also used by Wills in statue ferry service.

MEANWHILE, IN NEW YORK . . .

In the 1940s and 1950s, comfortable operation of the statue ferry required two medium-size passenger vessels. On most days, only one boat would actually be in service; the other would be held in reserve as backup. It would also supplement the primary vessel with extra trips when traffic was heavy, such as on weekends and on most summer weekdays.

One or more smaller boats were also useful for off-hour runs to Bedloe's Island. These vessels operated, according to the terms of the contract with the federal government, solely for the benefit of workers and their families. In a pinch, the smaller vessels could also carry revenue passengers if it were an off day and the tourists were not out in full force.

When Wills took over the service in late 1943, *Deepwater* became his principal vessel. Before 1943 was over, though, the federal government had requisitioned *Deepwater*. *Francis Scott Key* was sent north to take her place, and actually held down the run by herself for several months. *Mo-*

The excursion boat *Francis Scott Key* ran for Wills in Washington, Miami, Baltimore, Boston, and on the Statue of Liberty ferry run in New York.

hawk, which had been conscripted for military work early in the war but returned to Wills soon afterward, eventually joined *Francis Scott Key* in New York, and the two former Chesapeake Bay steamboats became Wills's regular vessels on the route in 1944.

Over the winter of 1945–46, *Deepwater*'s tour with the navy was finished, and she was conveyed back to Wills. The *Deepwater* that the navy returned to Wills, though, was in no condition to resume service. Her machinery had become completely disabled, and she needed serious yard work. By then, Wills owned a Baltimore shipyard—the former Spedden Yard on Boston Street that he had purchased in 1946 and renamed Wills-Spedden. He decided the proper thing to do was tow *Deepwater* there and put her through a substantial rehabilitation.[3] In February 1946, he wrote to the Curtis Bay Towing Company of Baltimore, inquiring if they would soon have a tugboat deadheading back to Baltimore from New York and could quote a "good price" for moving *Deepwater* south.[4] *Deepwater* eventually reached Wills-Spedden and after a lengthy stay emerged in early 1948 as *Liberty*. In place of her original steam engine, Wills had installed a pair of diesel engines obtained from the navy in lieu of a cash settlement for the wartime damages to *Deepwater*—"horse trading," he called it.[5] The vessel's largely wooden superstructure had also become badly deteriorated over the years, and *Liberty* emerged with new steel cabin work that gave her a modern, almost streamlined profile. She looked, certainly, nothing like the prewar *Deepwater*. As soon as ice in the upper Chesapeake Bay had cleared and she could reach the Chesapeake and Delaware Canal, she headed north to New York. *Liberty* made her first postwar trip as the statue ferry on March 15, 1948.

The vessel's entry into service in early 1948 allowed Wills to terminate a bareboat charter of Interstate Navigation's *Nelseco II*, a vessel that he had leased to work the statue ferry route while *Deepwater* was being rebuilt into *Liberty* in Baltimore. Because *Mohawk* and *Francis Scott Key* had been deployed north to Boston, in 1947 Wills purchased *Madisonville* and *Mayfair*, each of which also served on the statue ferry run. The 1878-built *Mayfair* was the onetime government lighthouse tender *Pansy*, which had been reconfigured many times over the years. Built in—and named after—Madisonville, Louisiana, *Madisonville* was a wooden hulled motor vessel that enjoyed an interesting career running for Wills in several different cities. Table 6-1 identifies the various boats that Wills used on the statue ferry run over the years.

TABLE 6-1
Vessels Used in Statue Ferry Work, 1943–53

Name	Type*	Gross tons	Years on run	Notes
Deepwater	st.s.	334	1943	1
Francis Scott Key	st.s.	462	1944–46	
Mohawk	st.s.	795	1944–45	
Nelseco II	ol.s.	237	1947–48	2
Liberty	ol.s.	413	1948–53	1, 3
Madisonville	ol.s.	141	1947, 1952	
Mayfair	ol.s.	302	1947–53	

*st.s., steam engine, screw propulsion; ol.s., diesel engine, screw propulsion
[1] *Deepwater* was requisitioned by the U.S. Navy in late 1943 and returned to service as *Liberty* in 1948 after being dieselized and thoroughly rebuilt; see text.
[2] Not a Wills-owned vessel, *Nelseco II* was bareboat chartered from the Interstate Navigation Company.
[3] Sold to Circle Line–Statue of Liberty Ferry, October 19, 1953.

B. B. Wills conducted his Statue of Liberty ferry operation using a number of different corporate entities. From the perspective of potential passengers, of course, it was simply the Statue of Liberty ferry that sold the tickets, ran the boats, and took people over and back to Bedloe's Island. From the perspective of an accountant, however—much less an auditor from New York City's Department of Docks—there was the Statue of Liberty Line, plus the Statue of Liberty Boat Line, two separate and different operating companies. In addition, vessels used on the statue ferry service were owned at various times by B. B. Wills himself; his wife, Gertrude; and two Baltimore-based companies controlled by Wills, Maryland Boat and Boat Sales, Inc. The vessels were then leased to one or another of the statue ferry operating entities. After 1948 a new company called Wills Lines owned at least one of the vessels used in the service.

Use of multiple companies to operate and lease vessels back and forth with each other was anything but an unusual modus operandi for B. B. Wills. But the practice may well have been carried to its extreme during the days that he ran boats between the southern tip of Manhattan Island and the Statue of Liberty.

A Touch of Scandal

While he was operating the Statue of Liberty ferry in New York, Wills found himself in a situation that can only be called unpleasant. The affair involved a perennial aspect of conducting maritime business in New York: hardball city politics. It would be tempting to characterize Wills as an unassuming country boy from Charles County, Maryland, who was totally out of his element in the rough world of Tammany Hall and sensationalist newspapers. In truth, however, he took his punches smartly—and survived nicely. More important, he kept his boats running back and forth across Upper New York Bay, even during bad times.

As noted earlier, in the early 1940s Wills became acquainted with George Sanders. It was from the Sanders-controlled Sutton Line, for instance, that Wills took over the Statue of Liberty ferry in 1943. Later, in 1946, Sanders became a principal in a venture that eventually became an all-time maritime success story in New York Harbor—Circle Line. The company's principal service was, and still is, three-hour sightseeing cruises around Manhattan Island.[6] In 1949, Sanders took over and reorganized the fabled Hudson River Day Line, keeping it in business for another fifteen years.[7]

Sanders, though, did not devote all of his time and attention to maritime activities. When William O'Dwyer was elected mayor of New York City in 1945, he asked Sanders, a longtime friend and traveling companion, to head the city's Department of Commerce. Salary was clearly not the reason anyone accepted appointment to this cabinet-level position; its incumbent was paid the munificent sum of one dollar a year.

As the O'Dwyer administration began to take control of city operations, charges of municipal corruption became anything but infrequent. One area of New York particularly prone to corruption was along the city's waterfront. Stories of racketeering among stevedores and longshoremen are legendary. Furthermore, because the municipal government itself had to serve as landlord in negotiating leases with private interests for the use of city-owned piers, opportunities for corruption abounded.

In the spring of 1947—with Mayor O'Dwyer beginning only his second year in office—the unmistakable stench of wrongdoing began to waft over the city's waterfront *again*. The reform era of the LaGuardia administration was over, as were the no-nonsense years of World War II. A New York County grand jury had been impaneled, and the district attorney, Frank Hogan, began a series of inquiries. Two separate sequences of events were under investigation. Because both dealt with waterfront-related matters, though, the newspapers tended to lump them together and treat the two as one. In shorthand fashion, journalists called both matters "the dock scandal."

The first issue was an inquiry into possible illegal practices by certain labor unions in the subleasing of space on various city-owned piers. The second was an investigation of possible improprieties by none other than George Sanders, who by then had resigned his dollar-a-year position with the O'Dwyer administration.

In the first inquiry, the grand jury handed down indictments and people were brought to trial and found guilty.[8] District Attorney Hogan took no action at all against Sanders, although from the middle to the end of May 1947, the Sanders name was as prominently featured in front-page headlines as those of the individuals who were eventually brought to trial and convicted. All city papers gave the matter serious coverage; the *New York Sun* appears to have been especially enthusiastic.

The allegation with respect to Sanders was that he used his position in the O'Dwyer administration to secure favorable pier-leasing arrangements for Sightseeing Around New York Waterways, a company in which Sanders reportedly owned a 50 percent interest. Some also suggested that Sanders was trying to force his way into an equity position with Circle Line not by buying stock or putting up cash as other principals did, but by awarding docking permits from the municipal government that he alone could promise to secure.[9]

Then matters took a strange turn. On May 27, 1947, the *New York Times* reported that Sanders had a "secret associate" in the previously unknown Sightseeing Around New York Waterways.[10] Emerging from an interview with District Attorney Hogan's staff, one witness told the assembled reporters: "You fellows find out who owns the other fifty per cent and you'll flush out a bird."[11] Suddenly the budding scandal had taken on an indispensable element of a big-time conspiracy: a real live mystery man pulling levers behind the scenes.

The next day the "bird" was indeed "flushed." The mystery man was none other than Benjamin Bowling Wills of Washington, D.C.[12]

Sanders and Wills had, in fact, formed a joint venture known as Sightseeing Around New York Waterways. In July 1946, Sanders wrote to Wills on Sutton Line stationery to tell Wills that it was important to open a bank account in the new company's name.[13] Earlier that year, on March 5, Wills had written to the New York City Commissioner of Marine and Aviation requesting docking rights for a new sightseeing company he was about to form.[14] He received a routine reply with the forms needed to file such a request.[15]

In retrospect, Sightseeing Around New York Waterways may well have been nothing but a ploy on Sanders's part—a perfectly legal ploy—to enhance his bargaining position for purchasing an equity in-

Sightseer, which may have operated for Sightseeing Around New York Waterways.

terest in Circle Line. Sanders eventually did make the purchase. In any event, Sightseeing Around New York Waterways probably never ran a single vessel in sightseeing service in New York. If it did run any, it certainly did not run many, and such tours could only have operated briefly during the 1946 excursion season. Sanders did join Circle Line after one of the five original founders, Jeremiah Driscoll, decided to leave the organization in 1946. Once Sanders became associated with Circle Line, Sightseeing Around New York Waterways faded quickly from the scene.

While there is no record that Sightseeing Around New York Waterways provided public sightseeing excursions in New York in 1946 or any time, there is evidence that a Wills-controlled company called Waterways Sightseeing was established in New York at about this time. In later years, Wills shifted Waterways Sightseeing to Washington to operate with various sightseeing bus ventures there.

In any event, some activity was apparently conducted in New York in 1946 under the corporate auspices of Waterways Sightseeing. A handwritten balance sheet for the company among The Wills Papers dated November 30 of that year showed an income of $18,001.38 and specified that repairs to the Wills-owned *Sightseer* were paid for by the company.[16] Certain operations of the statue ferry were likely charged to Waterways Sightseeing as well, since *Sightseer* was one of the smaller boats that Wills used for off-hour trips to Bedloe's Island for government workers and their families. Other than this single ledger entry, Waterways Sightseeing in New York, circa 1946, has left as little trace of itself as did Sightseeing Around New York Waterways.

Jeremiah Driscoll, whom Sanders had replaced at the Circle Line, proved to be rather outspoken about the line, George Sanders, the O'Dwyer administration, District Attorney Hogan, and numerous other individuals. He wrote a privately published book entitled *Crime Circles Manhattan*, which is long on vicious charges, quick to jump to conspiratorial conclusions, but unfortunately short on useful documentation.[17]

In addition to the 41-ton *Sightseer*, the 68-ton *Saltaire* was another Wills-owned excursion boat that Sightseeing Around New York Waterways could have used, or perhaps did use. *Saltaire*'s insurance policy was evidently endorsed to include mention of the new company, although the vessel's ownership did not change.[18] Like *Sightseer, Saltaire* was normally deployed in Wills's statue ferry service in New York, but more to transport workers between Bedloe's Island and Manhattan than to carry tourists.

Saltaire, a former Fire Island ferry, also became the subject of a protracted debate between B. B. Wills and several individuals, companies, and agencies, a debate as unclear and unfocused as it was lengthy. It involved a decision, by Wills, to replace *Saltaire*'s original Fairbanks-Morse diesel engines with a pair of Gray Marine diesels he had picked up on the war surplus market. Wills retained one of the preeminent naval architects associated with small-vessel diesel applications, a New Yorker by the name of Eads Johnson, to work up specifications for the conversion. Todd Shipbuilding was selected to perform the work.

But nothing Todd did would keep Wills happy. The Old Timer was continually pestering them, either directly or through Johnson, with suggestions, requests, and demands, not to mention challenging many of the shipbuilder's charges for work performed. *Saltaire* eventually had her engined replaced—at Todd—but it was an acrimonious piece of business. Letters flew back and forth for months between Wills and Eads Johnson, Johnson and the U.S. Coast Guard, Todd and Wills, and Wills and General Motors Acceptance Corporation, who played a role in the project's financing. Today, a half century later, the exact cause of the dispute is unclear. But like a kindergarten teacher who walks in on the aftermath of a food fight, a person reading the Wills Papers can easily see that people were in disagreement over something.[19]

Through all the unfortunate business in New York involving grand juries and talk of criminal malfeasance, Wills was never accused of doing anything wrong. Sanders, on the other hand, was the subject of an official grand jury investigation. Still, no formal charges were ever brought against him as a result of that investigation.

For all his years in the excursion boat business, B. B. Wills never saw his name in the newspapers as often as he did in May 1947, when the New York County district attorney was looking into possible illegalities on the New York waterfront. "New York, New York . . . it's one tough place to do business."

End of the Statue Ferry Service

The Statue of Liberty ferry service contract that Wills assumed from Sutton Line in 1943 was to expire in 1949 and then be put out for rebid. Except it was not; it was extended on a year-by-year basis after 1949, not at all unusual in the world of federal contracting. In 1953, though, the new Eisenhower administration decided it was time to put the statue ferry contract out for a fresh round of competitive bidding. By then, responsibility for Bedloe's Island and the Statue of Liberty had passed from the old War Department to the National Park Service of the Department of the Interior. The secretary of the interior, Douglas McKay, reportedly made the decision himself that it was time to rebid the contract.

There was some concern that under Wills's management, the statue ferry was not being run as well as it should be. In 1947, for instance, annual patronage on the route was 529,741; a year later, it had dropped to 504,023, a one-year loss of 4.6 percent. The small size and the relatively poor condition of the vessels that Wills assigned to the service were cited as one reason for the decline. *Liberty* was a reasonable enough boat, but the aging *Mayfair* was considered a distinct liability.

After the bids were opened and the results announced in late July 1953, Wills found himself in the same position as Daniel McAllister did back in 1939: Wills assumed that he would win the contract, except a new entrant submitted a better proposal. Wills's bid called for the federal government to receive 2 percent of the ferry's first $250,000 in annual gross revenues, 4 percent on the next $100,000, and 5 percent on anything over $350,000. The rival bid proposed a flat fee of $5,000 per year, plus a straight 4 percent of all gross revenues.[20]

Assuming $600,000 in annual revenues on the statue ferry for argument's sake, Wills was proposing to pay the Department of the Interior $21,500 per year, while the new bidder was prepared to pay $29,000. In addition, the new bidder said it would design and build a brand new vessel for the statue ferry service should it win the contract. In his entire excursion boat career, from 1934 through 1967, Benjamin Bowling Wills would never design and build a completely new passenger vessel.

The new entrant whose bid the Department of the Interior was pleased to accept was, effectively, Circle Line Sightseeing Yachts. The firm was headed by Francis J. Barry, a customs broker with Cambell and Gardner who had handled some vessel transactions for Wills in New York over the years. Frank Barry had been one of the five founding partners of Circle Line back in 1945 and was also called to testify before the New York County grand jury in the George Sanders matter in 1947.

Barry had been interested in taking over the statue ferry service from Wills for some time. In 1946, for example, he wrote Wills a letter on Cambell and Gardner stationery: "Some months ago you advised me that you may be interested in selling the Statue of Liberty run. If you are still interested I would appreciate your dropping me a line with reference thereto as I have been asked to write you with reference thereto by an interested party."[21] On the assumption the "interested party" was Barry's own Circle Line, he finally secured through a competitive bid in 1953 what he had been unable to buy in 1946.

Circle Line formed a separate company, Circle Line–Statue of Liberty Ferry, to handle its newly won contract. Wills agreed to remain on as contract operator until September 30 to ensure a smooth transition.

Something Wills could well have regarded as an evil omen with respect to his future with the statue ferry was that just about the same time the Department of the Interior was evaluating the bids to operate the service, his workers went out on strike. On June 17, 1953, members of Local 33 of the United States Marine Division of the International Longshoremen's Association walked off the job in a wage and contract dispute. All service to and from the Statue of Liberty was shut down, all except those special runs made solely for the convenience of government workers. These runs continued—with union personnel—despite the strike.

Wills flew to New York from Washington to play a more active role in the negotiations, and Commissioner T. G. Dougherty of the Federal Mediation and Conciliation Service brought his good offices to the dispute. Two days after it all began, the strike was over. "The union was victorious on most of the points in dispute," reported the *New York Times*.[22] Deckhands won a 35-cent hourly wage increase raising their pay to $1.53 an hour, while captains saw their wages increase from $1.77 an hour to $2.08. A pension and welfare system was to be established, the basic workweek was reduced to forty hours, and time and a half

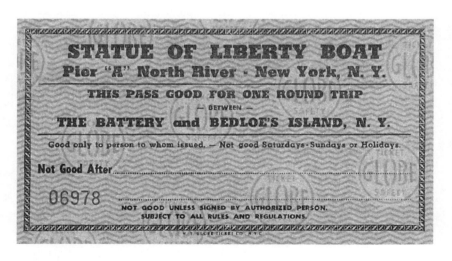

A round-trip pass for the Statue of Liberty boat.

would be paid for all work on Saturdays, Sundays, and holidays, not merely on Sundays as in the previous contract.

With the loss of the statue ferry in 1953, Wills sold *Liberty* to Circle Line, for which she continued to run out to Liberty Island for another decade. Wills retained title to *Mayfair*, though, and used her in various odd assignments in both Baltimore and Washington for the next several years. *Madisonville* had earlier been sold to interests in South Carolina, whereas the diminutive *Sightseer* migrated to Washington. Under the house flag Waterways Sightseeing, she sailed there for several seasons in cruises run in association with Gray Line sightseeing buses, another venture in which Wills held a substantial interest. *Saltaire* was sold in 1958, but not before heading north to Boston in 1947. The vessel worked for a spell on the Nantasket run, not in excursion service for large crowds heading for a day at Paragon Park and the beach, but in commuter service for Hull residents heading for their Boston offices in the early morning.

Finally, with Circle Line's advent on the Statue of Liberty ferry run, the company did design and build a new boat for the service. Diesel-powered *Miss Liberty* was delivered by Blount Marine, of Warren, Rhode Island, in the spring of 1954. She was a smart-looking three-decker that would enjoy a long tenure on the run and would lead to the construction of four similar-looking vessels in future years.

CHAPTER SEVEN

Excursion Boats after the War

The end of World War II saw the many inland and coastal passenger steamboats that had been taken over by the military for the duration returned to the civilian sector. B. B. Wills remained alert not only to the availability of such tonnage, but to its sometimes bargain basement prices. As a result, the immediate postwar years saw the Wills excursion boat empire expand and reach its all-time high-water mark. In the process, Wills again had to contend with his longtime rival, the Wilson Line, both on the water and in court.

Another Former Day Liner

In April 1947 Wills purchased from the U.S. Maritime Commission a former Maine coastal steamboat that had worked for the Hudson River Day Line in the years immediately before the war. The vessel was not, however, a large 300-foot-long classic Day Line sidewheeler like *Potomac*, which Wills had purchased in 1934 for Chapel Point service. She was instead a much smaller 185-foot propeller boat. The Day Line had used her for charter work and various other odd assignments, but certainly not as a regular vessel on its bread-and-butter route between New York and Albany.

Called *Rangeley* during her career in Maine, the vessel was renamed *Chauncey M. Depew* by the Day Line. The name honored a New York state senator who also served for a time as president of the New York Central Railroad, a company with which Day Line maintained a cordial working relationship over the years. For lack of a more appropriate name for his newest acquisition (another reason was that Wills was not really sure where he intended to use her), the name *Chauncey M. Depew* was retained. The name certainly had a distinctive ring to it.[1]

Chauncey M. Depew remained under Wills's ownership for a scant three seasons. He took possession of her in New York on March 31, 1947, and after having her reconditioned in the Marine Basin Shipyard on the shores of Brooklyn's Gravesend Bay, he dispatched her north to Boston on June 10, where she probably worked the Boston–Nantasket route during the rest of June. Then, on July 3, 1947, *Chauncey M. Depew* inaugurated a new service for B. B. Wills between Boston and Provincetown, at the tip of Cape Cod. The boat finished the 1947 season by running a number of special cruises between Boston and Plymouth, including several all-day tours through the Cape Cod Canal, before going into winter quarters in Boston.

Beginning in 1948, Wills leased the former Day Liner on bareboat charter to other steamboat companies. As a result, some have said that Wills himself was the operator of routes such as Providence–Block Island and New York–Atlantic Highlands. He was not. Although *Chauncey M. Depew* ran on both these services while she was *owned* by B. B. Wills, the routes were operated by Interstate Navigation and S. S. Sandy Hook, respectively, not Wills or any Wills-controlled company.

The charter to Interstate Navigation was for the 1948 excursion season. The contract specified that over and above a basic charter rate of fifteen thousand dollars for the season, Wills would also receive 50 percent of any profits that *Chauncey M. Depew* realized while working Interstate's Providence–Newport–Block Island route.[2] This certainly gave Wills more than a passing interest in the operation, but the service remained under the management and operation of Interstate Navigation, not Wills. After spending the summer of 1948 on the Block Island run, *Chauncey M. Depew* was returned to Wills at Boston, where she again spent the winter.

In the spring of the following year, 1949, the boat was dispatched south to New York on yet another bareboat charter. This assignment would end in a good deal of confusion and even litigation.

On March 15, 1949—the Ides of March—B. B. Wills signed a contract with a New York excursion boat company popularly called the Sandy Hook Line. Its formal corporate name was actually S.S. Sandy Hook, Incorporated. The agreement called for a five-year bareboat charter of *Chauncey M. Depew* to the Sandy Hook company to replace a vessel called *Sandy Hook*, which had been retired at the end of the previous season, 1948.

The *Chauncey M. Depew* came down from Boston in April and reportedly entered service between New York and Atlantic Highlands in late May. The basic charter rate was $10,000 per season, and while the

Sandy Hook Line was to retain the first $2,500 in profits earned by the vessel each summer, any profits above this amount would be shared on a fifty-fifty basis with Wills, a similar but not identical arrangement to the previous season's, when the boat was chartered to Interstate Navigation. The contract included a routine clause allowing the owner to repossess the vessel in the event of default, but it also went on to specify that "Such repossession by Owner may be with or without legal process and in connection therewith Owner and its Agents may enter upon any dock, pier or other premises where the vessel may be and take possession thereof." Another clause in the contract gave Wills the right to substitute *Francis Scott Key* for the *Depew* only during the 1949 season should Wills need *Depew* that season in Boston.[3] This option was never exercised, however.

The bareboat charter of *Chauncey M. Depew* to Sandy Hook Lines did not last the full five years specified in the contract; in fact, it did not even last for the full excursion season of 1949. Sandy Hook's key market was linked to the thoroughbred racing season at New Jersey's Monmouth

Chauncey M. Depew in Town Cut, St. George's, Bermuda. (Photograph by Bermuda News Bureau, courtesy of John H. Shaum, Jr.)

Park, located a short bus ride from the company's pier at Atlantic Highlands. Passengers found it convenient to travel to and from the track by this boat-and-bus combined service, and the company scheduled a morning departure from Manhattan to ensure that "Improvers of the Breed" would have ample time to line up at the two-dollar window well before post time for the first race.

In 1949, the racing season at Monmouth Park ended on August 10. Immediately afterward, *Chauncey M. Depew* was dispatched south to the Chesapeake Bay to fill in for Wills's regular Baltimore–Tolchester boat, which had developed a season-ending mechanical problem. With *Depew*'s departure to Chesapeake Bay, the five-year charter contract with Sandy Hook Lines was abruptly terminated. Details are lacking on the precise legal form of the termination. Among the Wills Papers, however, are letters between the Old Timer and his attorneys discussing over the next year the pending litigation with Sandy Hook Lines.[4] There is no information, however, about the subject or nature of the case, much less its outcome.

After her short stint on the Tolchester route, *Chauncey M. Depew* spent the winter of 1949–50 in Baltimore. The following spring, she was sold to a most unusual buyer. In need of a fair-sized vessel to serve as a tender when cruise ships too large to dock in Hamilton Harbor, Bermuda, had to anchor in Great Sound, the Bermuda government purchased the thirty-seven-year-old boat. A preliminary agreement was signed in Washington by Wills and James Hamilton Parker, the Bermuda representative, on March 20, 1950. The contract established the sale price of the vessel as ninety-thousand dollars.[5] Two days earlier, on March 18, Wills had filed an application with the U.S. Maritime Commission for permission to convey the vessel to British registry. The official Treasury Department bill of sale is dated May 23, 1950.[6]

Made ready for her ocean voyage at Baltimore, and pausing in Norfolk for final refueling, *Chauncey M. Depew* set out for Bermuda under her own power and steamed through Twin Rocks Passage into Hamilton Harbor on June 8, 1950. She served there for nineteen years before returning to the United States in 1970 and, eventually, a ten-year career as a shoreside restaurant near the New Jersey Turnpike in what is now called the Meadowlands.[7]

Through all her days working in Hamilton Harbor, the onetime Hudson River Day Liner continued to be called *Chauncey M. Depew*. Many who happened upon her during this phase of her career undoubtedly assumed that the name honored some venerable and since-departed personage from Bermuda's long and storied history. The name "Chauncey M. Depew" has indeed earned a place in Bermuda's maritime traditions, but it was a 185-foot steamboat that did the earning, not the man she was named after.

The vessel had a relatively short career with B. B. Wills, spending more time in bareboat charter to other operators than actually working for a Wills-controlled company. The years from 1947 through 1950, however, represent an important phase in the colorful history of this notable and interesting American steamboat.

The Strange Story of Virginia Lee

B. B. Wills purchased *Chauncey M. Depew* from the Maritime Commission rather conventionally. On the other hand, his postwar acquisition of a vessel originally called *Virginia Lee* was anything but conventional. The story of how *Virginia Lee* became an excursion boat in Wills's expanding empire contains enough adventure to fill a Hollywood movie. It could have been called "The Amazing Amazon Adventure of Indiana Wills."

The story began with World War II. While numerous American excursion boats were recruited for war-related duties, most of them stayed in U.S. waters. *Chauncey M. Depew,* for instance, ferried military personnel between Manhattan and Fort Hancock in Lower New York Bay. At least two flotillas of coastal steamboats, however, were dispatched overseas. Oddly enough, *Virginia Lee* was involved in both.

The more well known of the two flotillas has sometimes been dubbed the "Honeymoon Fleet." Nine steamboats were recruited and dispatched eastward across the North Atlantic to provide cross-channel logistical support between Great Britain and the continent during and after the Normandy invasion. When the flotilla paused at St. John's, Newfoundland, in mid-September 1942 before heading out on the longest leg of the journey, *Virginia Lee* was found to be suffering mechanical and structural problems that potentially put the whole fleet at risk in the submarine-infested waters. She was sent back to the United States, and the "Honeymoon Fleet," now down to eight steamboats and escorted by a pair of destroyers from the Royal Navy, set sail for Britain.[8]

Virginia Lee was a 2,158-ton, 291-foot twin-screw steamboat that had previously worked a route between Cape Charles and the Norfolk area across the mouth of the Chesapeake Bay for the New York, Philadelphia and Norfolk Railroad, a Pennsylvania Railroad (PRR) subsidiary. From a passenger's perspective, though, *Virginia Lee* was as much a part of the

Pennsylvania as the *Broadway Limited* or the Paoli Local. Her sailings connected at Cape Charles with PRR trains to and from Wilmington, Philadelphia, and New York, and she wore the PRR's Tuscan red and gold keystone logo on her stack.

A relatively new vessel, *Virginia Lee* was built in Quincy, Massachusetts, in 1928. Following her return to the United States after developing problems in Newfoundland, she was repaired and soon given a new overseas mission. In the spring of 1943, with five other coastal steamboats, *Virginia Lee* was sent south to Belém, Brazil, where increased rubber production was thought to be a strategic necessity given Japanese control of Far Eastern rubber sources. The inland location of potential and existing rubber plantations in Brazil required the expanded use of steamboats to transport workers up and down the Amazon River. Although the convoy to Belém was supposedly attacked by German U-boats on two different occasions, *Virginia Lee* completed the voyage to Belém successfully.

Belém is a Brazilian port city on the Bay of Guajara approximately 100 miles in from the sea and off the River Para, which is part of the enormous Amazon River estuary. Belém, the capital city of the Brazilian state of Para, is just below the equator and serves as a general distribution center for much of the interior Amazon valley.

The flotilla of steamboats dispatched to the Amazon was smaller than the Honeymoon Fleet. In addition to PRR's *Virginia Lee,* the flotilla included Wilson Line's *State of Delaware,* which once competed with Wills's *Tolchester* in Baltimore, and *Westchester* and *Belle Island,* two popular excursion boats that both worked Long Island Sound routes out of New York. The former had run for the Meseck Excursion Line between New York and Rye Beach, while the independently owned *Belle Island* ran to Roton Point, Connecticut.

In his book on the Wilson Line, Richard V. Elliott suggests that the whole Amazon adventure was flawed from the outset, and mismanaged besides. Furthermore, Elliott notes, the real substitute for Far Eastern rubber in the overall Allied war effort came not from tapping new natural sources but from the development of various kinds of synthetic rubber.[9]

In any event, at war's end, the U.S. government was anxious to liquidate the coastal steamboats that had been sent to Brazil. The vessels were put up for sale, "as is/where is." The problem was, of course, that thanks to the unyielding tropical climate in which the vessels worked, "as is" was a convenient code word for "extremely deteriorated." Furthermore, "where is" meant Belém, Brazil, over 2,500 ocean miles from the closest mainland point in the United States. Small wonder, then, that few American excursion boat operators gave the expatriate vessels even a second thought.

One man who did was Benjamin Bowling Wills. He sensed the possibility of obtaining some tonnage at bargain-basement prices, so in the spring of 1947 he booked passage to Brazil to see for himself.

Edward Maier, Wills's friend and associate from Columbia Steamship days, had been working in Brazil for several years and probably helped arrange meetings and introductions before Wills's arrival. In earlier correspondence with Maier, Wills spoke of the possibility of selling war-surplus electric-generating sets to rural villages in South America.[10] He also referred to the establishment of cargo and even passenger service by small ships—war-surplus vessels—between the United States and Brazil. Wills felt that if money were to be made by an upstart operator like himself on such a service, it would be a short-term proposition "before the established boat companies are able to rebuild their fleets and compete."[11] Although Wills did buy an excursion boat on his trip to Brazil, his correspondence with Maier clearly shows that he was thinking of other postwar business ventures in South America as well.

When Wills arrived in Belém in 1947, the vessel he primarily had in mind as a possible addition to his excursion boat fleet was *Belle Island*. In fact he had a signed agreement with Walter M. Drake, secretary-treasurer of the Steamer Belle Island Company, the vessel's prewar owner. The agreement authorized Wills to repurchase the vessel on their behalf, but also said that Drake's company would sell *Belle Island* to Wills once she was back in U.S. waters.[12] As a representative of the vessel's prewar owner, Wills could have negotiated *Belle Island*'s purchase in Brazil with considerably less red tape than would be involved in a transaction between himself and the U.S. government.

Unexpectedly, Wills did not buy *Belle Island* when he reached Brazil; he bought *Virginia Lee* instead. The sale was in the form of an auction, but as was the case when he bought *Albany* from the Day Line in 1934, it was undoubtedly a prearranged auction, with Wills the only bidder. *Virginia Lee* was transferred to Wills's ownership on April 11, 1947.[13] Nothing explains why Wills chose *Virginia Lee,* or why he rejected *Belle Island.* Perhaps *Virginia Lee* was in the better condition of the two after four years in the tropics. An even more speculative reason, though, lies in the vessel's overall size. Wills had long expressed interest in acquiring *large* excursion boats. An earlier chapter discussed, for instance, *Chester W. Chapin, Steel Pier,* and others that he considered purchasing at one time or another. At 2,158 gross tons, *Virginia Lee* became the largest excursion boat that Wills ever owned and operated. Perhaps that fact played some role in her selection.

Having purchased *Virginia Lee* "as is/where is" in Belém, Wills's next task was to get her back to Baltimore. As late as mid-April 1947, he still hoped that *Virginia Lee* could be returned and put in service that season. His hopes were not well founded. Not until two years later, in the excursion season of 1949, did the boat carry her first revenue passengers for her new owner.

When he purchased the vessel in April 1947, it had been at least two years since *Virginia Lee* was last under steam. Wills's initial plan was to fire up the boilers and let her proceed north under her own power. He hired a crew, and his onetime associate Fabian Noel was retained to skipper the effort. Past differences between Noel and Wills had apparently fallen under the rubric of bygones best forgotten. The former PRR flyer headed out to sea on May 21, 1947. No sooner was she away from port, though, than problems developed. Three of her four boilers quit, and she was forced to turn back, reaching Belém on May 24. By this time, the summer excursion season was approaching in the United States and Wills's various enterprises there demanded his full attention.

Virginia Lee remained in Brazil until early 1948, when Wills decided to tow her back to Baltimore. Under the aegis of a Panamanian company he had established at the end of the war called Wills Export Lines, SA, the Old Timer had purchased two war surplus submarine net layers, the AN-76 and the AN-77, at a cost of twenty-five thousand dollars each. He moved the two diesel-powered boats from a government facility along Virginia's James River up to Baltimore in April 1947. Flying the Panamanian flag and with an international crew aboard, AN-77 was dispatched from Baltimore to Belém on January 16, 1948, to bring *Virginia Lee* home. Capt. Eugene Feraldis was in command. While the "AN" designation is U.S. Navy notation and the vessels were built in the United States, both the AN-76 and the AN-77 were among five units of the ninety-two-vessel class that were transferred to the Royal Navy during the war under lend-lease. AN-77 came to be called HMS *Preventer* and served in Britain from late 1944 until late 1945, working on the Firth of Forth in Scotland, as well as around Holyhead, in Northern Wales.[14]

B. B. Wills was never one to overlook a chance to earn an extra dollar or two. When AN-77 set sail for Belém to tow *Virginia Lee* home, the net layer was carrying a cargo of eleven thousand bags of cement that Wills owned and planned to auction off in Brazil, plus two 1947 Plymouth four-door sedans neatly packed in crates. Wills's insurance carrier quoted a special rate of $308.25 to cover this cargo. Basic insurance coverage for AN-77's round-trip between Baltimore and Belém came to an additional $875.00.[15] The underwriters were adamant, though, that while under tow, *Virginia Lee* not be used to haul any cargo back from Brazil. The southbound journey was accomplished easily enough, although the market for cement reportedly collapsed rather suddenly and Wills's eleven thousand bags sat on a wharf in Belém—unsold—for several years.

In late January 1948, with *Virginia Lee* at the end of a towline, AN-77 was ready to set sail for North America. Prior to departure, according to U.S. insurance underwriters' requirements, the towing lines, the hookup between the two vessels, and the general seaworthiness of *Virginia Lee* were inspected and approved by a designated commercial agent in Belém. The inspection was completed, but Baltimore was 2,960 nautical miles away to the northwest across the open ocean. Assuming that the diesel-powered AN-77 could maintain a speed of between 6 and 8 knots with her tow—and that would be optimal—the journey would take about fifteen to eighteen days.

Captain Feraldis, though, did not set a direct course between Belém and Cape Henry at the mouth of the Chesapeake Bay. Instead he steered a more westerly route that would take him inside the Lesser Antilles and into the Caribbean Sea. While longer in both distance and time, such a course would afford a measure of protection from heavy seas and would also keep him within striking distance of several ports of call should trouble develop en route, or should any supplies be needed. It was a wise decision; serious trouble did indeed develop.

Several days out of Belém, as the AN-77 was off the coast of Venezuela, the towline parted and *Virginia Lee* was set adrift. It took almost a full day for Captain Feraldis to locate the lost steamboat and get a line aboard her. When he did, he could only take *Virginia Lee* under tow by the stern. Remaining at sea under such conditions—much less continuing on to Baltimore—was an invitation to disaster, so Feraldis set a course for Port of Spain, Trinidad, to take stock of his situation. Local residents lined St. Vincent Jetty in the harbor as AN-77 and a local Trinidad tug, *St. George,* maneuvered the steamboat alongside a vacant pier.

Wills had to address one immediate problem. Members of the crew were claiming that under traditional rights associated with "salvage at sea," they now *owned Virginia Lee.* He quickly flew to Trinidad and disposed of this matter by firing the entire crew on the spot. (Several years later the matter was brought to court, where Wills's action was sustained.) As soon as he heard about the diversion to Trinidad, though, Wills instantly realized that despite whatever problems had developed,

EXCURSION BOATS AFTER THE WAR 111

Virginia Lee at sea in January 1948. Photo was taken off the coast of Venezuela by a crew member aboard the onetime submarine net layer AN-77 that was attempting to bring the big vessel back to Baltimore.

a priceless opportunity had also washed up on his beach; he quickly seized it.

One of the improvements that Wills had in mind for *Virginia Lee* was replacing her original pair of four-cylinder, triple-expansion steam engines with a set of twin sixteen-cylinder General Motors diesels he had recently acquired on the war-surplus market. This was a reasonably technical job that Wills preferred to have done back in Baltimore. Besides, the two diesel engines he planned to install aboard the steamboat were themselves in Baltimore!

Virginia Lee's exterior and superstructure, though, were in terrible condition from her years in the tropics—years of operation, plus years of idleness. The hundreds of hours of chipping, painting, and basic carpentry work that would be required before she could reenter passenger service could not only be handled adequately by workers in Trinidad, it could be done far more cheaply in Port of Spain than in any U.S. shipyard. *Virginia Lee* stayed in Trinidad for the better part of three months, during which time Wills had forty thousand dollars' worth of work done to the vessel, primarily by a company called East End Foundries. Fifty local carpenters, mechanics, and painters were put to work on the vessel between January and April 1948.

When Wills flew to Trinidad upon hearing that *Virginia Lee* was forced to put in there, he was wearing a heavy winter overcoat, the lining of which secretly held the cash he would need to get *Virginia Lee*'s repairs under way. Customs officers on the tropical island raised no questions whatsoever, assuming that here was just another ignorant North American who lacked the common sense to learn even rudimentary facts about the local climate before flying down. Having *Virginia Lee* worked on in Trinidad was, by any standard, a serious bargain, even for a man whose entire career was spent in perpetual search of serious bargains.

In mid-April 1948, *Virginia Lee* again set sail for Baltimore. Her engines and boilers had been given sufficient work during the Trinidad layover that they could handle the rest of the trip north. She proceeded out of Port of Spain under her own power and after a short stopover in San Juan, Puerto Rico, successfully completed the two-thousand-mile voyage to Baltimore. The press in Trinidad praised the local craftsmen's

Once rebuilt, the former *Virginia Lee* entered Boston–Provincetown service as *Holiday*. (Photograph by R. Loren Graham, courtesy of B. B. Wills family.)

work in cleaning up what was originally described as a "gray ghost" back when she had suddenly materialized in Port of Spain at the end of a towline in January. The only serious error in the local account was that *Virginia Lee*'s prewar assignment for the Pennsylvania Railroad was described as running between Norfolk and Capetown, South Africa, rather than Cape Charles, Virginia.[16]

By early May 1948, *Virginia Lee* was back in Baltimore and the task of replacing her engines began; it would take almost a year to complete. Once the new diesels were installed and tested, Wills rechristened his latest acquisition *Holiday* and hastened to get her up to Boston. She was to take over the Boston–Provincetown run that *Chauncey M. Depew* had inaugurated in 1947, but which, for want of a proper vessel, Wills had not operated at all in 1948.

The AN-77, the former submarine net layer that towed *Virginia Lee* from Belém to Port of Spain was sold after she completed her assignment. Wills had disposed of her sister ship, the AN-76, even earlier. The two vessels had cost him $50,000 in 1947; he sold one for $45,000 and the other for $75,000 barely a year later, for a nominal profit of 140 percent.[17] One of the pair was transferred to British interests and eventually wound up in the Falkland Islands.

A New Tolchester Boat

In addition to *Chauncey M. Depew* and *Virginia Lee*, another excursion boat that Wills obtained after she served for the military during World War II is one that he renamed *Tolchester* (II). By a twist of circumstance, this vessel survived to become, two decades later, the last Wills-owned and -operated excursion boat to carry passengers.

Wills's acquisition of *Tolchester* (II) involved none of the theatrics associated with *Virginia Lee*. While the vessel did have a noteworthy pedigree, and while she was involved in some interesting episodes over the years, her time with Wills was characterized more by steady performance than by anything dramatic or unusual.

Unlike *Virginia Lee* and *Chauncey M. Depew*, *Tolchester* (II) was not purchased directly from the military or the U.S. Maritime Commission. After the war, she was first picked up by New Jersey interests who christened her *Asbury Park* and used her between lower Manhattan and Atlantic Highlands, New Jersey. She was sold to Wills at the end of the 1948 season, was put to work between Baltimore and Tolchester for the 1949 excursion season, and remained there for a number of years.

The boat was built in Wilmington, Delaware, in 1910 at the famous Harlan and Hollingsworth yard. Powered by a conventional three-cylinder triple-expansion steam engine, she was christened *City of Philadelphia* and was one of two sister ships launched at the same yard on the same day. Both were combination freight and passenger river steamers designed for all-weather service between Philadelphia and Wilmington for their owner, the Wilson Line.

In 1938, Wilson had *City of Philadelphia* rebuilt into an all-passenger seasonal excursion boat at the Maryland Drydock Company's Baltimore yard. She was given a new name in the process, *Liberty Belle*. Requisitioned for wartime service by the U.S. Navy, she served as a target towing vessel on the Chesapeake Bay for the duration.

The 1938 rebuilding included a measure of art deco streamlining. Except for some structural alterations to her upper works during her hitch in the navy, when she was acquired by Wills in late 1948, she looked much the way she had after Wilson Line's rebuilding ten years earlier in 1938. She did sport a new pilothouse after the war, though.

Interestingly, during her years of working out of Baltimore for Wills, *Tolchester* (II)'s principal competitor was Wilson Line's *Bay Belle*. Wilson Line never reinstituted service to Seaside Park after the war, but

The vessel that eventually became *Tolchester* (II) began life as Wilson Line's *City of Philadelphia*. (Photograph from the author's collection.)

Flyer publicizing a combined railroad and excursion boat outing from York, Pennsylvania, to Tolchester Beach, Maryland.

instead opened up a new route between Baltimore and Betterton, Maryland, a beach and picnic grove on Maryland's Eastern Shore a dozen or so miles north of Tolchester. *Bay Belle* herself had been rebuilt by Wilson Line in 1941 at Sun Shipbuilding in Chester, Pennsylvania. Formerly called *City of Wilmington,* she was the other Wilson Line sister ship launched at Harlan and Hollingsworth the same day as the boat that became *Tolchester* (II). While *Tolchester* (II) and *Bay Belle* were hardly similar looking on the outside thanks to their being rebuilt to different external specifications, the onetime sister ships were powered by identical Harlan and Hollingsworth–built three-cylinder, triple-expansion steam engines.

Tolchester Lines promoted their new vessel aggressively. Brochures and advertisements for the 1949 season featured a pen-and-ink likeness of *Tolchester* (II) that far overstated the extent of her streamlining and unhesitatingly called her "Baltimore's Favorite Boat," even though she had yet to carry her first passenger for Wills out of that city. A special flyer promoting group sales and charter excursions used this as its tag line: "Pleasure with Profit." As usual, Wills offered sizable discounts for groups and organizations prepared to handle the sale of excursion tickets to their members away from the wharf. The sale of 50 to 299 adult tickets resulted in a 20 percent discount, 300 to 399 earned a savings of 30 percent, and 400 or more translated to 40 percent. In 1949, a regular adult round-trip ticket between Baltimore and Tolchester Beach was priced at $1.25, weekdays as well as weekends. Children rode for sixty-five cents, while a ticket for a moonlight cruise cost $1.15.

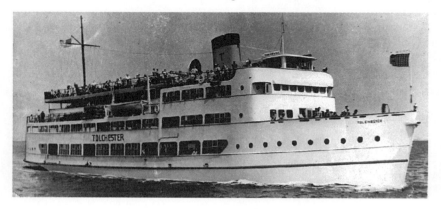

Wilson Line rebuilt the three-deck *City of Philadelphia* of 1910, shown on page 114, into the four-deck *Liberty Belle* in 1938. When B. B. Wills purchased the vessel in 1948, he christened her *Tolchester II*.

EXCURSION BOATS AFTER THE WAR

Shortly after putting *Tolchester* (II) into service, the company moved out of the old Light Street pier in Baltimore, Pier 16, which had been the departure point for Tolchester steamers for decades, and shifted operations to Pier 3 on Pratt Street. Early 1951 marked the initial phase of a total reconfiguration of Baltimore's Inner Harbor from a place whose shore was once lined with steamboat docks and wharves into today's bustling Harborplace development. The bulkhead line along Light Street was moved outward after the piers were removed, and the area behind the bulkhead was filled in. Today the place where steamboats like the two *Tolchester*s, *Bear Mountain*, and *Francis Scott Key* once docked is part of the northbound traffic lanes of a much-widened Light Street.

Old Services and New Ones

The immediate postwar years were steady ones for Wills and his various excursion boat enterprises. As discussed, the principal new service that was added during this period was across Massachusetts Bay from Boston to Provincetown.

The established operator on this route was Cape Cod Steamship, which used a veteran excursion boat that B. B. Wills was more than familiar

Wills was so pleased with *Holiday* that he had seasons greeting cards prepared featuring his new vessel.

with. The boat was *Steel Pier*, originally called *Miami*. As noted earlier, in 1947, Wills put *Chauncey M. Depew* into Boston–Provincetown service opposite *Steel Pier*, but lacking a proper vessel for the route in 1948, he let *Steel Pier* have the Boston–Provincetown run to herself. "Perhaps it will be just as well to be off the route," Wills wrote to Gerald Bruen, his attorney and colleague in Boston, toward the end of the 1947 season, "because there is not enough business for two boats, especially two large boats."[18] This was a telling observation whose accuracy would return to haunt Wills in the near future.

In 1949, *Virginia Lee*'s conversion was nearing completion and Wills was ready to get back into the Provincetown run in a serious way. Cape Cod Steamship and *Steel Pier* backed off in the face of the competition that *Holiday* would clearly provide. Although only *Holiday* now ran between Boston and Provincetown, the 1949 service was marketed as a cooperative venture between Wills's new Boston–Provincetown Line and

Holiday approaching the railroad bridge across the Cape Cod Canal at Buzzards Bay during a September cruise in 1950. (Photograph by R. Loren Graham, courtesy of B. B. Wills family.)

The Light Street waterfront in Baltimore during the winter of 1949–50. The two large vessels are *Holiday* (right) and *Tolchester* (II) (left). Of the two smaller boats sandwiched between the larger vessels, *Madisonville* is on the left, and *Chauncey M. Depew* on the right. (Photograph courtesy of John H. Shaum, Jr.)

the older Cape Cod Steamship Company, *Steel Pier*'s operator. Advertisements in the Boston newspapers boldly proclaimed that the new service with *Holiday* would begin on July 3.

Holiday set sail from Baltimore, and but for a broken steering cable that forced her to put in at Marine Basin in Brooklyn for repairs, she would have reached Boston in time for the July 3 inaugural. As matters turned out, she was only a few hours late and soon became a genuine favorite on the Boston–Provincetown run. She was the largest diesel-powered excursion boat in America and seemed to be proclaiming to all that the excursion boat empire of Benjamin Bowling Wills was poised for more seasons of growth and expansion. The proclamation, however, would prove to be far more illusory than real.

The large boat featured an attractive color scheme. Below the guards her hull was gray, below the waterline, red. Her upper works were white, with a thin red stripe between the first and second decks. Her stack, which had been shortened from her days as steam-powered *Virginia Lee,* was buff with a black top. Her ventilators were also buff on the outside, red on the inside. For her second season of service in 1950, the gray of *Holiday*'s hull extended up to the red stripe between the first and second decks. After her first summer in Boston, *Holiday* returned to Baltimore, and on two successive Sundays in September, she ran all-day excursions between Baltimore and Washington, down on one Sunday, back on the next.

Ship Brokering

The end of World War II saw Wills develop a new maritime business interest, the buying and selling of surplus vessels no longer needed by the military. Two Wills-controlled companies became the vehicles for his ship-brokering activities. One was domestic, the other was based offshore in Panama. Boat Sales was a Baltimore firm that once had its own yard at Key Highway and Williams Street. Under Wills's ownership, the firm conducted business out of the offices of Tolchester Lines at Light Street Pier 16 and later at Pier 3 on Pratt Street. Wills Export Line, SA, was the Panamanian company, and although nominally headquartered in the Central American country, it was in fact run out of Wills's home in Washington, D.C. Once, for instance, when a vessel owned by Wills Export Line was being sold to a buyer in Colombia, that is, transferred from Panamanian to Colombian registry, the paperwork crossed no international borders. It was simply hand-carried from Wills's home on Indian Lane in northwest Washington to the embassy of Panama, a short taxi ride away, for certification and filing. Wills Export Line allowed vessels to be registered outside the United States and operated under a flag of convenience using foreign crews, "because the cost of American labor is almost prohibitive," Wills wrote in 1946.[19] As discussed earlier, when the former submarine net layer AN-77 was sent to

FERRY BOAT FOR SALE

FERRY STEAMER "HOWARD W. JACKSON"

In Wonderful Condition Seen Little Service Used Only In Fresh Water
MUST BE SEEN TO BE APPRECIATED DOCKED AT FOOT OF BROADWAY

DESCRIPTION

OFFICIAL NUMBER : 224929 BUILDER: Maryland Drydock Company
DATE OF REGISTRY: 1925 PORT OF REGISTRY: Baltimore, Md.
REGISTERED TONNAGE: Gross 379 Net 238 RIG: Steam, Side Wheel
LENGTH OVERALL: 140'-0" LENGTH BETWEEN PERPENDICULARS: 126'-0"
BEAM MOULDED: 25'-0" BEAM OVER GUARDS: 45'-6"
DEPTH MOULDED: 11'-0" DRAFT MOULDED: 6'-7"
CONSTRUCTION
    Hull: Steel - 5 W. T. Bulkheads
    House: Wood
    Deck: Wood beams and planking covered with granolithic asphalt planks.
LIFE BOATS: Two - Metal - 18'-0"
PASSENGERS ALLOWED: One passenger for each ten square feet of deck space - main deck.
AUTOMOBILE ALLEYWAYS: Height: 10'-6" Width: 9'-0"
WATER CAPACITY: 2 - 1000 gal. tanks.
FUEL CAPACITY: 20 tons of coal.
Vessel heated by steam.
Vessel steers from either end. Two pilot houses on boat deck, each fitted with a carbon arc searchlight.

ENGINE

One single vertical cylinder beam engine.
VALVE GEAR: Stevens cut-off type. Fitted with four eccentrics and hook rods and starting bar.
CYLINDER DIAMETER: 28" INDICATED HORSEPOWER 350 STROKE: 84"

BOILER

One Scotch marine boiler 10'-0" diameter by 12'-3" long, fitted with 2 - 40" corrugated furnaces.
Maximum steam pressure allowed: 90 pounds. WORKING PRESSURE: 60 pounds
Built by Newport News Shipbuilding & Drydock Co.

Other equipment includes a filter box, feed water heater, condensate pump, connected air pump, surface condenser, duplex ram feed pump, donkey or fire pump, centrifugal circulator and a 5 K.W. electric generator.
    The vessel is in perfect condition, the entire superstructure as well as the main deck and guard were entirely removed and rebuilt, the work having been completed in July 1937. The vessel was then put in commission and operated until January 1, 1939, when it was tied up, machinery greased and necessary steps taken to preserve same in perfect condition. The vessel was drydocked in the summer of 1939 and the hull was painted.
    The vessel was built in 1925 at a cost of $135,179.50.

For further information communicate with
B. B. WILLS

Pier 16 Light Street Baltimore, Md.

Descriptive brochure to promote the sale of the ferryboat *Howard W. Jackson*.

Belém, Brazil, to tow home the *Virginia Lee,* she was owned by Wills Export Line and flew the Panamanian flag.

In all likelihood, Wills did not at first see his purchase of war surplus tonnage as particularly separate from his other various vessel operations. There is evidence, for example, that his motivation in buying two Canadian corvettes, HMCS *Whitby* (K-346) and HMCS *Hawkesbury* (K-415) in late 1945 was to refurbish the pair and put them into some kind of service himself, perhaps under a foreign flag.

Both vessels were built at the Quebec yard of the Morton Engine and Dry Dock Company, commissioned in June 1944, and belonged to the fifteen-ship revised *Flower*-class of Royal Canadian corvettes. (During World War II, Canada operated over a hundred corvettes in many different subclasses.) *Hawkesbury* and *Whitby* each displaced 970 tons, were 208 feet long, could maintain 16 knots, and were driven by a single four-cylinder triple-expansion steam engine built in Montreal by the Canadian Pacific Railway Company. Armament included one 4-inch and two 20-millimeter guns. Both vessels were active in convoy protection work out of Londonderry, Northern Ireland, and were mustered out of service in August 1945.[20] B. B. Wills purchased the pair shortly afterward.

Later that year, Wills contacted the Peninsula and Occidental Steamship Company in Jacksonville, Florida, inquiring if his two corvettes might be converted and used to establish a day passenger service between Key West and Havana.[21] Peninsula and Occidental was the principal steamship operator between Florida and Cuba and should not be confused, although it often is, with a British firm called the Peninsula and *Oriental* Steam Navigation Company. The latter firm's storied liners were once the principal link between England and those outposts of the Queen's empire located "east of Suez."[22]

An interesting question is how a passenger steamship service would have evolved between Florida and pre-Castro Cuba during the postwar era. The possibilities are endless. Perhaps when Mario Puzo later wrote *The Godfather,* he might have had Michael Corleone escaping from Havana not aboard a chartered airplane, but sitting comfortably in a deck chair on a Wills-operated passenger vessel!

In reality, neither HMCS *Whitby* nor HMCS *Hawkesbury* was ever converted into a day passenger vessel. Wills eventually sold off the two warships, but he never cited their acquisition as among his smarter, more lucrative deals. *Hawkesbury* eventually became the freighter *Campuchea,* whose owner was the Tan-Pa Company of Phnom Penh, Cambodia. She flew the flag of France, showed Saigon as her home port, and was broken up in Hong Kong in 1956. *Whitby* reportedly worked for many years as the freighter *Bengo,* but little is known of her later history.

Probably the first vessel that Wills bought and then tried to sell without ever putting into revenue service at all was the Baltimore harbor ferryboat *Howard W. Jackson,* which he purchased back in 1939. When the Norfolk County (Virginia) Ferry people contacted Wills with technical inquiries about the boat, Wills even gave them an option for purchasing her. But she proved to be much too slow for their purposes, and the option was never exercised.[23] When Wills's own Boston-Nantasket excursion boat service was getting back in high gear after the U.S. Coast Guard lifted wartime restrictions on Boston Harbor, the Old Timer inquired about the merit of deploying *Howard W. Jackson* on an over-and-back ferryboat route between downtown Boston and Logan Airport, given the expanding role of air transport. No chance, he was told, because the city's East Boston subway would soon be extended north and serve the airport directly.[24]

Over the years, the boat's wooden superstructure deteriorated, and a couple of small fires accelerated the overall decay. Wills eventually sold the vessel, but not to a potential ferryboat operator. Instead, on December 13, 1950, she passed into the hands of the Patapsco Scrap Corporation for $3,750, with the bill of sale identifying her as "the ferryboat hulk *Howard W. Jackson.*"[25]

Throughout the 1950s, Wills's purchase of vessels for resale was apparently more random than anything else. That is, he took advantage of opportunities that arose, but was not following any kind of strategic or long-range business plan. Having had no particular luck with the two Canadian corvettes, he tended to avoid large, steam-powered ships, concentrating instead on smaller, diesel-powered craft that offered a wider variety of conversion possibilities for their new civilian owners. In 1951, for instance, he purchased a onetime navy submarine chaser (SC 989, then called *Milbon*) and quickly sold the 107-foot vessel to South American interests. In 1959 he bought the 1916-built Coast Guard buoy tender *Palmetto* (WAGL-265) and effectively hung a "for sale" sign on her pilothouse. Various kinds and classes of former U.S. Navy landing craft were also owned by Wills at different times.

The full story of B. B. Wills's ship-brokering activities would be an interesting one to tell. It would also be a difficult one to report completely and accurately, since Wills sometimes served merely as a middleman—at a commission, of course—in a transaction involving two other parties, and he never took title to the vessel himself. Table 7-1 is a partial listing of various vessels that Wills is known to have once owned solely for the purpose of resale.

TABLE 7-1
Some Brokerage Vessels Owned by B. B. Wills

Name*	Off. no.	Type	Year built	Propulsion	Period of ownership by BBW	Comments
Howard W. Jackson	224929	Harbor ferryboat	1925	st.p.	1939–50	Sold for scrap by BBW; see text
(1) HMCS *Hawkesbury* (K-415) (2) *Campuchea*	None	RN (Canada) corvette	1944	st.s.	1945 to ca. 1949	See text
(1) HMCS *Whitby* (K-346) (2) *Bengo* (??)	None	RN (Canada) corvette	1944	st.s	1945 to ca. 1949	*See text*
AN-77 (HMS *Preventer*)	None	USN submarine net layer	194	ol.s	1947–49	Used to tow *Virginia Lee* out of Belém, Brazil; see text
AN-76 (HMS ??)	None	USN submarine net layer	194	ol.s	1947–48	Sold to British interests; see text
(2) *Benjamin Bros. II* (1) P 148 (US Army)	255041	Fishing boat	1943	ol.s	1952–53	
PCE(R) 848	None	USN submarine chaser	1943	ol.s	1948–51	Intended for conversion into day excursion boat; see text

Continued on next page

Table 7-1—Continued

(3) *Milbon*	256800	Freight boat; former USN submarine chaser	1942	ol.s.	1951–53	Sold to Colombian interests
(1) SC 989 (USN)						
(2) *Air Parakeet* (USCG)						
Palmetto (WAGL-265)	None	USCG buoy tender	1916	ol.s.	ca. 1960 to ??	
William T. Belt	282753	Tug/fireboat; ex-USN	1943	ol.s.	ca. 1964 to ca. 1965	Used by BBW as towboat; sold to Mobile, Ala. interests; see text
(2) USS *Maquinna* (YTB-225)						
LST 306	None	USN landing ship/tank	1942	ol.s.	mid-1960s	Participated in allied landings at Salerno and Normandy; given name USS *Barnalillo County* in 1955; possibly scrapped by BBW ca. 1965
LCU 1518	None	USN utility landing craft	1953	ol.s.	1962–65	Damaged in 1964 *Accomac* fire
City of Norfolk	208414	Overnight packet	1911	st.s.	1962–64	Former Old Bay Line; see text
City of Richmond	211710	Overnight packet	1913	st.s.	1962–64	Former Old Bay Line; lost at sea en route U.S. Virgin Islands; see text

*Numbers in parentheses indicate previous and/or subsequent names of the same vessel.

Abbreviations: st.p. = steam powered; propelled by paddlewheels; st.s. = steam powered; propelled by screw propeller(s); ol.s. = diesel powered; propelled by screw propeller(s); USN, United States Navy; RN, Royal Navy; USCG, United States Coast Guard.

Note: absence of an "official number" suggests that unit was never documented as a U.S. merchant vessel.

The High-Water Mark

With the inauguration of Boston–Provincetown service by *Holiday* in the summer of 1949, the excursion boat empire of B. B. Wills reached its all-time high-water mark. Six separate services were in simultaneous operation that summer in four major cities, with incidental excursions operated in additional cities at either the beginning or the end of the season. The same pattern prevailed in 1950 as well; table 7-2 lists the principal vessels assigned to each of the six services.

TABLE 7-2
The Excursion Boat Empire of B. B. Wills
1949–50

City	Service	Vessel(s)
Boston	Boston–Provincetown	*Holiday*
Boston	Boston–Nantasket	*Nantasket, Allerton, Francis Scott Key*
New York	Statue of Liberty ferry	*Liberty, Mayfair*
Baltimore	Baltimore–Tolchester	*Tolchester* (II)
Washington	Potomac River Line	*Bear Mountain*
Washington	Robert E. Lee Steamboat Co.	*Robert E. Lee*

"Muffled Drums for Albany-Potomac"

While the immediate postwar years were generally a time of expansion for Wills, one important element of his empire came to an end during this period. His original excursion boat, *Potomac*, was withdrawn from service following the 1948 season.[26] Built in 1880, the old sidewheeler had simply reached the end of her useful life. The same season, 1949, that the newly reconditioned *Holiday* began service for Wills in Boston was also the first season that *Potomac*'s walking beam would not rise rhythmically up and down as she headed downriver from Washington.

By her final season of 1948, *Potomac* was running nothing but nonstop cruises out of Washington. True enough, by prearrangement, an occasional cruise would also pause in nearby Alexandria, Virginia, to board additional passengers. Alexandria, though, was never a *destination* for *Potomac* like Chapel Point, Colonial Beach, and Liverpool Point

EXCURSION BOATS AFTER THE WAR

Excursion boats in winter quarters at Nantasket Beach between the 1947 and 1948 seasons. Starting at the left tip of the U and going around, the boats are *Francis Scott Key, Mohawk, Nantasket, Allerton,* and *Mayflower.*

in earlier days. It was simply a supplementary stop for boarding passengers on a downriver cruise.

After the war but before *Potomac*'s final season, officials in Colonial Beach wrote to Wills asking if he planned to resume steamboat excursions between there and Washington.[27] Wills, of course, had no desire to send *Potomac* on daylong cruises down the river, except for an occasional charter trip where the Potomac River Line would be at no risk. His reply to Norman Brewington, the acting mayor of Colonial Beach, was diplomatic, though diplomacy was hardly Wills's strongest suit over the years. He lamented how difficult it was to hire experienced steamboat crews those days and said he would give the town's request consideration in the future.[28]

Potomac's final day of service was Sunday, September 12, 1948. By coincidence, the Hudson River Day Line's *Hendrick Hudson* made her last trip that same day. *Potomac* actually ran three trips that Sunday. The first was a "midnight" trip that headed out of Washington at 12:56 A.M. with 289 passengers aboard and steamed downriver to Broad Creek; she returned to Washington at 2:58 A.M. There were 761 passengers aboard an afternoon cruise that left Washington at 3:07 P.M. and steamed south to Indian Head before returning at 6:55 P.M. Then there was the finale, designated as trip No. 161 of the season, which left the pier at 8:58 P.M. with 543 passengers aboard.[29] Table 7-3 lists all the time points that Captain Henry E. Slye, Jr., *Potomac*'s master since 1944, noted in the log for that trip. One can only wonder if even a single passenger among the 543 customers aboard that evening understood the wonderful steamboat heritage that *Potomac* represented, or sensed that she would never steam again.

TABLE 7-3
Potomac's Last Trip

Wind: south   Weather: warm and clear   Tide: ebb

lv.	Washington	8:58 P.M.
—	Haines Point	9:07
—	Jones Point	9:26
—	Broad Creek	9:40
—	Ft. Washington	9:48
—	Marshall Hall	10:04 (turn)
—	Ft. Washington	10:23
—	Broad Creek	10:31
—	Jones Point	10:47
—	Haines Point	11:07
ar.	Washington	11:35

On May 24, 1949, with the Washington fireboat *William T. Belt* assisting in the maneuver, *Potomac* was moved away from her Washington pier and, shortly afterward, towed away to a Baltimore scrap yard. There her graceful cabin work was cut away and she was converted into the unpowered barge *Ware River* for additional years of useful work on the Chesapeake Bay.

Her mighty walking beam has been preserved. It is today a major outdoor exhibit at The Mariners' Museum in Newport News, Virginia, a permanent memento of an era when vertical-beam steam engines played a central role in moving the nation's waterborne commerce.

A final irony associated with *Potomac*'s departure from Washington is this: the district fireboat *William T. Belt*, which helped move the inert sidewheeler away from her pier in May 1949, was a workboat that toiled for the U.S. Navy during World War II. In the 1960s she was purchased by Benjamin B. Wills and used in contract work hauling government-owned surplus merchant ships around the Norfolk area before Wills sold her to yet another operator.

The Potomac River Line itself, though, remained very much in business even after *Potomac* retired. Wills moved *Bear Mountain* down from Baltimore at the end of the 1948 season. The boat took over *Potomac*'s assignments at the start of the 1949 season, with *Tolchester* (II) picking up *Bear Mountain*'s work out of Baltimore.

Shrimp Boats

Like a cinematic folk hero of a later day—Forrest Gump—B. B. Wills's entry into the shrimp boat business was probably more accidental than anything else. Over the winter of 1951–52, he and his wife, Gertrude, were vacationing in Florida visiting old friends and avoiding the cold blasts of a typical northern weather. Since many of the people whom Wills visited were individuals he had run across in some maritime situation over the years, they would naturally invite their visitor down to the local docks to take a look at some new vessel they had just purchased, or were trying to sell, or were having trouble fixing up.

Wills, of course, always had a weathered eye out for a hull that could be easily and cheaply converted into an excursion boat. One day when Wills was in Fort Lauderdale, a gentleman name C. C. Bowers showed him a 104-foot-long war-surplus vessel, aboard which he had ingeniously constructed a complete below-deck refrigeration plant. This technological improvement promised to allow any fishing boat so equipped to remain at sea until the captain and crew had taken aboard a full catch. Bowers, though, lacked sufficient capital to outfit a complete fleet of boats with similar equipment.

At this point in his career, Wills was not looking for any new ventures that would require his own day-to-day managerial attention, but he did have some money to invest. Out of this chance meeting in Fort Lauderdale emerged a new Miami-based shrimping company known as Wills–Bowers. Table 7-4 provides a glimpse of Wills's Florida fishing boat fleet, circa 1954.

TABLE 7-4
The Miami Fishing Boat Fleet, Circa 1954

Name*	Off. No.	Hull	Gross Tons	Length	Place Built (year)
Dusky	247411	W	28	48.8	St. Augustine, Fla. (1945)
Mako	247360	S	30	51.5	Tampa, Fla. (1945)
(4) Sachem (1) Sachem (2) Ungava (3) Ivaneo	225427	W	77	71.3	Thomaston, Maine (1925)
(2) Susan (1) SC 1050 (USN)	251188	W	127	105.4	W. Atlantic City, N.J. (1943)
(3) Jay Bee (1) QS 78 (U.S. Army) (2) C-77455 (USN)	262728	Comp.	138	100.7	Daytona Beach, Fla. (1944)
(3) Camarones (1) QS-76 (U.S. Army) (2) C-77453 (USN)	262729	Comp.	137	100.8	Daytona Beach, Fla. (1944)

* Names in parentheses indicate previous and/or subsequent names of the same vessel.
Jay Bee and Camarones were owned by Wills-Bowers; all others were owned by B. B. Wills. Camarones was lost on January 21, 1953, when she went aground on a reef near Cayo Corker, 20 miles northeast of the city of Belize in a country then called British Honduras. Abbreviations: W, wood; S, steel; Comp., composition.

The Old Timer paid sufficient attention to the shrimp business, though, that he drew some conclusions about the pitfalls that boat owners must avoid. Never pay the captain of a shrimp boat straight wages, Wills believed; pay him only a commission on his catch. If you paid straight wages, the captain will be under too much temptation to put his boat into the nearest Caribbean port on the slightest pretext and draw pay while having a good time.[30] Writing to their sons Gene and Ben during that Florida vacation in early 1952, Gertrude had this to say about her husband's enthusiasm upon seeing a vessel equipped with a complete on-board refrigeration plant: "So it looks like we will be singing that song 'The Shrimp Boats Are Coming.'"[31]

CHAPTER EIGHT

Shadows Start to Fall

The excursion boat empire of Benjamin Bowling Wills reached its apogee at midcentury, with the capstone being the entry of the newly dieselized *Holiday* into Boston–Provincetown service in the summer of 1949. Wills began new ventures in subsequent summers, including some interesting and unusual ones. Nonetheless, the steady growth and expansion that Wills achieved in the 1930s, and to a lesser extent in the 1940s, did not carry forward into the 1950s. Instead, his excursion boat empire entered a period of contraction and decline.

The Overall Problem

Three noteworthy factors contributed to the decline. First, Wills himself began to devote more of his time and energy to various real estate interests, even using the sales proceeds from the disposition of certain excursion boats as investment capital for housing activities.[1] Second, his fleet of largely steam-powered excursion boats was getting old, but he never managed to put together a workable financing plan for a major investment in new, or at least *newer*, diesel-powered vessels. Finally, the excursion boat business itself was becoming a much riskier proposition overall as first affluent and then middle-class clientele were finding private automobiles a more attractive alternative for leisure travel. Excursion boat operators were thus forced to market their services largely to those who could afford little else.

Wills's interest in the real estate business went back to his own postcollegiate days and his moving to Miami to be a part of the Florida land boom of the 1920s. Even at the height of his excursion boat days, with vessels in operation all along the east coast, he spoke with longing of another career: "I often wish I was a real estate man instead of a small boat man."[2]

In the early fifties, when it became obvious that the domestic excursion boat industry was not poised for a new era of growth and prosperity, Wills began to dabble again in real estate ventures. Living as he did in Washington, D.C., the Old Timer was quick to see the potential in the undeveloped tracts of land in nearby Fairfax County, Virginia. In 1953 he formed a partnership with his second cousin, home builder James Burch, to construct several private dwellings in Annandale, Virginia. Other real estate ventures followed until in 1957, Wills, together with his sons J. Eugene and a man by the name of Alfred Van Metre, formed a partnership that went on to become one of the major forces in home-building throughout the Washington suburbs. By 1960, the firm of Wills and Van Metre was building two hundred new units a year, and Wills's youngest son, P. Reed, had also started a successful real estate business.

Wills clearly understood that a fleet of old steamboats represented a serious cash drain on his overall excursion boat enterprise. The entrepreneur once succinctly described the problems of companies operating steam-powered excursion boats: "The main reason these vessels have gone out of business is due to the large consumption of fuel and heavy labor costs involved in taking care of large steam vessels."[3] He also noted that an active steam-powered excursion boat required a licensed engineer and crew of three others to be aboard twenty-four hours a day to care for the boilers and other equipment. In contrast, once a diesel-powered vessel was shut down for the evening, the only requirement was a low-paid night watchman—or maybe even just a good padlock.[4] Wills needed new boats, and they had to be diesel powered.

More than once, Wills drew up plans for a major fleet upgrade, but none of the schemes ever came to fruition. The lack of action may have come from Wills's own increasing attention to his real estate business, or the difficulties in arranging financing for such an upgrade, or simply a lack of motivation. In any case, the upgrade never happened. *Holiday* and *Liberty* were exceptions to the rule. But after all the aggravation of converting the steam-powered *Virginia Lee* into the diesel-powered *Holiday*, Wills understandably had little desire to repeat the experience.

Wills did raise some capital after the war by taking out a $245,000 loan from the Reconstruction Finance Corporation (RFC), a loan against which he was prepared to pledge his entire excursion boat fleet. The RFC was uncomfortable, however, with the multiple ownership of Wills's fleet by so many different subsidiary companies. In 1948, nine vessels were reregistered under the name of a unified Wills Lines, hailing port, Baltimore, Maryland.[5]

Wills Lines never became an operating company of any kind; it was simply an entity of convenience to facilitate the securing of an RFC loan. The proceeds of the loan, however, were not used to underwrite a serious program of fleet replacement or upgrading. Although some money was used for completing the conversion of *Holiday* from steam to diesel, the remainder served as routine working capital to keep the old boats in passable operating condition.

Wilson Line after the War

Wills's principal competitor over the years, the Wilson Line, did move ahead after World War II with precisely the kind of fleet upgrade that Wills knew was necessary, but was either unwilling or unable to accomplish. Wilson Line never brought *State of Delaware* back from the Amazon; she was replaced by a totally new excursion boat the company had built and christened *Delaware Belle*. The new vessel was, obviously, of all-steel construction and was powered by a pair of eight-cylinder diesel engines. Licensed to carry 3,400 passengers, she entered service for Wilson during the 1947 excursion season.

Over the next six years, Wilson Line added three additional diesel-powered excursion boats to its fleet. They were not totally new vessels like *Delaware Belle*, but converted U.S. Navy "submarine chasers" built during World War II. Two vessels were former PC-class, while one was a PCE(R). Although called submarine chasers, the diesel-powered vessels performed a variety of general-purpose functions during the war.

PCE(R) 854 was launched in the Calumet Harbor section of Chicago in 1943. As an indication of how completely the nation's industrial capability had been converted to war-related production, all thirteen of the navy's PCE(R)s were built by Pullman-Standard, a company that normally turned out railroad cars, not vessels of any kind.

Wilson Line crafted a thoroughly modern-looking, four-deck excursion boat out of the onetime sub chaser PCE(R) 854. She was given the name *Liberty Belle* and effectively replaced Wilson Line's earlier, steam-powered *Liberty Belle*, formerly *City of Philadelphia*, which the navy had requisitioned during the war. Wilson Line felt that the older *Liberty Belle* was not worth rehabilitating and returning to service afterward. This older *Liberty Belle* was the same vessel that Wills had purchased in 1948 and renamed *Tolchester* (II). In 1949 Wilson Line converted PC-1258 into a three-deck vessel it called *Boston Belle*, and three years later, the company turned PC-1207 into the roughly similar-looking *Sea Belle*.[6]

In contrast to the Wilson Line's successful conversion of three navy submarine chasers into modern passenger vessels, Wills was not so successful with a similar venture. He had also purchased a PCE(R)-class vessel after the war—the 848. Both the Wilson Line and the Wills Line PCE(R)s served with distinction in the Pacific during the war. PCE(R) 848 was cited for its participation in the landings at Leyte and Lingayen Gulf, while PCE(R) 854 was honored for mine-sweeping operations in the East China Sea.[7]

After Wills took title to PCE(R) 848 in San Diego on January 21, 1947, and a west coast ship surveyor had certified her seaworthiness for an ocean voyage—as required by Wills's insurance agent—she departed under her own power for Baltimore. The trip down the Pacific coast, through the Panama Canal, and up to the Chesapeake Bay took almost seven weeks.

On several occasions Wills spoke about converting PCE(R) 848 into an excursion boat. The year before he bought the sub chaser, 1946, he

The U.S. Navy's PCE(R) 853. Wilson Line converted her sister ship PCE(R) 854 into the excursion boat *Liberty Belle*. Wills purchased PCE(R) 848, but never managed to turn her into a passenger vessel. (Photograph courtesy of U.S. Naval Institute.)

put together a reasonable enough plan for converting two war-surplus vessels into excursion boats as the backbone of his postwar fleet.[8] But the only action to emerge from this plan was the conversion of *Holiday*, and Wills eventually sold PCE(R) 848, presumably to foreign interests.

Hand in hand with the upgrading of the Wilson Line fleet, the company's plans for service expansion also moved forward. In 1946, the line dispatched the 1885-built steamboat *Dixie*, originally named *Brandywine*, north to inaugurate a new service in Boston. Out of deference to northern sensibilities, *Dixie* was renamed *Pilgrim Belle* for her assignment in New England. In 1948, Wilson Line replaced *Pilgrim Belle* in Boston with the newly converted *Liberty Belle*, which was replaced a year later by *Boston Belle*. The latter two boats worked a new Boston–Plymouth route, not the nonstop sightseeing service that *Pilgrim Belle* had inaugurated in 1946. Then in 1950, thanks to a lease that Wilson Line negotiated with town officials in Provincetown for dock space there, *Boston Belle* went to work not between Boston and Plymouth but in direct competition with Wills's *Holiday* on the Boston–Provincetown run.

In the entire history of the American excursion boat industry, the Boston–Provincetown run in the summer of 1950 was apparently the first and the last time that two large diesel-powered passenger vessels competed with each other over the same route for a full season. ("Large" is defined as a two-thousand-passenger capacity, or more.) Newspaper advertisements placed by each company tried to position its own service in the best possible light:

- "Largest and fastest" *(Holiday)*
- "Ultra-modern and stream-lined" *(Boston Belle)*
- "Outdraws its Rival 2-to-1" *(Holiday)*
- "World's greatest excursion liner" *(Boston Belle)*

In reality, however, the two vessels, between them, were providing far more daily capacity than the Boston–Provincetown route warranted. Wills himself had recognized this market reality years earlier, when *Steel Pier* was running to Provincetown. Furthermore, because competitive pressure tended to restrain the level of fare that either company could charge, neither operator—Wilson nor Wills—enjoyed a terribly profitable season that year.

B. B. Wills decided that one way to counter the Wilson Line was politically. Calling on old contacts from his undergraduate days at Holy Cross College, he mounted an effort in the Massachusetts state legislature to have a rather self-serving bill enacted into law. In simple terms,

House Bill No. 230, introduced over the winter of 1950-51, would have given any steamboat operator important rights to any intrastate route that operator was running on a specified date—a date conveniently prior to Wilson Line's advent on the Boston–Provincetown service.

The proposed law did not give Wills exclusive rights to any service; it merely gave the older operator primary rights and required any newer operator to demonstrate that its proposed additional service was required by public necessity.[9] The law would have established Wills's monopoly on the Boston–Provincetown and Boston–Nantasket routes. With a perfectly straight face, Wills claimed that the legislation would benefit Wilson Line equally, since the Wilmington company would be given primary rights to the Boston–Plymouth service. The problem was, of course, that the Wilson Line had no interest at all in retaining the Boston–Plymouth route. The line saw it as largely a placeholder in the Boston market, and was far more interested in Boston–Provincetown, and even Boston–Nantasket.

Wills enlisted the support of Massachusetts state senator Maurice Donohue, of Holyoke, in his effort. Donohue later became president of the Massachusetts senate and one of the most influential and respected Democratic politicians in the state. Even with such heavyweight political support and an intense letter-writing campaign mounted on Wills's behalf by the Holy Cross Club of Boston, his bid failed and the bill was defeated.

Wilson Line, of course, marshaled its own lobbying effort in opposition to the proposed legislation, and by all objective standards, Wilson Line's position was much more reasonable than that of B. B. Wills. Elmer P. Atherton, Wilson Line's counsel, put it this way: "Under the thin guise of a routine regulatory measure, this bill asks you to summarily discard American free enterprise and free competition which made this country the greatest producer and consumer in the world."[10]

For all intents and purposes, Wills had tried to have the state legislature enact a law that would ban a perfectly reputable excursion boat company from operating vessels over routes that Wills preferred to operate alone. Ironically echoing why Wills himself was kept from purchasing the assets of the Nantasket–Boston Steamboat Company back in 1941, the letter that the Holy Cross Club of Boston sent to its members had characterized Wilson Line as a group of *outsiders!* The letter spoke of "a formidable outfit from Delaware" and "the powerful, multimillionaire Wilson Line" that was attempting to out-muscle and displace a venerable New England businessman—namely Benjamin Bowling Wills.[11]

Holiday *in Trouble*

While this drama was playing itself out in the halls and chambers of the Massachusetts statehouse on Beacon Hill in Boston, drama of a different sort was occuring elsewhere. Events on the high seas south of Cape Hatteras, North Carolina, would have an even more decisive impact on the future of the Boston–Provincetown excursion boat service.

Because competition from the Wilson Line had severely reduced *Holiday*'s revenue during the 1950 season, Wills decided to look for winter work for his big diesel during the off season. "We have such a heavy investment in this vessel," he said, "that a short season of sixty days in Boston isn't sufficient to make ends meet."[12] Following her first season on the Boston–Provincetown run, 1949, *Holiday* ran a successful Baltimore–Washington round-trip, down on one September Sunday, back on the next. But by 1950, Wills felt that a more extended off-season assignment was needed. He quickly developed a plan that would send *Holiday* south to Tampa on Florida's Gulf coast, where she would run a series of day trips and moonlight cruises on Tampa Bay from late January through March.[13]

With Capt. Winfield H. McKown of Boston in command and a crew of seventeen others aboard, *Holiday* left Baltimore early on February 2, 1951, in ballast, for her winter assignment in Florida. She cleared Cape Henry and entered the Atlantic Ocean later that day. At 1:00 A.M. the next morning, February 3, she passed the Currituck buoy north of Cape Hatteras.

By 3:30 A.M., though, the vessel was rolling in a thick northerly sea; at 4:55 A.M., with the weather worsening, the starboard cable on her steering gear snapped. Captain McKown had an auxiliary gear quickly rigged and put in place. It was working within minutes. At 5:45 A.M., however, this auxiliary system also failed. No on-the-spot repairs were possible this time; *Holiday* was in serious trouble.

McKown hove the vessel with her stern into the sea and held this position by calling for slow astern on both engines. This stabilized matters somewhat, except that *Holiday* started taking water over her stern and the force of it began to damage her after cabin work. At 6:30 A.M., with no improvement in the weather, *Holiday* radioed the Coast Guard for assistance. A search plane was immediately sent out to assess the situation, and merchant vessels in the vicinity were asked to stand by.

Captain McKown maintained reasonable stability for the rest of the day on February 3. The next morning the Coast Guard cutters *Marion* and *Cherokee* arrived and took *Holiday* in tow. She arrived in Morehead

City, North Carolina, the next day, February 5. Even before she made port, B. B. Wills was telling the press back in Washington that *Holiday* would be repaired quickly and would continue on to her winter assignment in Tampa.[14] After a quick inspection at Morehead City, though, the Coast Guard withdrew *Holiday*'s permit for continuing her coastal journey to Florida.[15]

If *Holiday*'s entry into Boston–Provincetown service in July 1949 can be regarded as the apogee of the Wills excursion boat empire, the same vessel's being towed ignominiously into Morehead City a mere nineteen months later can be just as correctly regarded as the beginning of a steady but relentless decline. *Holiday* herself, for instance, would never carry another revenue passenger for B. B. Wills.

The damage to *Holiday* was not severe enough to render her a total loss. The full insurance estimate came to $38,024.55, but that included everything—piloting fees for the arrival at Morehead City, for instance, and replacing broken furniture and dinnerware.[16] From Wills's perspective, however, there was not only the casualty loss. He also could not recoup any of the year's operating losses by a successful winter season in Tampa. Adding to his problems was the uncertainty of the next summer, since his competitor, the Wilson Line, would again be running to Provincetown.

Wills quickly realized that it would be foolish to spend good money repairing *Holiday*, only to lose even more during the 1951 season competing against *Boston Belle.* Though dejected, Wills was willing to sit down with his adversary and negotiate the sale of *Holiday* to them. Wilson Line was interested in the vessel not as an addition to its summertime excursion fleet, but for conversion into a roll-on/roll-off automobile-carrying ferry for its Virginia Ferry Company subsidiary. The sale was completed in the spring of 1951, and the vessel that began life as *Virginia Lee* was reconditioned by the Newport News Shipbuilding and Dry Dock Company.[17]

Then, with new doors and loading stages built into her bow and stern, and a second stack added to give the vessel a more balanced look, *Holiday* was renamed *Accomac* and put to work on August 31, 1951, across the mouth of the Chesapeake Bay between Little Creek and Kiptopke Beach. The route was virtually the same one she had worked for the Pennsylvania Railroad as *Virginia Lee* before World War II. The main difference was that in keeping with the country's changing travel habits, she no longer offered connecting service to and from PRR passenger trains. Now she was rigged to haul people and their automobiles across the mouth of the Chesapeake, a service she would continue to operate

Holiday at the Newport News Shipbuilding and Dry Dock Company being converted into the automobile-carrying ferry *Accomac*, June 1951.

until 1964, when the Chesapeake Bay Bridge/Tunnel was completed and open-water ferries were no longer needed between the lower end of the Delmarva Peninsula and the greater Norfolk area.

What Might Have Been

Around the same time that B. B. Wills was selling *Holiday* to Wilson Line, his wife, Gertrude, wrote a letter that leaves some interesting questions. In writing to their son Gene, who, like his father, was a student at Holy Cross College in Worcester, Massachusetts, Gertrude Wills expressed concern over the stress that the pending sale of *Holiday* was causing her husband. "Daddy is going through some very trying days," she wrote. She also suggested that the Old Timer would prefer not to sell the vessel to the Wilson Line at all, and that her husband was talking to another potential buyer, the Hudson River Day Line.[18]

Wilson Line/Chesapeake Ferry, of course, eventually purchased *Holiday*. But the notion that the Day Line, then controlled by Wills's former associate and longtime friend, George Sanders, was even passably interested in *Holiday* allows for some marvelous speculation. For instance, would the Day Line in 1951 have run *Holiday* in addition to its three steamboats, *Robert Fulton, Alexander Hamilton,* and *Peter Stuyvesant*? Or would the advent of *Holiday* into Day Line service have led to an earlier retirement for the company's last walking-beam sidewheeler, *Robert Fulton*, a vessel that actually remained in regular Hudson River service through the 1954 excursion season? These are hypothetical questions, of course, whose answers will never be known.

No More Nanny Boats

With the departure of *Holiday*, Wilson Line and *Boston Belle* had the Boston–Provincetown run all to themselves when the 1951 excursion season got under way. Wills, for his part, continued to run a fleet of turn-of-the-century steamboats, *Allerton, Nantasket,* and *Francis Scott Key*, back and forth between Boston and Nantasket.

Unfortunately, matters would not remain stable for Wills and his "Nanny boats." In 1951, the Wilson Line filed a petition in Suffolk County Superior Court against the selectmen of the town of Hull and

B. B. Wills. The company sought a writ of mandamus to prohibit the town from continuing its exclusive lease of the town pier in Hull to Wills's Nantasket Boat Line.

Superior Court Judge John V. Sullivan ruled that the 1941 state legislation that authorized the town to acquire the pier at Nantasket did not authorize an exclusive lease of the facility to Wills and his company, or to anyone, for that matter. There could be an exclusive lease for a certain number of years, Judge Sullivan said, but such an agreement must be put out for public bid by all qualified steamboat companies at reasonable intervals. The town agreed that it would do so before the start of the 1952 excursion season. Wills realized that the future of the Nantasket Boat Line was anything but secure. Wilson Line would certainly make a spirited effort to earn a place on the Nantasket route in 1952, and if he intended to retain the service, he would have to provide something better than *Nantasket*, *Allerton*, and *Francis Scott Key*.

In the face of all this uncertainty, instead of putting his fleet into winter quarters at Nantasket once the 1951 season was over as had been the custom, the three boats were sent south to Baltimore. *Francis Scott Key* and *Nantasket* steamed under their own power, *Allerton* arrived at the end of a towline.

When the town of Hull sought proposals over the winter of 1951–52 for a new multiyear lease of the town pier in Nantasket, Wills put together a halfhearted proposal that called for sending *Bear Mountain*, and possibly even the 1878-built *Mayfair*, north to Boston the following summer. But on February 6, 1952, Hull officials awarded a five-year franchise to the Wilson Line for seasonal service between Nantasket and Boston. Thus, when the 1952 excursion season began, Wilson Line was operating the Boston–Nantasket service. The three boats that had worked for Wills's Nantasket Boat Line had been sold to the North American Smelting Company of Wilmington, Delaware, and were on their way to that company's scrap yard in Bordentown, New Jersey.

Wills-owned excursion boats can hardly be called a Boston fixture or a tradition on the same scale as, say, Old North Church or the swan boats in the Public Garden. Nevertheless, for seven marvelous summers from 1945 through 1951, the Old Timer kept the venerable "Nanny boats" running, and that, by any standard, is no insignificant accomplishment. Strangely enough, B. B. Wills would return and make one last stand on both the Boston–Provincetown and Boston–Nantasket routes some years down the road.

See You in Court

Although Wills was politically and competitively outmaneuvered in Boston by his arch rival, the Wilson Line, the Old Timer felt that Wilson's business tactics presented him with a different kind of opportunity. On April 13, 1952, his attorneys filed suit against the Wilson Line in federal court in Baltimore, claiming that Wilson Line's pricing policies on the Boston–Provincetown run during the summer of 1950 drove him out of business and thus represented "monopolistic practices." Wills sought compensatory damages of $3.75 million on behalf of both the Wills Lines and the Nantasket Boat Line. Named in the suit were three Wilson Line officials, George B. Junkin, the company's president; Lawrence C. Campbell, the vice president and general manager; and Frank Weber, the traffic manager. Wills was represented by a pair of attorneys, Vernon H. Wiesand, of Baltimore, and Thurman Arnold, of Washington.[19]

In later years, Wills would boast that he had "won" this case.[20] In fact, though, attorneys for the two sides reached an out-of-court agreement that saw Wilson pay Wills $44,000. While not an insignificant sum of money, in light of the $3.75 million originally sought, the smaller amount seemed more of a nuisance settlement on Wilson's part. With this payment, Wilson Line could avoid the time and money that a prolonged litigation would entail, and need not admit guilt or liability on the matter of "monopolistic practices."

Wills's civil action against the Wilson Line in 1952 was perhaps the most notable litigation to emanate from his various excursion boat companies over the years. He was a party to many other court cases, though, most of them totally routine. A passenger might trip and fall aboard one of his vessels and bring suit to recover damages, for instance. Wills himself took an intense interest in even the most trivial of claims filed against his companies. The Wills Papers contain interesting correspondence between Wills and his various attorneys discussing legal strategies, often involving individual claims for less than a hundred dollars.

As far as can be determined, only one case involving B. B. Wills and his excursion boats ever made its way to the Supreme Court of the United States. It was a civil matter whose facts were not in dispute. On January 15, 1953, when Wills ran the Statue of Liberty ferry service in New York, *Mayfair* was preparing to make a 3:30 P.M. departure from the Statue of Liberty to Manhattan. Sixty-one passengers were aboard when a thick blanket of fog descended and made navigation impossible. The fog had come and gone all day long and was sometimes so severe that it caused several mishaps between other vessels in the harbor. The unusual weather merited front-page coverage in the next morning's newspapers. Twelve people suffered minor injuries, for instance, when the municipal ferryboat *Gold Star Mother* collided with the United States Lines freighter *American Veteran* near Governors Island.[21]

Mayfair remained tied up to the pier at Bedloe's Island until after eight o'clock in the evening, when the captain decided that the fog had lifted sufficiently to allow him to proceed. Lines were cast off and *Mayfair* moved away from the small wharf at Bedloe's Island, only to become quickly surrounded by fog again. "Stop engines" was the command, and the boat began to drift . . . right into a pier owned by the federal government but leased to a company called Tankport Terminals.

The damage was minimal. There was none whatsoever to *Mayfair*, and relatively minor damage to the pier. When the boat smashed into some oil delivery pipes on the pier, the broken pipes began to leak oil into the harbor. Members of *Mayfair*'s crew quickly jumped onto the pier after the accident, found the proper valves, and shut off the flow.

The litigation was less about who was liable and more about the application of a principle of admiralty law that had been codified in the Shipowners Limitation of Liability Act. It states, in simple terms, that a vessel owner will not be held liable for damages caused by his or her vessel to an amount greater than the value of the vessel itself. Wills argued that his liability should have been capped at the fifteen-thousand-dollar figure he paid in 1947 for the 1878-built *Mayfair*, or as she was called in court documents submitted by Wills's attorney, "the ancient *Mayfair*." Tankport Terminals found this grossly insufficient, claimed Wills was being "fraudulent" and "schemeful," and attempted to impose a different procedure that would double the vessel's true value and would therefore raise the limit of Wills's liability in the case. Lower courts found for Tankport, and Wills appealed to the Supreme Court's October term in 1957 for a writ of certiorari to the lower court's ruling.[22]

In his petition, Wills put forth what was undoubtedly a smokescreen. Before addressing the technical arguments over the limitation of liability statute, the real heart of his case, he asserted that the owner of a stationary pier should be held liable when a vessel adrift in fog smashes into it. Furthermore, Wills's attorney argued that Tankport Terminals should have put warning signals on the pier or have stationed personnel at the end of the pier when the fog rolled in, just as Wills had stationed lookouts in *Mayfair*'s bow. At the time of the collision, Wills's petition states, "respondent's watchman . . . was enclosed in its main office ashore, about a mile away from the point of collision, having lunch with his dog."[23] One is left to wonder if Benjamin Bowling Wills is the only petitioner in all of American history who ever called the attention of the highest court in the land to the fact that a man "was having lunch with his dog."

On April 28, 1958, the Supreme Court issued its ruling in the case. The petitioner's request for a writ of certiorari to the earlier ruling of the U.S. Court of Appeals for the Second Circuit was denied. The ruling of the lower court was let stand.[24] In other words, Wills lost.

Sunset on the Potomac

For dedicated steamboat enthusiasts, *Bear Mountain*'s running out of Washington for the Potomac River Line after 1948 was a poor substitute for *Potomac*, the vessel that had launched B. B. Wills into the excursion boat business back in 1934. The latter was a classic American steamboat with a most impressive lineage. Although the former was also a steam-powered sidewheeler, she was not nearly as distinguished or as storied a vessel as the one she replaced.

Far more contributory to the economic decline of the Potomac River Line than one steamboat replacing another, though, was a steady but inexorable shift in the line's clientele. Gone were the gasoline-rationing days of the war, when fashionable couples would ride the trolley car to the Washington waterfront to board the *Potomac* and dance the night away to the music of some of the most famous orchestras in the world. Instead, year after year, *Bear Mountain* found herself serving a much less stylish clientele. Furthermore, the restricted confines of an excursion boat exacerbated the kinds of misunderstandings that all too easily develop when young and energetic people are socializing after dark around a dance floor, and the bartender gets paid by the number of drinks sold, not the number of fistfights avoided. As stories of drunken encounters aboard *Bear Mountain* spread, they only served to reduce the vessel's potential customer base to those inclined to find the prospect of such behavior appealing.

Bear Mountain last sailed in 1952. In subsequent years Wills put the onetime Statue of Liberty ferry *Mayfair*—the "ancient *Mayfair*" of Supreme Court fame— into Potomac River Line service. But if *Bear Mountain* was a comedown from *Potomac*, then *Mayfair* was a downright insult after *Bear Mountain*.

Furthermore, as the Potomac River Line's service continued to deteriorate in the 1950s, Wilson Line's Washington operation managed to thrive. Before the war, Wilson had replaced its 1888-built *City of*

Mayfair, which once operated on the Statue of Liberty ferry run in New York, eventually took over the Potomac River service for Wills. The vessel is shown at Washington in April 1955. (Photograph by the author.)

Washington with *Mount Vernon*, built in 1916 as *City of Camden* and rebuilt in 1940 at Sun Shipbuilding, in Chester, Pennsylvania, to the same general specifications as *Bay Belle*. *Mount Vernon* operated for a long season, from early spring through mid-fall, and served both Mount Vernon on the Virginia side of the river and Marshall Hall amusement park in Maryland, plus ran moonlight dance cruises. The Potomac River Line, of course, ran nothing but nonstop cruises.

By the time the 1954 season rolled around, the only excursion services that Wills still had in operation were *Tolchester* (II), steaming regularly out of Baltimore; *Mayfair*, showing the flag on a much curtailed Potomac River service; and incidental operations like the diminutive *Sightseer*, running out of Washington in conjunction with Wills's Gray Line sightseeing bus service.

Then, just when the days seemed numbered for the entire Wills excursion boat empire and real estate interests might have occupied the remainder of the man's days, the Old Timer turned around and inaugurated a brand new excursion boat service in a port where he had never operated.

Wilson Line's *Mount Vernon,* which became the principal Potomac River excursion boat after the demise of the Potomac River Line. (Photograph by the author.)

CHAPTER NINE

The Battle of *San Jacinto*

Although B. B. Wills saw the major northeast cities such as Boston, New York, Baltimore, and Washington as the best seaports in which to concentrate his excursion boat operations, he was never averse to sending vessels on extended tours to other places. In the manner of a traveling road show, his boats might work a local market for a few days or weeks before moving on to someplace else.

Barnstorming

As mentioned earlier (chapter 3), even after she was permanently based in Washington, D.C., *Robert E. Lee* often spent several weeks each year running excursions out of Virginia cities such as Norfolk and Richmond. *Francis Scott Key* worked in Miami during the winter of 1941–42. Similarly, *Holiday* was en route to a winter assignment in Tampa when she was damaged off Cape Hatteras and had to be towed into Morehead City, North Carolina, by the U.S. Coast Guard.

Another vessel that did a fair amount of "barnstorming" was the wooden-hulled motor vessel *Madisonville,* which Wills purchased from Charles Sutton's partner Guy Moon in 1947.[1] *Madisonville* had earlier worked the Statue of Liberty ferry for Sutton Line, and Wills purchased her with his own statue ferry needs primarily in mind. But she proved to be a versatile vessel for Wills and worked in several different cities.

For example, on December 14, 1951, she left Baltimore for New York and a stint on the statue ferry run. Rough weather in Delaware Bay forced her to return to the east end of the Chesapeake and Delaware Canal that afternoon. As a result she did not reach North River Pier A in New York until 1:10 A.M. on Tuesday, December 18, almost four days after casting off from Baltimore.

It would be over a month before *Madisonville* performed any revenue work at New York. On January 25, 1952, she made nine trips out to Bedloe's Island. Then, except for an early February trip to a fuel dock in Bayonne, New Jersey, she made no more runs until April 7. Through the end of June she worked as the relief boat on the statue ferry, occasionally substituting for *Liberty*, the principal vessel, but primarily working as the second boat on weekends.

On Monday, June 30, 1952, with *Mayfair* now available to run with *Liberty* on the statue ferry, *Madisonville* headed south. She left New York at lunchtime, but once beyond *Ambrose* lightship and the start of the coastal trip south to Delaware Bay, the weather worsened. The boat was forced to turn back and seek shelter inside the Rockaway breakwater. She tied up at Beach Channel Drive in Rockaway Beach at 7:15 that evening.

The next morning, July 1, she again put to sea. *Madisonville* made port for several hours later in the day in southern New Jersey, and the next afternoon, after transiting the Chesapeake and Delaware Canal, she paused briefly at Tolchester to receive orders for the rest of the journey. By late afternoon she was tied up at the Pratt Street pier of Tolchester Lines in Baltimore.

Later in the month, *Madisonville* left Baltimore and continued south to Savannah, Georgia, where she arrived on July 17. Two days later she handled her first revenue work in almost six months, a moonlight cruise around Savannah Harbor. She remained working along the Georgia and South Carolina coasts for the next five years.[2]

The boat's ownership while she worked in the Charleston–Savannah area is a little difficult to sort out. Technically and legally, Wills sold the boat to John W. Tobin of Charleston in 1952. Tobin was in business with Walter A. O'Brien, also of Charleston, who served as the vessel's master. Wills, however, held a substantial first preferred mortgage on the vessel and insinuated himself, after the sale, into all kinds of details associated with the day-to-day operations to protect his interest. The Wills Papers contain lengthy correspondence between Wills in Washington and various actual and potential charter customers in both Savannah and Charleston. He bickered over minor details and costs associated with past and future cruises aboard *Madisonville*, even though he no longer owned the boat.[3] There is also extensive correspondence over insurance matters.[4]

Madisonville, renamed *Dixie Queen* by Tobin and O'Brien in 1953, remained working along the Georgia and South Carolina coast for several years until around 1958. She was then returned to Washington and reverted to more direct control by Wills, even though still owned by Tobin and company, doing business for the Dixie Boat Company.

B. B. Wills Invades the Sun Belt

One of the more unusual excursion boat services that Wills ever instituted was in Houston, Texas. The year was 1954, and Houston had yet to become home to a dozen or more citizens whose business travels would one day take them to the surface of the moon. This was a city whose sports fans would have laughed just as hard as anyone else at the suggestion of playing major league baseball indoors on a field of plastic grass. In fact, from the perspective of 1954, the Astrodome and indoor baseball may very well have been more implausible than astronauts and travel to the moon.

Just as he had recognized Florida real estate as an important growth sector in the late 1920s, B. B. Wills was ahead of the curve when he saw Houston as a potential market for his excursion boats. Again, he proved that his business instincts were sharp and sound. He corresponded with officials of the Houston Chamber of Commerce in 1953, and they were enthusiastic about his proposed venture.[5]

Unfortunately, as was earlier the case in Florida, Wills's venture did not work out. The point, though, is that Wills knew that if his excursion boat enterprise were to generate a new burst of enthusiasm and experience genuine growth, he would have to move into new and unconventional markets. Hello, Houston.

For his new Texas venture, Wills secured a surplus navy landing craft known as an LCI(L) (Landing Craft Infantry, Large). The design philosophy behind the LCI(L) was this: Instead of moving battle-ready troops across open water in a large transport ship and then transferring them to smaller landing craft immediately before the assault on an enemy-held beachhead, why not carry fewer soldiers—about two hundred per boat—in a smaller vessel that could make the entire trip from friendly harbor to hostile shore without any need for transferring en route? In addition, the new landing craft should be designed and built to make maximum use of off-the-shelf hardware from the U.S. industrial sector. The specialized suppliers of marine equipment could then concentrate their skills on heavier tonnage.

The LCI(L) had a 130-foot all-welded hull that was severely straight and angular. The vessel was powered by eight diesel engines that were adaptations of the power plants used commercially in mass transit buses. Its electrically operated rudder was controlled not by a conventional ship's wheel, but by a streetcar-like control handle that must have made quartermasters feel like seafaring motormen.

The basic LCI design had some variations. Some vessels were reconfigured as gunboats under the designation LCI(G), while others were outfitted as platforms for launching rockets and were called LCI(R)s. Most of the 869-boat fleet, though, were LCI(L) landing ships; they contributed to the success of Allied assaults on enemy-held beaches in various theaters of operation from Anzio to Normandy to Okinawa.

Because of its modest size and conventional components, the LCI(L) adapted well to peacetime uses after the war. Converted to civilian purposes, LCI(L)s have performed many maritime functions for various postwar owners. In 1995, for example, when the world at large was celebrating the fiftieth anniversary of the end of World War II, three veteran LCI(L)s were still active as sightseeing boats around Manhattan Island for New York's Circle Line.[6]

Circle Line put its first converted LCI(L) into sightseeing service in 1952. Even before this, though, the company began to acquire former LCI(L)s for such conversion work.

For use in service around Manhattan Island, the LCI(L)s had to undergo extensive rebuilding. The original pilothouse, located high up amidships and looking menacingly like the conning tower of a submarine, was removed and replaced with a new structure lower and closer to the bow. This was necessary because the original LCI(L) pilothouse would not clear the many bridges along the Harlem River that the sightseeing boats had to transit. For service in markets where the height of the original pilothouse was not a liability, though, such extensive rebuilding was not necessary and conversion of the old landing craft simply involved some structural, but largely cosmetic, changes. That is what the Dolphin Excursion Corporation did in 1949 with an old LCI(L) they put in service out of Pittsburgh as the passenger boat *Dolphin*. The vessel was likely one of 270 LCI(L)s ordered by the U.S. Navy during the war, but canceled before they were ever commissioned. *Merchant Vessels of the United States* shows no LCI(L) designation as a "former name" for *Dolphin*, but she was clearly built to U.S. Navy LCI(L) specifications.[7]

From a business perspective, *Dolphin* was a flop in Pittsburgh. Two years after her purchase there, she was sold to Circle Line for fourteen thousand dollars. For whatever reason, Circle Line turned around and immediately resold *Dolphin* to B. B. Wills. The sales contract contained these stipulations: the sale was "as is/where is," and just about the only thing Circle Line was willing to guarantee was that *Dolphin* existed and

THE BATTLE OF SAN JACINTO

that she was docked in Bayonne, New Jersey. Furthermore, the purchaser had to agree that the vessel would not be used in sightseeing service around Manhattan Island for at least five years.[8]

At first, Wills thought that his newly acquired LCI(L) would be assigned to his Statue of Liberty ferry operation. It is unlikely, though, that *Dolphin* ever carried a single passenger out to Bedloe's Island. She was soon sent south to Baltimore and saw little if any service for many months. Some evidence indicates that she may have been chartered by Wills on a bareboat basis to an operator in the Jacksonville, Florida, area in the early 1950s, but if so, it was only for a short period.[9]

A few years later, however, *Dolphin* moved to center stage. She was renamed *San Jacinto* and used by Wills to inaugurate the new Texas service in the summer of 1954. Basically, Wills had in mind both day and evening nonstop cruises along the Houston Ship Canal, as well as charter service to interested business, social, civic, and religious organizations. He even once thought about using *San Jacinto* to run a basic point-to-point passenger and freight transport service between Houston and Galveston, but nonstop cruises turned out to be her dominant fare.

Ticonderoga, a former LCI (L) that ran on New York's Lake George. Because *San Jacinto* was not yet ready for promotional photographs, Wills published photos of this vessel to promote *San Jacinto*'s new Houston service. (Photograph from author's collection.)

Because *San Jacinto* was not yet presentable enough for proper promotional photographs, Wills unashamedly used pictures of another former LCI(L) in his early advertisements. She was *Ticonderoga*, a vessel then toiling for the Lake George Steamboat Company in upstate New York. Visually, she was not a bad stand-in for Wills's own vessel.

The press in Houston welcomed the pending arrival of *San Jacinto*, pointing out that the city had not had any excursion boat service since the mid-1920s when two such vessels, *Ethel B.* and *Nicholaus*, supposedly caught fire and burned.[10] Each was a small gasoline-powered passenger boat considerably less than 100 feet long. (*Merchant Vessels of the United States* records no destructive fires in the 1920s, though, and shows both vessels surviving until roughly the time of World War II.)

As had long been his custom in the excursion boat business, B. B. Wills established a new and separate company to operate his Houston service. While Wills himself was the principal stockholder in the new San Jacinto Boat Line, he recruited two businessmen, Norman W. Charlton and S. Castra, as associates. Capt. Bill Helwig, a local Houston mariner, was hired to skipper *San Jacinto* on her cruises along the Ship Canal. To raise fifteen thousand dollars in working capital for the venture, Wills arranged for a local bank, the Harrisburg National Bank of Houston, to issue a second mortgage on *San Jacinto*.[11]

THIS ADMITS ONE ADULT

50 *Mile Galveston Bay Cruise*

Sunday, 2 to 7 p.m.

THE SAN JACINTO

"Houston's Modern Excursion Vessel"

DEPARTS DOCK 1, FOOT OF 75TH ST.

Ticket for a ride aboard *San Jacinto*.

While Wills was unquestionably correct that Houston was a city with a solid future, the Houston Ship Canal has never been confused with, say, the Rhine Valley or the fjords of Norway as a beautiful and picturesque waterway. True, an after-dark cruise back from the battlefield was dramatic enough, with lights glowing from all the chemical factories and oil refineries along the shore. Although the darkness could hide some of the visual ugliness that was apparent during daylight, it did nothing whatsoever to mitigate the unavoidable olfactory assault from the Port of Houston, day, night, or in between. Many years later, when asked why the Houston venture was not successful, Wills's son Eugene put it rather bluntly: "You couldn't do anything about the smell of the water."[12] In any event, the new Houston service got under way with a day cruise aboard *San Jacinto* on Sunday, May 23, 1954.[13]

Two untoward incidents marred the Houston venture during its first year, although neither was major. Early in the morning on Tuesday, September 7, 1954, thieves broke into the company's offices at the foot of Seventy-fifth Street and stole $350 from an office safe. A week and a half later, on Sunday, September 19, *San Jacinto*, with Capt. Bill Helwig in the pilothouse, was forced to make a hard turn and wound up grounding on a mud bank in an effort—a successful effort—to avoid a collision with the tugboat *Earl E.* and a barge she was towing. Captain Helwig later said that there had been a mix-up in whistle signals.

Although Houston is now, and was in 1954, a major American seaport, the city itself did not grow up around the port. Downtown Houston and the port are separated by many miles, and the Houston Ship Canal over which *San Jacinto* sailed was not a waterway that downtown office workers could stroll along during lunch hour. Ports on America's eastern seaboard featured harbors intimately associated with the growth and development of the various cities themselves and immediately adjacent to business and commercial districts. Simply enough, Houston and its seaport enjoyed no such relationship. *San Jacinto*'s dock at the foot of Seventy-fifth Street, for all intents and purposes, could only be reached by automobile. For certain selected sailings, passengers were encouraged to ride the No. 76 bus to Avenue P and Seventy-fifth Street, where a "courtesy car" would take them to the pier. Stated differently, *San Jacinto*'s dock in Houston was not nearly as "user friendly" as Light Street Pier 16 in Baltimore or Rowes Wharf in Boston.

One interesting sidelight on Wills's Houston adventure was how the Wilson Line reacted to it. Wills approached Houston in his typical fashion—a second-hand boat and minimal investment, so when the operation ultimately failed, he was saddled with no serious long-term

San Jacinto, a diesel-powered excursion boat converted from a U.S. Navy LCI (L)-class landing craft that B. B Wills ran in Houston, Texas.

debt. By 1955, the Wilson Line was under new ownership, the City Investing Company of New York. Apparently, they felt that Wills was on to something with his Houston venture. They pulled *Sea Belle*, their newest vessel, off the Boston–Nantasket route after the 1954 excursion season and spent virtually the entire 1955 season getting her ready at the company's Wilmington base for a new service in Houston. *Sea Belle* was replaced in Boston by a veteran Wilson Line vessel renamed *Pilgrim Belle II*. The replacement vessel was, in fact, the company's old *City of Washington*, which had sailed the Washington–Chapel Point service in conjunction with B. B. Wills a quarter century earlier in 1930. The 1888-built steamboat's 1955 tour in Boston, however, proved to be her swan song, and she never sailed again.[14]

By the time *Sea Belle* arrived in Houston in late 1955, Wills was finishing up his second season and had determined that the excursion market there was soft, at best. Perhaps without the arrival of the Wilson Line, Wills might have kept *San Jacinto* operating in Houston for another year or more, and the old LCI(L) might have eventually achieved profitability. Realizing that the newer, larger, and recently air-conditioned

The motor vessel *General*, *San Jacinto*'s running mate in Houston. The vessel later ran sightseeing service on the Potomac River out of Washington.

B. B. Wills welcomes a charter group aboard *San Jacinto*.

Sea Belle would take too many customers away from his decidedly lesser-scale vessel, he withdrew from the market entirely. Wills had no desire whatsoever to repeat along the Houston Ship Canal the kind of destructive head-to-head competition with Wilson Line that he waged on the Boston–Provincetown run in the summer of 1950. After the 1955 season, B. B. Wills called it quits in Texas.[15]

In the end, *Sea Belle* fared no better in Houston than did *San Jacinto*, and the Wilson boat was back on the Boston–Nantasket run mere months after her arrival in Houston. The whole episode represented a terrible financial blow to the new owners of the Wilson Line. Wills actually had added a second boat to his Houston operation in 1955, his second season in Texas. She was a diminutive vessel that bore the name *General* and that had previously worked out of Paducah, Kentucky. Wills used her both for public trips along the Ship Canal and in charter work for groups of between 150 and 200 passengers. *San Jacinto,* in comparison, could accommodate between 500 and 600 passengers. Despite her small size, *General* will always retain a distinction among all the excursion boats owned by B. B. Wills. Purchased in 1954, the 1952-built *General* remains the youngest excursion boat Wills ever owned.[16]

San Jacinto and *General* were brought back to Baltimore, and in 1956 Wills sold the former LCI(L) to Jeremiah Driscoll of New York, but retained a hefty first mortgage on the boat himself. Driscoll, a founder of the Circle Line (chapter 6), had in mind converting *San Jacinto* into an around–Manhattan Island sightseeing yacht for his Panorama Line, but provisions written into Wills's contract with Circle Line in 1951 had put a five-year restriction on such use, and five years had yet to pass. Consequently, Driscoll ran *San Jacinto* between Battery Park and Coney Island for several weeks in late 1956 and converted her for the Manhattan Island service over the winter of 1956–57.[17] *General*, on the other hand, remained under Wills's ownership for several more years, operating in charter and sightseeing service out of Washington. She also worked under bareboat charter for a period, on the Patuxent River in the Solomons Island, Maryland, area. Eventually, Wills sold *General* to a party in Saint Paul, Minnesota.[18]

CHAPTER TEN
Twilight on the Bay

Despite the many skirmishes between B. B. Wills and the Wilson Line over the years, the business dynamo was willing to cooperate with his arch rival if and when it appeared to be in his own business interest.

Changes in Baltimore

By the mid-1950s, both the Wilson Line and B. B. Wills knew that Baltimore could no longer support two excursion boat services. At the time, Wilson's *Bay Belle* was operating to Betterton, and Wills's *Tolchester* (II) was holding down the run to Tolchester Beach. Over the winter of 1956–57, the two lines reached an agreement that called for *Bay Belle* to run a regular public trip each morning from Baltimore to Tolchester, and then continue on to Betterton before returning to Baltimore, via Tolchester, in the evening. *Tolchester* (II) would be held in reserve and used for any charter trips the new venture booked. The longtime rivals and competitors would become partners.

The agreement between the Wilson Line and Tolchester Lines was signed on March 1, 1957, and was on the complicated side. It involved an exchange of notes between the two companies, with Wilson Line's parent company also agreeing to forego payment on a $1.5 million debt owed to it by Wilson Line to enhance the value of a note that Wilson was giving to Wills.[1]

After the agreement was negotiated and signed, Wills peppered the Wilson Line management with a series of letters claiming that *Bay Belle* was not in good enough shape to meet the service specifications their agreement called for. Perhaps, he suggested, it would be a better idea to use *Tolchester* (II) as the regular boat instead, with, of course, additional payments to Tolchester Lines. Wilson Line executives patiently answered each letter, calmly rejecting Wills's claims, but perhaps wondering if it had not been a good deal easier having this man as an adversary than as an ally.[2]

While *Bay Belle* became Baltimore's principal excursion boat and served both Betterton and Tolchester in 1957, *Tolchester* (II) did get a chance to strut her stuff during that summer of unprecedented cooperation. Late in the season, *Sea Belle* suffered a bent shaft while working Wilson Line's Boston–Nantasket route. Wills's 1910-built steamboat was dispatched north to fill in for her for the rest of the season. It was the vessel's first visit to Boston. Oddly enough, it would not be her last.

The Wilson–Wills cooperative venture on the Baltimore–Tolchester run lasted but a single season, 1957. Neither partner was willing to continue the relationship into 1958; each participant was ready to exit the Chesapeake Bay excursion boat business entirely.

Over the winter of 1957–58, Wills sold both the amusement park at Tolchester Beach and the steamboat *Tolchester* (II) to a new corporation associated with the Annapolis Bus Line. Wilson Line leased *Bay Belle* to the same company. Some confusion has surrounded this development, however, since the new firm elected to call itself the Wilson–Tolchester Steamship Company, even though it was a completely new and independent entity with no corporate ties to the older Wilson Line.

Wills claims that he received $125,000 for both his boat and the park, with the sales contract giving him an option to buy back *Tolchester* (II) for $25,000, which he immediately did.[3] Wilson Line, on the other hand, was in the process of dismantling all its excursion boat operations. Two of its converted submarine chasers, *Boston Belle* and *Liberty Belle*, were sold off to foreign interests. *Boston Belle* found a new home in Argentina in 1961, and *Liberty Belle* was delivered to Cuba in 1958 on the eve of the Castro revolution. B. B. Wills even tried to earn a dollar or two during the breakup of his onetime competitor. In 1965 he attempted to broker a deal for the sale of Wilson Line's *Bay Belle* and *State of Pennsylvania*. "You have confirmed to me this date that you will pay me a 5% commission fee for selling either of these vessels," he reminded company officials.[4]

Wilson-Tolchester Steamship Company continued to operate *Bay Belle* out of Baltimore to Tolchester Beach through the 1962 excursion season, after which the old amusement park was closed and never opened for business again. It was left to deteriorate on the Kent County shore of the Chesapeake Bay, occasionally becoming the subject of wistful Sunday supplement articles in the Baltimore press recalling the glories of yesteryear.[5] Eventually, after a fire or two made it completely impossible for anyone to consider rehabilitating the old resort, bulldozers were called in and the park was leveled. A quarter century after *Bay Belle* cast off from the pier at Tolchester Beach for the last time, a simple marina is all that occupies the old property.

Bay Belle herself would have a few more active seasons, though. In fact, in 1966 she found herself again competing with an excursion boat owned and operated by Benjamin Bowling Wills, an encounter that will be described later in this chapter.

In the years immediately following 1957, Wills turned even more of his attention to the real estate development business. He celebrated his sixtieth birthday in 1957 and, after the sale of Tolchester Beach, frequently characterized himself as a former excursion boat owner and operator. But like those reports of the death of an earlier American steamboat man—Mark Twain—Wills's protestations that he was no longer active in the excursion boat business proved to be greatly exaggerated.

The Freestone *Fiasco*

Freestone Point is on the Virginia side of the Potomac River between Nebasco Creek and Powells Creek, roughly 15 miles south of Washington, D.C. In the late 1950s, a group of investors had in mind the development of the Freestone Point area into a combination resort, marina, and light industrial park. Although it was not necessarily central to their plans, the investors nevertheless hoped to have a permanently moored gambling ship at the end of a short pier near Freestone Point. They got an early start on the project by converting *Tolchester* (II), which they had bareboat-chartered from B. B. Wills.

Critical to the whole business was the fact that the Maryland–Virginia state line does not run down the middle of the Potomac, but rather is at the low-water mark on the Virginia side of the river. What rendered this seemingly inconsequential piece of geography important was the difference in Maryland's and Virginia's laws on alcohol and gambling. In the 1950s, certain forms of gambling were legal in three southern Maryland counties, but illegal in Virginia. The sale of liquor by the drink was also permissible in Maryland, but prohibited in the Old Dominion.

Thanks to the location of the Maryland–Virginia state line, then, a boat moored at the end of a short pier on the Virginia side of the Potomac was, in actuality, under Maryland jurisdiction and subject to Maryland law. In late 1957, *Tolchester* (II) was renamed *Freestone;* fitted out with slot machines, roulette wheels, and similar accoutrements; and declared open for business as a gambling ship on the Potomac River, a ship that also featured liquid refreshment of several styles . . . and vintages.

Colonial Beach exploited this same set of circumstances in the late 1950s, and for several years gambling flourished there on piers built out into the Potomac. Back in the 1930s, when B. B. Wills was running *Potomac* to Colonial Beach, Maryland law was not as permissive as it would later become and Wills's passengers had to content themselves with less risky amusements.

B. B. Wills himself was not part of the syndicate seeking to develop Freestone Point, even though real estate ventures were occupying more and more of his time in the late fifties. His sole relationship to the venture was this: he continued to own *Freestone,* and he also put a small excursion boat named *Dixie Queen* to work on a newly established Washington–Freestone Point route.

From a purely excursion boat perspective, the *Dixie Queen* angle may be the more interesting aspect of the Freestone Point venture. The vessel was the former *Madisonville,* which Wills once ran to the Statue of Liberty and then sold to Charleston, South Carolina, interests in 1952. *Dixie Queen* remained—technically and actually—under the ownership of John W. Tobin and Walter A. O'Brien and their Dixie Boat Company while she was running to Freestone Point, but Wills had stepped in and seized effective control of the vessel to protect his interest as mortgage holder. Wills and O'Brien exchanged heated correspondence, each accusing the other of being responsible for just about all the ills of humankind, and then some.[6] In any case, the thirty-year-old, wooden-hulled *Dixie Queen* was approaching the end of her useful life. After her trips to Freestone Point, she faded from the scene, eventually being converted into a shoreside restaurant in tidewater Virginia.

Nor was *Dixie Queen* the only vessel Wills ran between Washington and Freestone Point. *Sightseer,* a launch he purchased in 1945 to carry government personnel back and forth to Bedloe's Island, was also deployed there. Commenting on Wills's latest waterborne service, *Steamboat Bill* characterized *Sightseer* as "an overgrown motorboat."[7]

A gambling ship on the Potomac River, though, was an idea whose time had not yet come and, many hope, never will. Strong public protests were voiced over the prospect, with Virginia interests especially upset over what they saw as the use of a mere technicality in the law to conduct a business—gambling—that Virginia state law expressly prohibited. The riverboat gambling attempt at Freestone Point ended in 1958, the year after it began. Maryland eventually rescinded the legislation that permitted certain kinds of gambling in the southern part of the state, but even

Promotional photograph for *Sightseer*'s Potomac River cruises.

before this, statutory restrictions were enacted in Annapolis to prohibit gambling in Maryland waters on the Virginia side of the river.[8]

The resort and industrial park idea at Freestone Point fared no better than the gambling ship. The area has since become a picturesque piece of public land called Leesylvania State Park. The Lee family, Light Horse Harry and his son, Robert E., once owned property at Freestone Point. Today the old pilings of the dock where *Freestone* was once moored are still visible, and along a walking trail at river's edge in today's state park is a historical marker that tells of when an old excursion boat was turned into a gambling ship and tied up at the end of the pier. For many visitors, it is as remote an event as those associated with the Civil War and depicted on other markers in the park.

Fortunately, the Freestone Point gambling ship project was done on the cheap and no structural harm was inflicted on the old steamboat. While she remained stationary, her engines were neither removed nor disabled, and she was still a potentially active excursion boat. *Freestone* did not operate in 1959 and 1960, but in 1961 Wills sold her to a new owner, a group headed by a Washington attorney, Timothy Casey. The

Advertisement run by Wills in the maritime trade press in the late 1950s in an effort to find a buyer for *Tolchester* (II).

purchase price for a steamboat that had been launched fifty-one years earlier was a robust $150,000, with $145,000 of that sum—96 percent of the purchase price—in the form of an eight-year, 6 percent preferred mortgage held by B. B. Wills. The mortgage instrument was a very limiting document for Casey and company: no structural or mechanical alterations could be made without Wills's prior approval, nor could Casey even change the name of the vessel, or her home port, without the written consent of the mortgage holder. The mortgage also stated that in the event of default, Wills was free to "[r]etake the vessel without legal process at any time wherever same may be."[9] Casey planned to run her out of Washington on moonlight and charter trips.

SS Potomac: *Phase One*

B. B. Wills played no formal management role with the Casey-led organization, a venture that called itself the Potomac River Line.[10] Whether any consideration was paid to Wills for the use of the name remains an unanswered question.

With approval from Wills, the vessel was renamed *SS Potomac* for her new Washington career. The designation "SS" was a formal part of the boat's name, not a descriptive preface. During the years she was so named, the vessel was found under the letter "S," not "P," in the U.S. government's annual publication, *Merchant Vessels of the United States*.

Casey's new Potomac River Line was anything but a smashing success. To protect his interest in the vessel, Wills stepped in and contacted his old friend, Joseph Stone, the owner of Paragon Park in Nantasket Beach, Massachusetts, and before the 1961 season was over, *SS Potomac* was running between Boston and Nantasket. Wills advanced most of the working capital needed to shift the aging steamboat north. The understanding was that half of the profits that Casey might earn would go to pay off the mortgage that Wills was holding.[11] Wilson Line had abandoned all of its service out of Boston after the 1960 season—Provincetown as well as Nantasket—so the route was effectively there for the taking.

Because of her late arrival, *SS Potomac* did not have a banner year in Boston in 1961. The year 1962 turned out to be a little better, though, and both Casey and his mortgage holder had high hopes that 1963 would be even better. Unfortunately, it was not. In fact, *SS Potomac* never ran at all in 1963. Casey's Potomac River Line went into receivership, and Wills was forced to buy back the vessel at a marshal's sale to protect his interest. When he sent his people aboard to prepare for a return trip to Baltimore—the boat had stayed in Boston since arriving there in 1961—they found her to be in such poor condition that a coastal journey under power was out of the question. SS *Potomac* eventually wound up back in Baltimore in mid-1963, but on the end of a tugboat's hawser.

A dispute developed between Wills and the Coast Guard over this tow. They called him to task afterward for failing to have the vessel inspected before leaving Boston. Wills wrote back—appropriately contrite—saying that in all his thirty-odd years in the excursion boat business, he was never aware of a need to secure Coast Guard inspection of a vessel prior to a coastal tow. He promised that it would never happen again.[12]

Wills was upset with Casey over the SS *Potomac*'s demise. In a 1964 letter Wills wrote: "As to Casey, I would like to find his bank account or some asset of his that I could attach. . . ."[13] But however upset the Old Timer was with Timothy Casey in 1964, it did not stop him from doing business with him again three years later.

Once Wills had SS *Potomac* back in Baltimore, he amazingly turned around and put her back in operating condition. Wills had to spend over seventy thousand dollars getting the old steamer in shape, and she passed her annual Coast Guard inspection in May 1964.

A Former Old Bay Liner

In the midst of Wills's involvement with SS *Potomac,* in 1962, a Chesapeake Bay institution came to a quiet end. The Baltimore Steam Packet Company, more commonly known as the Old Bay Line, discontinued overnight steamboat service between Baltimore and Norfolk. The demise of this storied company marked the end of overnight packet service not merely on the Chesapeake Bay, but in the entire United States, but is beyond the scope of this book. Of interest, however, is that after the Old Bay Line suspended operations, B. B. Wills purchased all three of the company's passenger vessels, *City of Norfolk, City of Richmond,* and *District of Columbia* (table 10-1).

Wills's intentions in buying these vessels remain unclear. He also took title to certain piers and waterfront property in Baltimore as part of the transaction, and while these would seem to be secondary to the sale of the three boats, perhaps the opposite is true. Was the purchase of the three Old Bay liners principally orchestrated by Wills-the-real-estate-tycoon, a transaction that only accidentally gave Wills-the-excursion-boat-operator, and Wills the second-hand-boat-seller, an opportunity to practice his old trades?

TABLE 10-1
Old Bay Line Vessels Purchased by B. B. Wills, 1962

Vessel	Gross tons	Dimensions	Place built (year built)
City of Norfolk	2,379	297.5 × 46.5 × 16.2	Sparrows Pt., Md. (1911)
City of Richmond	1,923	261.6 × 53.1 × 14.1	Sparrows Pt., Md. (1913)
District of Columbia*	2,128	297.8 × 51.0 × 16.3	Wilmington, Del. (1925)

* *District of Columbia* was originally owned by Norfolk and Washington Steamboat Company; she was sold to Old Bay Line in 1949.

Practice them he did, though. Wills put both *City of Norfolk* and *City of Richmond* on the market and, after some false starts, sold both vessels to parties who intended to convert the pair into permanently moored shoreside attractions.[14] Neither vessel was ever so converted, though. *City of Norfolk* was eventually scrapped, while *City of Richmond* was lost at sea off Cape Hatteras en route to her new assignment in Charlotte Amalie in the U.S. Virgin Islands.

Wills put *District of Columbia,* the newest of the trio, into Bethlehem Steel's Baltimore yard, tore out many of her staterooms so she might better serve as a day excursion boat, and then sent her north to work the Boston–Provincetown run for two delightful summers, 1962 and 1963. For her new and altogether surprising assignment she was rechristened *Provincetown.*

Wills had signed a contract with town officials in Provincetown to provide service to and from Boston midway through the previous season, 1961. But lacking a vessel of his own to use on the route, he chartered the onetime Nantucket and Martha's Vineyard steamer *Martha's Vineyard* from her owner, Capt. Joseph Gelinas, and ran her across Massachusetts Bay that summer.[15] Wilson Line, as noted earlier, had deserted Boston after the 1960 season.

As she left Baltimore and headed north to Boston in the spring of 1962, *Provincetown* became the twenty-second excursion boat put into service by B. B. Wills since *Potomac* first steamed to Chapel Point in the spring of 1934. Nobody knew it then, but there would never be a twenty-third.

Steamboat enthusiasts, of course, were delighted to see *Provincetown* sailing out of Boston Harbor. With *SS Potomac* working the Nantasket run for a summer or two, and the former Old Bay liner operating to Provincetown, thanks to B. B. Wills, Boston had become something of a steamboat Valhalla, at least for a few seasons.

What happened next is both interesting and curious. *Provincetown* never returned to Boston after the 1963 excursion season. Wills had agreed to operate a boat to Provincetown for at least another summer, and lacking one of his own he chartered the motor vessel *Yankee* from

Brochures promoting Chesapeake Bay Line's proposed cruise service.

District of Columbia at Washington in 1952 while operating for the Old Bay Line. The vessel moored behind her is Wills's *Robert E. Lee*.

Interstate Navigation for the 1964 season. After this, though, Wills never operated an excursion boat in Boston again.

Provincetown returned to Baltimore after the 1963 excursion season, but there was still a long list of deferred repairs that the Coast Guard required before she could ever hope to steam again.[16] Then, in December 1964, after the boat had lain idle for over a year, Wills signed an agreement to sell *Provincetown* to a newly created organization called Chesapeake Bay Line. The purchase price was $147,815, of which $55,000 was to be paid in cash and $92,815 in the form of a new five-year second mortgage at 6 percent simple interest that Wills would hold. The buyer also agreed to assume an existing first mortgage on the vessel of $150,000.[17]

Chesapeake Bay Line was headed up by Charles C. Hoffberger, of an old-line Baltimore family. Another family member, Gerry Hoffberger, a cousin of Charles C., later became the owner of the Baltimore Orioles. There were six stockholders in Chesapeake Bay Line: Hoffberger; two of his associates, Suzanne H. Nasdor and Alan D. Hoffberger; B. B. Wills; and two of his longtime associates, Mrs. Elmore E. Egan and Edward F. Mitchell. Whether all six individuals held equal shares in the new company is not known. Mrs. Egan served as Wills's secretary and general business manager for many years, whereas Mitchell began his association with Wills in the mid-1940s, when he managed the Nantasket Boat Line.

Chesapeake Bay Line hoped to get *Provincetown* back in shape as an overnight steamboat. That meant restoring the staterooms that Wills had earlier torn out and operating her on two- and three-night cruises out of Washington, D.C., with shore excursions to places like Jamestown and Colonial Williamsburg. It would have been the same kind of short-cruise service that later became so popular aboard oceangoing cruise ships out of places like Miami and Port Everglades. Brochures were printed, a reservation office began to accept bookings, and the former Old Bay liner was to be given a new name, *Chesapeake*.

Clearly, Wills, by then almost seventy years old, did not envision playing a major or full-time role in the day-to-day operations of the new company; it was to be Hoffberger's venture. But Wills was a stockholder, he was experienced in the passenger boat business, and, since he also had time on his hands, he pitched in and lent a hand with preliminary tasks such as attempting to secure wharf space for the new company in both Washington and Norfolk.[18]

Wills also took the lead in getting *Provincetown* inspected and approved by the Coast Guard for her new service. Indeed his sales contract with Hoffberger and Chesapeake Bay Line stipulated as a condition of the sale that *Provincetown* had to be approved for service by the Coast Guard before the transaction could be regarded as complete.

Wills had anticipated some $40,000 in repair work on the vessel in order to satisfy all the Coast Guard's requirements; this figure was even written into the sales agreement between Wills and Hoffberger as the maximum that Wills would have to spend to prepare the vessel for service.[19] By the time Coast Guard inspectors had completed their review, though, the "punch list" of items that required attention and correction before the vessel could be certified for passenger service was so extensive that the cost was estimated to exceed $300,000, not $40,000.[20] On the strength of this disappointing development, the sale was canceled, the Hoffberger-led venture collapsed, and *Provincetown* never steamed again.

Wills insisted that he had been misled by the Coast Guard, and claimed that a preliminary inspection led him to believe that $40,000 was a reasonable figure to get the vessel certified for service. He argued that only the second and followup inspection—by different Coast Guard personnel—resulted in the more lengthy list of necessary repairs and corrections.[21] The bottom line, however, was that the Chesapeake Bay Line was out of business before it ever carried its first revenue passenger.

Provincetown lay idle in Baltimore Harbor for several years until a tentative deal was struck that would have seen her converted into a shoreside restaurant in New Jersey. But on June 4, 1969, before she could be towed away, the boat caught fire at Pratt Street Pier Three. Over 230 firemen, thirty-nine pieces of land apparatus, and the Baltimore fireboats *J. Harold Grady* and *P.W. Wilkinson* fought the six-alarm blaze for most of the afternoon. Afterward, the burned-out hulk was towed to the Curtis Bay section of Baltimore Harbor and there, over the years, she continued to deteriorate until she eventually disappeared beneath the water's surface.[22]

Virginia Lee *Redux*

In April 1964, the Commonwealth of Virginia completed a massive $200 million public works project, an 18-mile "bridge-tunnel" across the mouth of the Chesapeake Bay. For most of its length, the new crossing is a conventional causeway built on concrete piers. But where the roadway approaches the two deep-water channels that link the Chesapeake Bay and the port of Norfolk with the open sea, Chesapeake Channel to the north, Thimble Shoal Channel to the south, man-made islands were constructed and the "bridge" burrows underground, and underwater, to become a tunnel. Traveling from one end to the other, one drives across a section of bridge, through a tunnel, across another bridge, through another tunnel, and finally across yet another bridge.

Once the project was complete and open for business, the Chesapeake Bay Ferry District's Little Creek–Kiptopeke route across the mouth of the Chesapeake Bay was no longer needed; its seven vessels were put up for sale. The Chesapeake Bay Ferry District was a public agency formed in 1956 to take over a service previously operated by the Virginia Ferry Corporation, a private company that once had corporate ties with the Wilson Line.[23]

Whether he was motivated more by business or more by sentiment, in early 1964 Benjamin Bowling Wills proved to be a ready and willing buyer for *Accomac,* one of the seven ferries the commission had put up for sale. *Accomac,* of course, was built in 1928, ran for Wills as *Holiday* in 1949 and 1950, and was the vessel whose trip north from Belém, Brazil, in 1948 involved such high adventure.

Wills purchased the vessel from the Chesapeake Bay Ferry District for seventy-thousand dollars. He also attempted to play the role of broker—for a commission, of course—on the sale of two other district vessels, *Northampton* and *Old Point Comfort,* a pair of former navy LSTs that had been converted into ferries after the war. He had no luck on this score, though, and the district sold the former landing ships with no help from Wills.

One published report suggested that Wills intended to use *Accomac* on the Boston–Provincetown run during the summer, and have her substitute for *Chesapeake* on those two- and three-day cruises out of Washington the rest of the year.[24] The Wills Papers contain several strong suggestions that the market the Old Timer primarily had in mind for *Accomac* was New York.

New York still had a strong and stable excursion market for charter work. The market was anchored in a longstanding tradition of area high schools, of which there were hundreds, chartering an excursion boat at the end of the academic year for a day's outing. By the mid-1960s, this market was quite under-served as older and more established companies had fallen by the wayside. Both the Wilson Line and the Meseck Line were no more; even the Hudson River Day Line, since 1962, a subsidiary of Frank Barry's Circle Line, had reduced its fleet to just one vessel, the 1924-built sidewheeler *Alexander Hamilton,* and the company was thus unable to handle the volume of charter business that it once did.

There was also a world's fair upcoming in New York during the summers of 1964 and 1965, which Wills felt would generate a decent volume of new charter business. While he primarily foresaw conventional single-day round-trip outings to nearby destinations up the Hudson or out on Long Island Sound, Wills also considered *Accomac* a perfect vessel for reinstituting a maritime tradition that had disappeared after the 1948 excursion season: daylong trips up and down the Hudson between New York and Albany. It would not be a daily service, but there might be a half-dozen or so trips over the course of a full excursion season.

In late 1963 Wills wrote to the Albany Chamber of Commerce outlining his plan.[25] He received many supportive endorsements from business interests in Albany, since Wills's idea called for passengers to spend the night in an upscale Albany hotel and enjoy a meal or two in Albany restaurants before heading back downriver for New York aboard *Accomac*.[26] Wills was not as fortunate, though, in finding financial institutions anxious to lend him money to underwrite the restoration of New York–Albany passenger boat service. The Marine Midland Trust Company, for example, expressed the view that because there had been no such service for almost two decades, they doubted that it was an enterprise worthy of investment.[27]

Returning *Accomac* to any kind of excursion service, however, proved to be a far more difficult proposition than Wills ever imagined. First of all, there were myriad new Coast Guard regulations to contend with. Understandably, by 1964 newly constructed passenger vessels had to be built to much more demanding specifications for fire-prevention and general safety than had vessels launched thirty years earlier. By virtue of her age, *Accomac* was exempt from many of these newer and more stringent requirements. The federal government's general policy was predicated on a long view: sooner or later, older tonnage would be retired, and the new requirements would then achieve universality.

What Wills quickly discovered, though, was that *Accomac* would swiftly lose her exempt status if her enrollment were changed from "ferry" to "passenger" vessel. If she remained in ferry service, she could remain as is. If, on the other hand, Wills did any work at all on the vessel's interior to render her more appropriate for day excursion service, and if he then changed her enrollment status from ferry to passenger, a whole range of new fire and safety requirements would automatically be triggered. *Accomac*'s entire wooden superstructure, for example, would have to be torn out and replaced with steel construction.[28]

TWILIGHT ON THE BAY 173

The cost of such work was extreme, but Wills was not yet ready to call it prohibitive. At this point, the Old Timer probably toyed with various ways of retaining *Accomac*'s technical status as a "ferry," despite her primary function as a passenger vessel. Perhaps Wills was thinking of the way *Southport* ran as a combination automobile ferry/excursion boat between Baltimore and Tolchester in the late 1930s. The matter was settled in a different fashion, however, on May 27, 1964.

Work was proceeding on *Accomac* in the Pinners Point section of Portsmouth, Virginia, at a pier once owned by the Atlantic Coast Line Railroad, when fire erupted and raged out of control for most of the night. In addition to *Accomac*, a Wills-owned ex-navy LCU and the motor vessel *Sightseer* were damaged in the fire.[29]

Whether *Accomac* was beyond repair was uncertain. One thing was absolutely clear, though. She was in no condition to travel to New York for the 1964 excursion season that was only weeks away. Despite the small size of his fleet compared to decades earlier, Wills did have another vessel available to take her place, *SS Potomac*.

Accomac, after the 1964 fire.

One can speculate that had *Accomac* been successfully reconverted into a day excursion boat, B. B. Wills might well have become a permanent force on the New York excursion boat scene in the mid-1960s and for a number of years afterward. With the big diesel—Wills planned to name her *Holiday* once again—joining forces with SS *Potomac*, he might have created a dominant presence there just when older excursion boat companies were cutting back their operations. If *Accomac* had returned to service, Wills clearly planned to operate her the year around, as he had attempted to do in 1951. He had identified at least two warm-water assignments as potential winter deployments. One was a route from the eastern end of Puerto Rico somewhere near Roosevelt Roads to Charlotte Amalie on Saint Thomas in the U.S. Virgin Islands. Another was a day service between Palm Beach on the Florida mainland and Freeport in the Bahamas, where it was reliably reported that gambling casinos would soon be opening.

The fire in Portsmouth in May 1964 ended all such possibilities, of course, though Wills continued to profess that *Accomac*, even in her damaged condition, could be repaired and returned to service. "It is my intent to rebuild the boat and this is a tremendous job because it will take some time to make the architectural plans as well as to fight every detail through the Coast Guard," he said.[30] He also remained open to the possibility of selling the fire-damaged *Accomac* to a third party. At one point Wills contacted California interests and made a pitch that a restored *Accomac* would make a perfect vessel for service to Catalina Island.[31]

The boat was neither restored nor sold to Californians, though, and Wills eventually disposed of *Accomac* to the Waterman Steamship Company. The firm regarded the damaged hulk as a convenient way to qualify for a federal ship subsidy program that allowed U.S. flag operators to purchase surplus vessels from the government as long as they had a vessel—any vessel—over a certain minimum gross tonnage to trade in as part of the deal. Many inland and coastal steamboats were purchased by oceangoing firms to satisfy this bureaucratic requirement. This unusual provision laid the groundwork, perhaps, for decades of confusion among future maritime historians, who may wonder why a twentieth-century steamboat that spent most of her life working on the Hudson River, for example, wound up being owned by a company whose specialty was hauling cargo between San Francisco and Hong Kong.

Wills actually reacquired *Accomac* from the U.S. Maritime Commission after this transaction and later claimed that he sold her twin diesels to a tugboat operator, and was about to turn a few extra dollars on the sale of her bronze propellers.[32] *Accomac* herself was eventually towed to a ship's graveyard at Mallows Bay on the Potomac River south of Washington, and there she has remained for thirty years. Less than a mile further down the Potomac on the Maryland shore from the place where *Accomac* sits quietly rusting away is Liverpool Point, a picnic grove where *Potomac* once landed excursionists seeking a day's respite from the heat and humidity of summertime Washington.[33]

SS Potomac: *Phase Two*

In the mid-1960s, when B. B. Wills returned to the excursion boat business, most of the steamboat companies he once controlled lacked active corporate charters and thus could not be used to conduct business. One company was an exception, though, and so when *Provincetown* operated out of Boston in 1962 and 1963, and when *SS Potomac* later sought charter business in New York, they operated under the house flag of Tolchester Lines. In addition, Wills used two of his real estate companies, Wills Homes and Wills Development Corporation, to conduct excursion-boat-related work in the 1960s.

Speaking of corporate names and entities, Wills also formed a brand-new excursion boat company in 1962 that was called Maryland Boat Lines. Maryland Boat Lines of 1962 should not be confused with an earlier Wills-owned company, the Maryland Boat Corporation, that was founded in 1944. The new company was established when the city of Baltimore decided to compensate for the loss of *Bay Belle* by designing and building a new municipal excursion boat, a vessel whose day-to-day operations would be handled by a private company under contract to the city. The vessel was the diesel-powered *Port Welcome.* Unfortunately, Wills was defeated in his effort to win the operating contract since the Wilson–Tolchester Steamboat Company submitted a better proposal than Maryland Boat Lines.

When Wills decided to substitute *SS Potomac* for the fire-gutted *Accomac* in charter service out of New York during 1964, he immediately ran into several new bureaucratic obstacles. The first involved the U.S. Coast Guard. Uncertain about what impact recent changes to the vessel's superstructure might have on overall stability, in early 1964 the Coast Guard lowered *SS Potomac*'s passenger capacity from 1,850 to 1,500 as a safety measure, pending the outcome of a new stability test. Wills put *SS Potomac* through such a test in Baltimore on May 7, 1964, but the results were not certified by the Coast Guard until late June. As a result the vessel was only permitted to carry a maximum of 1,500 passengers through the height of the late spring high school outing season in New York. Wills claims that he had to cancel several charter contracts with high schools that had no interest in an excursion boat unable to accommodate their entire student body. By late June, though, *SS Potomac*'s legal capacity had been reestablished at 1,850 passengers.[34]

The second obstacle that Wills faced involved a complexity long associated with excursion boats operating in and around New York, namely, the Interstate Commerce Commission. In bygone years, there were many popular excursion boat destinations within convenient round-trip distance of New York. By the 1960s, however, most charter groups were interested in one or two such places—Rye Beach on Long Island Sound, about 25 miles from the Battery and the site of a popular amusement park, and Bear Mountain, a park and picnic grove located 45 miles up the Hudson River from midtown Manhattan. With its rides and concessions, Rye Beach was generally more popular with high school charters at the end of the academic year. Bear Mountain had more appeal as a destination for family-oriented church, civic, and social organizations throughout the excursion season.

For an excursion boat operator, though, the two destinations had another difference: To provide service between New York City and Bear Mountain—either regularly scheduled public service or purely charter operations—a company had to receive authorization from the ICC. No such permission was required to operate to Rye Beach.

The rationale behind this distinction is complicated. Service to and from Rye Beach, as long as it originated from a point within New York Harbor, was exempt from ICC jurisdiction because Rye Beach itself was defined as being within a "contiguous harbor zone" associated with New York.[35] An actual trip to Rye Beach could even originate from a point in New York Harbor that was in the state of New Jersey, such as Hoboken, Jersey City, or Bayonne; a trip was exempt from ICC jurisdiction even though it linked, for example, Jersey City, *New Jersey*, and Rye Beach, *New York*.

Service between New York and Bear Mountain, on the other hand, was fully subject to ICC control. Bear Mountain was beyond the "contiguous harbor zone" associated with New York. Although an excursion boat trip between Manhattan and Bear Mountain was arguably a journey within a single state and not subject to ICC jurisdiction, because the New York–New Jersey state line runs down the middle of the Hudson River for a portion of the distance between Manhattan and Bear Mountain, the ICC had previously determined that waterborne commerce on the river was interstate in character and subject to its control, irrespective of whether a vessel ever made port in more than one state.[36]

In summary, then, excursion boat service between any point in New York Harbor and Bear Mountain was subject to the full gamut of ICC regulatory control, while excursion boat service from New York Harbor to Rye Beach was not. To add a historical dimension to this matter, during World War II, Frank Russel, the district director of the U.S. Office of Price Administration in New York, issued a Solomon-like decision. Faced with requests for Bunker C fuel from two oil-powered excursion boats, Russell said yes to Sutton Line's *Claremont*, but no to Meseck Line's *Americana*. He explained that because *Claremont*'s New York–Bear Mountain route required ICC certification and *Americana*'s service to Rye Beach did not, the former was part of the nation's basic intercity transportation system and thus deserved a wartime fuel allocation, while the latter was not.[37]

SS Potomac arrived in New York from Baltimore in May 1964. Because her capacity was limited until the results of the new stability test were certified, Wills did not enjoy a robust high school charter season in May and June that year. He was looking forward to July and August, though, when the Bear Mountain trade would be at its height. Unfortunately, both the Hudson River Day Line and the Keansburg Steamboat Company registered their opposition with the ICC against Wills's petition for approval to operate charter service between New York and Bear Mountain, and the federal agency failed to award Wills the authority he sought. *SS Potomac* spent the summer of 1964 in New York. In late August Wills brought her south to Baltimore, where she ran a few additional charters before being laid up for the off season.

While denied the right to operate to Bear Mountain, *SS Potomac* did serve as an official spectator boat for New York's Operation Sail in July 1964, but not without a bit of controversy between the project's sponsor and Wills. When Wills and Op Sail reached an agreement for chartering *SS Potomac*, it was on the understanding that the vessel's passenger capacity was 1,850. In reviewing all aspects of Op Sail, however, the Coast Guard remembered that *SS Potomac*'s capacity had been an issue earlier in the season. Given that passengers for a one-time event like Op Sail might tend to flock to the vessel's rails to watch the tall ships go by, the Coast Guard decided to lower her capacity by several hundred people for this event.[38]

Wills, however, neglected to tell the Op Sail people about this development. On the day of the pageant, more people showed up to board *SS*

Potomac—with paid tickets in hand—than were permitted to board and were turned away. Nasty correspondence flew back and forth for weeks afterward, replete with threats of lawsuits.[39] Eventually, as many such things inevitably do, everything settled down.

SS *Potomac* was back in New York the following year, 1965, a much better year for her. With no early-season capacity limitations she enjoyed a vigorous May and June running high school charters, primarily to Rye Beach. And while the ICC was not prepared to rule on Wills's request for permanent authority to operate New York–Bear Mountain, he was given a temporary permit pending a full review of his petition for unrestricted authority.

SS *Potomac*'s first New York trip that year was a charter from Battery Park to Rye Beach on May 17. Her final excursion was on September 6, Labor Day, when she took a party from Battery Park to Rockaway Beach and back. Between these two excursions, the boat ran sixty-seven charter trips that summer on sixty-three different days. Between her first and last trip in New York that summer, she was inactive for a total of forty-eight days.[40]

All but four of SS *Potomac*'s twenty-four round-trips to Rye Beach originated at New York's Battery Park. She sailed up the Hudson to Bear Mountain nineteen times, and all but three of these trips also originated at Battery Park. Of the four Rye Beach trips that did not begin at Battery Park, one was out of Bayonne, another left from the Lackawanna Terminal in Hoboken, the third originated at the foot of Noble Street in the Greenpoint section of Brooklyn, and the fourth departed from Brooklyn's Erie Basin, where the vessel tied up between assignments. Of the Bear Mountain trips not starting from Battery Park, one originated at North River Pier 80, the other two at West 125th Street. To show what a typical charter trip entailed that summer, Table 10-2 presents details from two of SS *Potomac*'s trips.

The boat had two other destinations for round-trip excursions in 1965. One was Rockaway Beach, a site she visited on four different occasions, twice from Battery Park and twice from Yonkers. The other was perhaps her longest, busiest trip of the entire summer. On Saturday, August 21, she left Erie Basin at 5:10 A.M. and steamed out into Long Island Sound. Then, entering Hempstead Harbor, she docked at Glenwood Landing at 8:00 A.M. and boarded 1,387 passengers for a round-trip to Whitestone Point, Queens, with the return trip leaving Whitestone at 5:57 P.M. The New York Mets played a home game at Shea Stadium that afternoon, and perhaps some of SS *Potomac*'s passengers were in the stands. (The hapless Mets, then firmly ensconced in last place, managed to beat the visiting Cardinals, 6 to 2.) The 1964–65 world's fair was also running that summer in nearby Flushing Meadows, and undoubtedly many passengers spent the afternoon wandering around the fairgrounds. In any event, it was almost midnight when the boat returned to Erie Basin.

TABLE 10-2
Two Trips of SS *Potomac* in the Summer of 1965

Sunday, May 30, 1965*		Master: E. R. LeBlanc	Pilot: James O'Driscoll
	lv.	Pier 46/Brooklyn (Erie Basin)	7:15 A.M.
	—	Battery Place	7:25 A.M.
	ar.	125th Street	8:30 A.M.
	lv.	125th Street (1,744 passengers)	9:42 A.M.
	—	Tappan Zee Bridge	10:55 A.M.
	—	Stoney Point	11:57 A.M.
	ar.	Bear Mountain	1:07 P.M.
	lv.	Bear Mountain (1,744 passengers)	5:50 P.M.
	—	Stoney Point	6:14 P.M.
	—	Tappan Zee Bridge	7:12 P.M.
	ar.	125th Street	9:00 P.M.
	lv.	125th Street	9:28 P.M.
	—	Battery Place	10:20 P.M.
	ar.	Pier 46/Brooklyn (Erie Basin)	10:50 P.M.
Tuesday, June 1, 1965		Master: E. R. LeBlanc	Pilot: Ben S. Parrillo
	lv.	Pier 46/Brooklyn (Erie Basin)	9:55 A.M.
	ar.	Battery Park	10:15 A.M.
	lv.	Battery Park (1,048 passengers)	10:33 A.M.
	—	Hell Gate	11:00 A.M.
	—	Stepping Stones	11:50 A.M.
	—	Buoy 38A	12:28 P.M.
	ar.	Rye Beach	12:45 P.M.
	lv.	Rye Beach (1,048 passengers)	5:20 P.M.
	—	Buoy 38A	5:28 P.M.
	—	Stepping Stones	6:20 P.M.
	—	Hell Gate	7:04 P.M.
	ar.	Battery Park	7:50 P.M.
	lv.	Battery Park	8:15 P.M.
	ar.	Pier 46/Brooklyn (Erie Basin)	8:50 P.M.

Information from *SS Potomac* logbook, 1965, Wills Papers.
*The log also includes the following notation: "Slowed to allow Day Line steamer to unload at Bear Mountain."

The log for the June 1 excursion to Rye Beach notes "minor damage" to the pier at the beach while the boat was docking. In subsequent months, Wills engaged in protracted correspondence with Westchester County officials over this incident as he attempted to have the pier repaired by his own carpenters rather than submit a routine claim through his insurance carrier.

SS Potomac was not an especially fast vessel, at least not in 1965. Her running times for a half-dozen random Battery Park–Bear Mountain trips that year averaged a little over 3 hours and 45 minutes, or roughly 12 miles per hour. The Hudson River Day Line long advertised a 2-hour, 50 minute, running time from Pier 81 to Bear Mountain. While Pier 81 is about 4 miles closer to Bear Mountain than Battery Park, the Day Line's faster performance included two scheduled stops en route, West 125th Street and Yonkers. *SS Potomac,* on the other hand, made no stops at all.

SS Potomac, the last excursion boat owned and operated by Wills. (Photograph by Alexander Shaw, courtesy of John H. Shaum, Jr.)

Besides round-trip excursions, *SS Potomac* also operated numerous nonstop cruises that summer. Most were moonlight sails out of Battery Park, but there were a few interesting daylight cruises, as well. On Thursday, June 17, *SS Potomac* boarded 546 rabbinical students from Brooklyn at Battery Park, headed north to where the ocean liners docked above West 42nd Street, and then paced RMS *Queen Elizabeth* down to the Narrows so the students could wave farewell to their rabbi, who was on his way to Europe. Five days later, *SS Potomac* took a group from Port Newark, New Jersey, on a Hudson River cruise as far as Ossining, New York, before returning.

The vessel stood for a Coast Guard inspection during a layover at Rye Beach on Friday, May 28. She also conducted three fire and boat drills during the summer, all on off days at Pier 46, Erie Basin. Then, on Tuesday, September 7, the day after her final New York charter for the season, the log contains this notation: "Crew engaged in making preparations for sea."[41] The next day, September 8, *SS Potomac* cast off from Erie Basin and headed for Baltimore. John B. Donohue was the master, and William F. Crosson the pilot. The boat reached Baltimore without incident (table 10-3).

TABLE 10-3
SS Potomac Cruise, Brooklyn to Baltimore, September 8, 1965

lv.	Pier 46/Brooklyn (Erie Basin)	6:03 A.M.
—	Verazzano-Narrows Bridge	6:37 A.M.
—	Buoy No. 1, Sandy Hook channel	7:47 A.M.
—	Barnegat Light Vessel	11:57 A.M.
—	Cape May Jetty Buoy	6:42 P.M.
—	Delaware Bay Buoy No. 4	7:47 P.M.
—	enter C&D Canal	12:50 A.M.
—	Chesapeake City	2:10 A.M.
—	Tolchester	5:20 A.M.
ar.	Broadway Pier/Baltimore	7:30 A.M.

SS Potomac returned to New York in 1966 with Wills hoping to improve on his performance of the previous year. Early in the year, though, he was dealt a fatal blow. Wills had hoped that the ICC would convert the temporary New York–Bear Mountain authority it had issued the previous year into a permanent certificate. Instead, the commission rejected the Tolchester Lines petition and withdrew the temporary permit. The ICC examiner assigned to the case contended that "existing carriers are first entitled to handle any additional traffic which might become available." He added that he was "inclined to the conclusion that Wills is interested in keeping [his] vessel profitably occupied until it can be disposed of."[42] Wills and *SS Potomac* could operate New York–Rye Beach, New York–Rockaway Beach, and nonstop cruises. But the lucrative Bear Mountain run was ruled off limits.

Keansburg Steamboat was even more opposed to Wills's petition in 1966 than in 1964. Through the excursion season of 1965, its *City of Keansburg*, the company's only active excursion boat, had primarily been deployed on a regular route between lower Manhattan and Atlantic Highlands, New Jersey, and was not especially active in summertime charter work. Over the winter of 1965–66, however, its pier at Atlantic Highlands was destroyed during a storm, and Keansburg quickly realized that charter work would play a larger role for its vessel. The company accordingly voiced strong opposition to Wills's application. Additional competition also materialized in New York in 1966, when a company doing business as Sound Steamship Lines began running *Bay Belle* in charter service there. *Bay Belle*, of course, was the former sister ship of *SS Potomac* back when both vessels ran for the Wilson Line.

Wills retained S. Harrison Kahn, a Washington attorney with considerable experience arguing cases before the ICC. On February 7, 1966, Kahn filed exceptions to the ICC examiner's report and, on June 20, petitioned for reconsideration of the decision of the full commission.[43] The effort was to no avail, though; the appeal was rejected. With no prospect of operating to Bear Mountain, there was no sense retaining an active excursion boat in New York. And so, at 5:53 A.M. on August 15, 1966, *SS Potomac* cast off from Pier 46 in Brooklyn's Erie Basin and headed south to Baltimore. With William F. Crosson at the helm, the boat reached Baltimore at 6:15 A.M. the next day. This trip from Brooklyn to Baltimore took 1 hour and 5 minutes less than the same run the previous September.[44]

SS Potomac handled four late-season charters in Baltimore in September 1966, three to the head of the Bay and the entrance to the Chesapeake and Delaware (C&D) Canal, the fourth an all-day round-trip to Cambridge, Maryland, on September 5. An untoward incident occurred during the second canal trip on September 11. An elderly woman traveling with a church group from Baltimore began to experience chest pains as the vessel headed across the Chesapeake Bay. The master called ahead, and a launch came out to meet *SS Potomac* when the steamboat reached the Eastern Shore. The woman was transferred to the launch and taken to a hospital in Kent County, Maryland. Because of the emergency, the *SS Potomac* had found herself off Tolchester Beach, Maryland, where she had first run for B. B. Wills in 1949 as *Tolchester* (II).

The final trip of the year on Sunday, September 12, 1966, was another cruise to Town Point at the mouth of the C&D Canal, with 1,738 passengers aboard. The pilothouse log is unfortunately incomplete for this trip; the final notation shows *SS Potomac* off Turkey Point at 2:40 P.M. en route back to Baltimore. Presumably she reached port around seven o'clock that evening.[45]

The next year, 1967, *SS Potomac* ran a short schedule of cruises out of Baltimore in August, and in September she headed north to Newport, Rhode Island, to work as a spectator boat for the America's Cup yacht races held there that year. For this final assignment, *SS Potomac* was a last-minute replacement for *City of Keansburg*, which was unable to serve for some reason.

Interestingly, many other vessels recruited to provide "grandstand seats" for the offshore yacht races between *Intrepid*, the U.S. defender, and *Dame Pattie*, a challenger from Australia, have played some role in the excursion boat empire of B. B. Wills. Steaming out of Providence each day was *Bay Belle*, Wilson Line's longtime Baltimore excursion boat. Taking on passengers in Newport with *SS Potomac* was *Martha's Vineyard*, which Wills operated to Provincetown under charter in 1961. Interstate Navigation's *Yankee*, another boat that Wills once ran on the Boston–Provincetown route under charter, sailed from Block Island each day of the race.

After *Intrepid* beat *Dame Pattie* four matches to none, *SS Potomac* headed back to Baltimore and tied up at Pier 3, Pratt Street. Much uncertainty surrounds *SS Potomac*'s work during the 1967 excursion season. Were her trips run by B. B. Wills and Tolchester Lines, or was the vessel bareboat chartered to someone else? There is no documentation about any of these 1967 trips among the Wills Papers. Newspaper advertisements promoting the various Baltimore excursions in August mention a company called Washington Excursion Line.

There were six cruises scheduled out of Baltimore to the C&D Canal between August 2 and August 30, one round-trip to Cambridge, Maryland, on August 13, and three moonlight cruises. All were open to the public. Chesapeake Bay steamboat historian Jack Shaum recalled riding *SS Potomac* on one of the C&D Canal trips: "The ship was pretty run down. There were obvious canvas patchings in the deck covers and the paintwork was sloppy. Her engine kind of wheezed the whole way to the canal and back and she certainly broke no speed records."[46]

B. B. Wills in the 1970s.

One August charter trip in addition to the regularly scheduled trips resulted in a bit of unfavorable publicity for *SS Potomac*. Washington attorney Timothy Casey, the same man who once owned *SS Potomac* and headed up the "second" Potomac River Line in the early 1960s, chartered the vessel for an all-day cruise from Baltimore to Washington. As in earlier days, when excursion boats like *Bear Mountain* and *Holiday* ran such trips at the end of an excursion season, *SS Potomac* was scheduled to leave Baltimore at 9:00 A.M. on Thursday, August 16, reach Washington by 9:00 P.M., with buses at the ready for a swift return trip to Baltimore.

SS *Potomac* lies partially sunk at an abandoned pier along Boston Street in Baltimore, January 1973. (Photograph by *Baltimore News American*, courtesy of John H. Shaum, Jr.)

The boat was over an hour late leaving Baltimore that day, and that set the tone for the rest of the trip. The problem was that the poor old vessel's aging steam engine was simply in no condition to make a trip to Washington from Baltimore in anything remotely like 12 hours. By 9:00 P.M., the time she was due to dock in the nation's capital, the old steamboat was still south of Chapel Point battling her way up the Potomac. Casey told the press that the vessel had to fight a strong tide. A Coast Guard spokesman noted, however, that the Potomac River was actually at flood tide most of the time SS *Potomac* was steaming upstream toward Washington, and hence was assisting the struggling vessel, not impeding it.[47] In the end, SS *Potomac* never made Washington at all. She put in at Alexandria, Virginia, at 3:30 A.M. where the buses had been repositioned, and the sun was coming up before most people reached their Baltimore homes. Many passengers were quoted in the press as being upset over the whole experience. Wisely, Casey canceled a planned return cruise out of Washington, and SS *Potomac* deadheaded back to Baltimore to resume her schedule of 1967 charter trips.

Because Casey was probably the force behind *all* the *SS Potomac*'s trips in 1967, not just the ill-fated Baltimore–Washington cruise, it is unclear exactly when the last B. B. Wills–operated excursion boat made its final voyage. Perhaps the trip up to Newport and back for the yacht races was operated by Tolchester Lines with a Tolchester crew. In that case, the curtain came down on the excursion boat empire of B. B. Wills in September 1967, when *SS Potomac* returned from Newport and tied up at Pier 3, Pratt Street, in Baltimore. On the other hand, if *SS Potomac* operated under a bareboat charter arrangement in 1967 to Casey or anyone else, the real finale would be different. Her final Wills trip would have been the last trip of the previous season, 1966, when the onetime Wilson Line vessel made that cruise to Town Point at the mouth of the C&D Canal and back on Sunday, September 12.

In any event, *SS Potomac* never steamed again after the summer of 1967, nor did any other B. B. Wills–owned excursion boat. She remained tied up in Baltimore Harbor at a Pratt Street pier until early 1973, when she was moved to a location along Boston Street. On January 13, 1973,

TABLE 10-4
The Excursion Boats of B. B. Wills

Largest	2,158 gross tons	*Holiday*
Smallest	41 gross tons	*Sightseer*
Longest	314 feet	*Potomac*
Shortest	54 feet	*Sightseer*
Oldest	Built in 1878	*Mayfair* and *Tolchester*
Newest	Built in 1952	*General*
Longest tenure	19 years 1948 to 1967 (not continuous)	*Tolchester* (II)
Longest continuous tenure	14 years 1934 to 1948	*Potomac*
First vessel	1934	*Potomac*
Last vessel:		
Last acquired	1962	*District of Columbia*, formerly *Provincetown*
Last operated	1966 or 1967 (see text)	*SS Potomac*, formerly *City of Philadelphia*, etc.
Number of excursion boats owned and operated	22	(See roster in appendix A)

one of her aft plates developed a bad leak, and she went down at the stern and settled into the harbor's soft mud bottom.[48] In subsequent months she was repaired, raised, and eventually towed north to Camden, New Jersey. And there, in the same Delaware Valley where she was launched sixty-three years earlier as the Wilson Line's *City of Philadelphia*, *SS Potomac* was scrapped.

Table 10-4 summarizes the excursion boat empire of Benjamin Bowling Wills by identifying vessels that qualify as "record-setters" in various categories, oldest, smallest, longest, and so forth.

EPILOGUE
Was It Really the End?

After completing a handful of charter assignments during the summer and fall of 1967, *SS Potomac* never sailed again. Nor did any other Wills-owned or Wills-operated excursion boat, for that matter.

The finale was totally unremarked at the time. No television camera crews waited at the dock when *SS Potomac* pulled in for the last time; no reporters interviewed the crew to ask questions about what it was "really like" to work aboard an old-fashioned steamboat. There was no B. B. Wills standing on the wharf reminiscing about days gone by.

One reason for the lack of fanfare may well be that the seventy-year-old Wills never regarded *SS Potomac*'s service in 1967 as the end of his excursion boat activity. A maritime venture in which Wills did remain briefly active after *SS Potomac*'s final cruise was the Island Transportation Corporation. The mission of this Caribbean firm was to supply fresh drinking water—by tanker—to the U.S. Virgin Islands. Wills's role was that of mortgage holder, member of the board of directors, and constant supplier of unsolicited advice.

The company's principal vessel was *Islander,* originally called Y6-60, a 177-foot diesel-powered bulk carrier built in Rochester, New York, in 1943 for military purposes. Wills purchased her in 1959 through his Boat Sales company and sold her to Island Transportation the following year. In 1968, after a protracted flap between the company's president and Wills, *Islander* was sold off and transferred to British registry. She then found a home for herself in Bermuda for the next twenty years or more.

Islander was not a passenger-carrying excursion boat. Two pieces of correspondence among the Wills Papers, however, hint that the Old Timer was perfectly willing to stay active in the excursion boat business if the right opportunity presented itself. The first is found in an August 1970 letter to Wills from the people who were then operating the overnight sternwheeler *Delta Queen* on the Mississippi and Ohio Rivers. New federal safety regulations banning wooden cabin work on overnight vessels were about to go into effect, and the steamboat's ability to survive was in serious doubt. She was eventually granted a statutory exemption from the rules by Congress, since her inland routes were considered a unique case that set her apart from the seagoing vessels the new law was primarily attempting to regulate.

During the period of uncertainty about *Delta Queen*'s fate, Rita Heintz of Greene Line Steamers responded to an earlier inquiry from Wills. Her words suggest that Wills was considering yet another venture in the excursion boat business: "The *Queen* could be operated as a day excursion boat and carry over 1,000 passengers."[1]

Delta Queen's many loyal fans might feel a twinge of horror at the thought of turning the venerable American institution into a day excursion boat. Had the steamboat not been "rescued" by legal exemption, however, Wills might have staved off her pending doom by converting her into an excursion boat.

Another series of correspondence involved a vessel not nearly so fortunate as *Delta Queen*. She was *Carib Star*, a smaller, diesel-powered passenger vessel built by Blount Marine in 1970 for a customer in Puerto Rico. Her service there did not prove to be profitable, however, and she was reported to be en route back to the mainland and very much on the market.

Wills was in communication with Blount Marine about *Carib Star* in the early 1970s.[2] Whether he was interested in the vessel merely for its brokerage possibilities or for his own revenue service somewhere is not clear. In any case, the purchase was never made.

Carib Star eventually migrated to the Pacific Coast and entered service between Catalina Island and the California mainland. An on-board explosion in San Pedro Harbor in the late 1970s—thought to be the work of terrorists—put her out of commission. She was eventually repaired, renamed *Royal Star*, and moved north to the San Francisco area.

Was B. B. Wills still interested in owning and operating an excursion boat in the years after *SS Potomac* made her final cruise? Beyond the correspondence about *Delta Queen* and *Carib Star*, there is no further evidence that Wills pursued other excursion boat ventures in the 1970s and beyond. The Wills Papers contain no follow-up inquiries or financial estimates, much less draft contracts, proposed business plans, or anything more formal. Quite possibly, these various letters are little more than inquiries of idle curiosity from a retired excursion boat operator, a man with time on his hands and stenographic services at his disposal. Nevertheless, his correspondence with the *Delta Queen* and *Carib Star* owners shows a man of endless personal drive and business acumen, who even in his seventies, could not resist the possibility of a "good bargain." And on this note, the story of the excursion boat empire of Benjamin Bowling Wills comes to an end.

Gertrude Gosnell Wills died on April 9, 1981. B. B. Wills himself passed away in his home on Indian Lane in Washington, D.C., on Thursday, October 9, 1986.[3] He was eighty-nine. Five days later, on October 14, Mass was celebrated for the repose of his soul in Saint Ignatius Church at Chapel Point, Maryland. After the Mass, his coffin was carried outside. He was laid to rest in a family plot in the hillside churchyard overlooking the spot where the Port Tobacco River gently flows into the wider Potomac, fifty-odd miles downriver from Washington. It was twelve noon, just about the time, many decades earlier, when a long, white paddlewheel steamboat with three side-by-side funnels would come into view on the Potomac and, giving a long, deep salute on her whistle, come around to port and slowly head in toward an open wharf that jutted out from the shore down below the cemetery.

> Kitty especially remembered when the *Potomac* would come in. Her brother would take you, Marcella, Ben and herself—all holding hands—down to the boardwalk to see the boat come in. What a sight that would have been.[4]

It all began at Chapel Point . . . and it ended there, too.

The church yard at St. Ignatius Church, Chapel Point, Maryland.
(Photograph by the author.)

APPENDIX A

Roster of Passenger-carrying Excursion Boats Owned and Operated by B. B. Wills and/or Wills-controlled Companies

Note: The numbers preceding the vessel names signify the order in which the names progressed; at the top of the column is the name of the vessel during its ownership by B. B. Wills.

Name	(2) *Potomac* (1) *Albany*	(1) *Southport* (2) *Col. Frank H. Adams*	(2) *Robert E. Lee* (1) *Dorchester*	(3) *Tolchester* (1) *St. Johns* (2) *Bombay*
Off. no.	105908	208730	224518	115633
Gross tons	1,415	245	612	1,098
Dimensions (feet)	314 × 40 × 10.1	125.6 × 21.2 × 8.8	192 × 36.2 × 10.2	250 × 38 × 12.5
Type	st.p.	st.s.	st.p.	st.p.
Hull	Iron	Wood	Steel	Iron
Year built	1880	1911	1912	1878
Place built	Wilmington, Del.	Boston	Sparrows Point, Md.	Wilmington, Del.
Shipyard	Harlan & Hollingsworth	Wm. McKie	Maryland Steel	Harlan & Hollingsworth
Engine	1-cylinder VB	3-cylinder TE	2-cylinder inclined	1-cylinder VB
Cylinder dimensions (inches)	73 × 144	10.5, 17.5, 28 × 18	30, 30 × 96	66 × 144
Acquired from (year)	Hudson River Day Line (1934)	Eastern SS Lines (1934)	Baltimore & Virginia S/B (1936)	Tolchester Beach Improvement Co. (1937)
Disposition (year)	Out of service (1949)	To U.S. government (1941)	Scrapped (1953)	Lost (fire) (1941)
Principal assignment(s)	Potomac River	Potomac River; Tolchester	Potomac River; barnstorming	Tolchester
Notes	1, 2	—	—	1

Abbreviations. **Type:** st.p. = steam powered, paddlewheel propelled; st.s. = steam powered, propelled by screw propeller(s); ol.s. = diesel powered, propelled by screw propeller(s). **Engine:** VE = vertical beam (steam); TE = triple expansion (steam); comp. = compound (steam); GM = General Motors (diesel); FM = Fairbanks-Morse (diesel); Gray = Gray Marine (diesel).

APPENDIX A

Name	(2) Francis Scott Key (1) Susquehanna	(2) Mohawk (1) Anne Arundel	(4) Bear Mountain (1) William G. Payne (2) Bridgeport (3) Highlander	(5) Liberty (1) Boothbay (2) USS Grampus (USN) (3) Boothbay (4) Deepwater (6) Provincetown
Off. no.	116827	201088	81809	204233
Gross tons	462	795	941	413
Dimensions (feet)	157.7 × 38 × 9	174 × 36 × 10.2	243.3 × 36.9 × 14.6	126 × 33 × 10
Type	st.s.	st.s.	st.p.	ol.s.
Hull	Iron	Steel	Steel	Steel
Year built	1898	1904	1902	1907
Place built	Baltimore	Baltimore	Wilmington, Del.	Philadelphia
Shipyard	C. Reeders & Sons	Baltimore S/B & Drydock	Harlan & Hollingsworth	Neafie & Levy
Engine	2-cylinder comp.	3-cylinder TE	2-cylinder comp.	Single diesel
Cylinder dimensions (inches)	20, 38 × 28	13, 21, 34 × 34	35, 72 × 72	n/a
Acquired from (year)	Sound SS Lines (1940)	Stony Creek Improvement Co. (1942)	Mandalay Line (1943)	Sutton Line (1943)
Disposition (year)	Scrapped (1954)	Dismantled (1951)	Scrapped (1953)	To Circle Line statue ferry (1953)
Principal assignment(s)	Tolchester; Boston–Nantasket; statue ferry	Tolchester; statue ferry; Boston–Nantasket	Tolchester; Potomac River	Statue ferry
Notes	—	—	—	3,6

APPENDIX A 193

Name	(2) *Allerton* (1) *Homer Ramsdell*	(2) *Nantasket* (1) *Newburgh*	*Mayflower*	*Saltaire*
Off. no.	95920	130350	92291	219549
Gross tons	1,181	1,034	778	68
Dimensions (feet)	225 × 32.5 × 11.8	200 × 32 × 11	202.5 × 32.5 × 10.7	73.5 × 19 × 6.3
Type	st.s.	st.s.	st.p.	ol.s.
Hull	Iron	Iron	Wood	Wood
Year built	1887	1886	1891	1919
Place built	Newburgh, N.Y.	Philadelphia	Chelsea, Mass.	Wareham, Mass.
Shipyard	T.S. Marvel	Neafie & Levy	Montgomery & Howard	n/a
Engine	2-cylinder comp.	2-cylinder comp.	1-cylinder VB	2 Gray diesels
Cylinder dimensions (inches)	28, 52 × 36	26, 45 × 36	48 × 108	n/a
Acquired from (year)	Nantasket-Boston S/B (1944)	Nantasket-Boston S/B (1944)	Nantasket-Boston S/B (1944)	Village of Saltaire, N.Y. (1945)
Disposition (year)	Scrapped (1954)	Scrapped (1954)	Out of documentation (1948)	To A. Hempstead of Key West, Fla. (1958)
Principal assignment(s)	Boston–Nantasket	Boston–Nantasket	Boston–Nantasket	Statue ferry; misc.; see text
Notes	—	—	2, 4	—

APPENDIX A

Name	(4) *Sightseer* (1) *Evelyn* (2) *Ruby* (3) *Karibou*	(2) *Alura* (1) *Symphonia*	(2) *Chauncey M. Depew* (1) *Rangeley*	(2) *Holiday* (1) *Virginia Lee* (3) *Accomac*
Off. no.	214079	222567	211290	228015
Gross tons	41	195	652	2,158
Dimensions (feet)	54.2 × 15.6 × 5.7	112.6 × 20.2 × 9.2	185.1 × 35.6 × 13.5	291 × 50.1 × 16.5
Type	ol.s.	ol.s.	st.s.	ol.s.
Hull	Wood	Steel	Steel	Steel
Year built	1916	1922	1913	1928
Place built	Miami, Fla.	New York City	Bath, Maine	Quincy, Mass.
Shipyard	n/a	n/a	Bath Iron	Bethlehem
Engine	n/a	n/a	4-cylinder TE	2 16-cylinder GM diesels
Cylinder dimensions (inches)	n/a	n/a	16, 26, 30, 30 × 24	8.75 × 10.5
Acquired from (year)	Southey Truitt of Cambridge, Md. (1945)	David Mitchell of Reedville, Va. (1946)	U.S. government (1947)	U.S. government (1947)
Disposition (year)	Abandoned (ca. 1967)	To H. W. Ward of Crisfield, Md. (1954)	To government of Bermuda (1950)	Lost (fire) (1964)
Principal assignment(s)	Misc.; see text	Misc.; see text	Boston–Nantasket; Boston–Provincetown	Boston–Provincetown
Notes	—	—	—	5, 6

APPENDIX A

Name	(2) *Mayfair* (1) *Pansy*	(3) *Madisonville* (1) *Madisonville* (2) *Monhegan* (4) *Dixie Queen*	(5) *Tolchester* (II) (1) *City of Philadelphia* (2) *Liberty Belle* (3) USS *Liberty Belle* (USN) (4) *Asbury Park* (6) *Freestone* (7) SS *Potomac*
Off. no.	232885	226632	207201
Gross tons	302	141	618
Dimensions (feet)	145 × 25 × 10.4	114.6 × 26 × 6	200.6 × 38 × 11.6
Type	ol.s.	ol.s.	st.s.
Hull	Composite	Wood	Steel
Year built	1878	1927	1910
Place built	Philadelphia	Madisonville, La.	Wilmington, Del.
Shipyard	Baird & Huston	Madisonville Industries	Harlan & Hollingsworth
Engine	2 8-cylinder FM diesels	Single diesel	3-cylinder TE
Cylinder dimensions (inches)	10 × 12.5	n/a	19, 29, 44 × 24
Acquired from (year)	U.S. government (1947)	G. Moon & C. Sutton of New York City (1947)	Jersey Shore Lines (1948)
Disposition (year)	Scrapped (1967)	To J. W. Tobin of Charleston, S.C. (1952)	Out of service (1967)
Principal assignment(s)	Statue ferry; Potomac River	Statue ferry; barnstorming; see text	Tolchester; misc.; see text
Notes	8	—	6, 9

… APPENDIX A

Name	(2) *San Jacinto* (1) *Dolphin* (3) *Manhattan II* (4) *Manhattan*	*General*	(2) *Provincetown* (1) *District of Columbia*
Off. no.	253076	265441	224391
Gross tons	226	163	2,128
Dimensions (feet)	151.5 × 22.8 × 7.7	63.7 × 25 × 4.6	297.8 × 51 × 16.3
Type	ol.s.	ol.s.	st.s.
Hull	Steel	Steel	Steel
Year built	1944	1952	1924
Place built	Barber, N.J.	New Orleans	Wilmington, Del.
Shipyard	Federal	Alexander	Pusey & Jones
Engine	8 6-cylinder GM diesels	2 6-cylinder Gray diesels	4-cylinder TE
Cylinder dimensions (inches)	4.5 × 5	4.5 × 5	23.5, 37, 43, 43 × 42
Acquired from (year)	Circle Line (1951)	Harry Schroeder of Baton Route, La. (1954)	Old Bay Line (1962)
Disposition (year)	To J. Driscoll of New York City (1956)	To St. Paul Yacht Club, Minneapolis (1968)	Lost (fire) (1969)
Principal assignment(s)	Houston Ship Canal	Houston Ship Canal; misc.; see text	Boston–Provincetown
Notes	7	—	—

1. Hull converted to unpowered barge following career as an excursion boat.
2. Engine by W. & A. Fletcher.
3. Originally steam powered; 3-cylinder TE (11, 18, 32 × 22); converted to diesel by B. B. Wills.
4. Converted to a land-locked night club at Nantasket Beach, Mass., following career as an excursion boat.
5. Originally steam powered; two 4-cylinder TE (18, 30, 34, 34 × 27); converted to diesel by B. B. Wills; see text.
6. Not continuously owned by Wills or a Wills-controlled company, in the period between acquisition and disposition; see text.
7. Built as a U.S. Navy LCI (L)-class landing craft, but possibly never commissioned by the navy; see text.
8. Originally steam powered; two 1-cylinder engines (22 × 27).
9. Last vessel to operate in excursion service for Wills or a Wills-controlled company.

APPENDIX B

The Financial Empire of B. B. Wills

It would take an intense analysis by trained accountants to conduct a precise and sophisticated statistical review of the finances of Benjamin Bowling Wills, for any year, or over his entire career. His various business holdings were many and varied. While the focus of this book has been Wills's excursion boat empire, various real estate ventures in which he participated in his later years were far more remunerative than his earlier maritime exploits.

In any event, Wills began with a $5,000 cash down payment on the $200,000 Chapel Point property in 1926, which he eventually lost. He put forth another $5,000 cash outlay in 1934 to initiate the purchase, for $25,000, of the sidewheeler *Albany* from the Hudson River Day Line. From these modest investments his empire grew.

In 1926, the opening year of Chapel Point Park, Wills had an annual income of $688. Four years later, with Wilson Line's *City of Washington* helping bring customers to Chapel Point, Wills's income had risen to $4,193.

By 1941, the year-end balance sheet shows the total value of the assets held by B. B. Wills to be $137,379, primarily consisting of stock in three excursion boat companies: Potomac River Line, Inc., Robert E. Lee Steamboat Corp., and Tolchester Lines, Inc. In addition, Wills's net worth in 1941 included the ferryboat *Howard W. Jackson*, the steamboat *Mohawk*, and other miscellaneous items.

By war's end in 1946, Wills's net worth had grown substantially. He and his wife, Gertrude G. Wills, wholly owned seven different corporations and one unincorporated company:

    Potomac River Line, Inc.
    Robert E. Lee Steamboat Corp.
    Nantasket Boat Line, Inc.
    Boat Sales, Inc.

Wills Export Line, S.A.
Statue of Liberty Line, Inc.
Wills-Spedden Shipyard, Inc.
Bay Ridge Beach, Inc., a resort property on Chesapeake Bay near Annapolis
Statue of Liberty Boat Line (unincorporated)

Finally, the Willses controlled four corporations, although they were not their sole owners:

Maryland Boat Corp.
Tolchester Lines, Inc.
Waterways Sightseeing, Inc.
Wil-Mar Corp., an entity created in 1937 to be the owner and operator of the amusement park at Tolchester Beach

While most vessels were owned by one or another of the various corporations, two excursion boats were owned by either B. B. himself or Gertrude in 1946. These were *Francis Scott Key* and *Deepwater*. By the end of 1946, the couple had total assets of $845,358.

Two years later, in 1948, their total assets had increased to $870,364. The principal holdings that were added since 1946 were four companies primarily associated with the operation of sightseeing bus tours in and around Washington, D.C.:

Anchorage Transportation, Inc.
Blue and Gray Motor Tours, Inc.
Gray Line Auto Rental, Inc.
Boat Concessions, Inc., a company originally formed to handle the sale of food and drink aboard excursion boats, but which also became a holding company of sorts for sightseeing bus ventures

At the beginning of the 1960s, and with the golden era of Wills-owned excursion boats long since past, Wills and his wife could claim total assets of $1,132,098. Less than 20 percent of this sum was attributable to maritime activities or holdings. There was $29,478 in a secured note from Wills-Bowers, Inc., the Florida-based fishing boat company; $96,096 from Jeremiah Driscoll in remaining mortgage payments on the vessel that Wills once operated as *San Jacinto;* and almost $70,000 in the value of three excursion boats—*SS Potomac, Mayfair,* and *General*.

COLLEGE SELLING AGENCY

B. B. WILLS, MANAGER

| Pennants, Banners and Pillows
Photo Books in College Colors
Laundry and Brief Cases
Die-Stamped and General Stationery
Christmas Seal Cards | From Factory Direct to College Store | Twinpoint-Pen and Pencil in One
Rugs Woven with Name and Design in College Colors
College Mascot Dolls
Neckties in College Colors
College Souvenirs and Novelties |

BEL ALTON, MARYLAND

PHONE { WASH. MAIN 1444
HOME LA PLATA 57-F-31

B. B. WILLS, PROP.

CHAPEL POINT
THE PRIDE OF THE POTOMAC
MARYLAND

Home Address:
Bel Alton - Maryland

Washington Office:
903 National Press Building

B. B. WILLS
PRESIDENT
F. P. NOEL
VICE-PRES. & GEN'L MANAGER

Potomac River Line, Inc.
7th and Water Streets, S. W.
Washington, D. C.

District 5611
5612

NAtional 8-7722

MARYLAND BOAT CORP. T/A

Potomac River Line

7th & Main Ave., S. W.   Washington 4, D. C.

B. B. WILLS, President

BOSTON, MASS.
ROWES WHARF
HUBBARD 2-1000

WILLS LINES, INC.
Operators of Passenger and Excursion Vessels
CHANDLER BUILDING -:- 1427 EYE Street, N. W. -:- Washington, D. C.

WASHINGTON, D. C.
7TH & MAINE AVE., S. W.
NATIONAL 7722

NEW YORK, N. Y.
PIER A, NORTH RIVER
BOWLING GREEN 9-6217

REPUBLIC: 3456

BALTIMORE, MD.
PIER 16, LIGHT STREET
LEXINGTON 3450

BOSTON-PROVINCETOWN LINE

Largest, finest, fastest coastal excursion vessel under the U. S. flag.

INDIA WHARF
310 ATLANTIC AVE.—Tel. HU 2-4800
operators of the
MOTOR VESSEL **HOLIDAY**

Letterheads from various companies controlled by Benjamin B. Wills.

Fifteen years later, in 1975, the assets of B. B. Wills had a recorded value of $4,830,800. Of this impressive sum, the only line item of value that recalled his excursion boat days was a small matter of $25,000, described as follows: "G.M. Diesel Engines (2)—1600 H.P. with 5-1 Reduction Gears." These were the engines from *Accomac,* whose colorful career is highlighted throughout the book.

In summary, the man who began his excursion boat career in the depths of the Great Depression with a modest cash outlay of $5,000 had successfully parlayed that investment into an estate worth many millions of dollars.

APPENDIX C

Chronology: The Life of B. B. Wills

Year	Event
1897	B. B. Wills born in Bel Alton, Maryland
1922	Graduates from College of Holy Cross; embarks on career as traveling salesman
1924	Moves to Miami, Florida; begins new career in real estate development
1926	Leaves Miami and returns home to Bel Alton; purchases land at Chapel Point, Maryland, from the Jesuit Fathers and opens picnic grounds and bathing beach
1928	Wed to Gertrude Clementine Gosnell
1930	Builds dock at Chapel Point; contracts with Wilson Line to provide daily excursion boat service to and from Washington; expands Chapel Point Park
1931	Builds bus terminal at T.B., Maryland
1932	Wilson Line abandons Chapel Point service at end of summer season
1934	Wills purchases *Albany* from Hudson River Day Line for $25,000; renames her *Potomac* and establishes Potomac River Line; begins service between Washington and Chapel Point, plus evening dance cruises
1935	Purchases *Southport* and establishes Columbia Steamship Line to provide segregated charter excursions out of Washington for African Americans
1936	"Defaults" on mortgage and returns Chapel Point property to Jesuit Fathers; closes Chapel Point Park so *Potomac* can concentrate on evening dance cruises
1936	Establishes Robert E. Lee Steamboat Company with Fabian P. Noel; deploys *Robert E. Lee* in barnstorming-type service in tidewater country of Virginia

1938	Establishes Tolchester Lines and takes over assets of Tolchester Beach Improvement Corporation; begins operation of *Tolchester* between Baltimore and Tolchester Beach; charters *Chelsea* from Reading Company for Baltimore–Tolchester ferryboat service
1938	Returns *Chelsea* to Reading Company; shifts *Southport* to Baltimore to handle cross-Chesapeake ferry business; moves *Robert E. Lee* to Washington, D.C., to serve African American market
1941	Unsuccessful effort to take over Nantasket–Boston Steamboat Company
1941	*Tolchester* lost in fire at Baltimore; replaced by newly purchased propeller steamboats *Francis Scott Key* and *Mohawk*
1941–42	*Francis Scott Key* sent south to inaugurate winter service in Miami; boat returns to Baltimore via Intracoastal Waterway because of submarine threat on coastwise route
1942	Wills purchases *Bear Mountain* from New York's Mandalay Line for Tolchester service
1943	Takes over Statue of Liberty ferry in New York from George Sanders
1944	Purchases assets of Nantasket–Boston Steamboat Company after the 1944 excursion season
1945	Establishes Nantasket Boat Line to operate Boston–Nantasket service
1945	Establishes Wills Export Line, SA, a Panamanian company that will allow vessels to sail under "flag of convenience" with foreign crews
1945	Through Wills Export Line, purchases two "revised *Flower*-class" corvettes from the Royal Canadian Navy
1946	Purchases Spedden Shipyard on Boston Street in Baltimore; renames it Wills-Spedden
1947	Purchases former Pennsylvania Railroad passenger steamboat *Virginia Lee* from U.S. government in Belém, Brazil
1947	Purchases former Hudson River Day Liner *Chauncey M. Depew* from U.S. government and operates her between Boston and Provincetown
1947	Grand jury inquiry in New York about dock leases associated with Sightseeing Around New York Waterways, a firm Wills formed in 1946 in partnership with George Sanders
1948	Wills uses former navy submarine net layer AN-77 to tow *Virginia Lee* north out of Belém, Brazil; AN-77 and *Virginia Lee* forced to put in at Port of Spain, Trinidad

1948	Last season of operation for *Potomac*; replaced in 1949 by *Bear Mountain*
1949	*Virginia Lee* dieselized and renamed *Holiday*; operates Boston–Provincetown
1950	*Chauncey M. Depew* sold to government of Bermuda for tender service in Hamilton Harbor
1951	*Holiday* damaged off Carolina coast en route to proposed winter assignment in Tampa, Florida; *Holiday* sold to Wilson Line–affiliated company for ferry service across the mouth of the Chesapeake Bay and renamed *Accomac*
1951	Final season for Nantasket Boat Line; service taken over by Wilson Line in 1952
1952	Last season of service for *Bear Mountain* on the Potomac River
1952	B. B. Wills files $3.75 million suit in federal court against Wilson Line; receives $44,000 following a negotiated out-of-court settlement
1952	Becomes investment partner in a Miami-based shrimp boat company called Wills-Bowers
1953	Circle Line–Statue of Liberty Ferry replaces B. B. Wills as contract provider of service to Bedloe's Island
1954	Excursion service inaugurated on the Houston Ship Canal with converted LCI(L)-class landing craft *San Jacinto*
1955	Houston service terminated after its second season
1957	Wilson Line and Tolchester Lines merge Baltimore excursion operations
1958	Joint Wilson–Wills service not repeated and both companies abandon excursion service out of Baltimore; amusement park at Tolchester Beach sold
1958	*Tolchester* (II) renamed *Freestone* and chartered for use as a stationary gambling ship at Freestone Point on the Potomac River; venture ends quickly in the face of public protests
1958	Wills now devoting majority of his time to real estate development business, primarily in the Virginia suburbs of Washington, D.C.
1961	*Freestone* sold to new company intending to operate Potomac River Cruises; renamed *SS Potomac*, but venture is unsuccessful; Wills arranges for *SS Potomac* to be moved to Boston to take over Boston–Nantasket excursion service after abandonment by Wilson Line
1961	Wills arranges resumption of Boston–Provincetown service using chartered vessel *Martha's Vineyard*

1962	Purchases three overnight passenger steamboats from Old Bay Line; puts one of the three, *District of Columbia,* into Boston–Provincetown service as *Provincetown*
1963	Second and final season for *Provincetown* on Boston–Provincetown run
1963	Wills operates Boston–Provincetown service with *Yankee,* under bareboat charter from Interstate Navigation; last Wills-operated service in Massachusetts
1963	Reacquires *Accomac*
1964	*Accomac* damaged in shipyard fire while being reconverted into day excursion boat
1964	*SS Potomac* begins short career as charter boat in New York
1965	*Provincetown* to become *Chesapeake* and run two- and three-day cruises out of Washington; venture fails when *Provincetown* is unable to pass Coast Guard inspection
1966	*SS Potomac* withdrawn from New York when ICC rejects application for permanent certificate of public convenience and necessity for New York–Bear Mountain route
1967	Series of charter cruises out of Baltimore, followed by assignment as spectator boat for America's Cup races off Newport, Rhode Island, and *SS Potomac* marks the final operation of any B. B. Wills–owned excursion boat
1981	Death of Gertrude Wills
1986	B. B. Wills dies; buried in family plot at Chapel Point, Maryland

APPENDIX D

Albany and the Hudson River Day Line

Albany, the steamboat that B. B. Wills would purchase in 1934, was an iron-hulled, three-deck passenger vessel built in 1880 for a company whose formal corporate name changed a bit in the final decades of the nineteenth century but is best known as the Hudson River Day Line. She was the first of a new generation of boats designed for an era when railroads had clearly become the principal form of basic transportation up and down the Hudson Valley, while the Day Line deliberately appealed to a different and specialized market. One did not use Day Line steamers to travel from New York to Albany if the press of business made speed a controlling factor. In such cases, a fast train on the New York Central and Hudson River Railroad was a far better choice. On the other hand, if one's travel plans were flexible and a full day's cruise up the river from New York to the state capital had some appeal—with a tasty meal or two en route—then the Hudson River Day Line's seasonal service was made to order.

From the outset *Albany* was designed with this style of travel in mind. Consequently, every portion of her three decks was laid out to provide comfortable accommodation for passengers. Her design had no compromises dictated by the need to serve multiple markets or functions; no sections of the main deck were reserved for freight, much less livestock. There was no need to wall off precious space for overnight cabins. *Albany* was a day passenger boat, pure and simple.

Launched in Wilmington, Delaware, at the famous Harlan and Hollingsworth yard, she was powered by a single-cylinder vertical-beam engine, built by Fletcher-Harrison. The firm later evolved into the W. and A. Fletcher Company and was, by any name, the premiere builder of such power plants on the East Coast, and perhaps the entire world.

The engine's single cylinder was positioned vertically amidships with the piston rod emerging from the cylinder at the top. The cylinder was big; *Albany*'s had a diameter of 73 inches and a stroke of 12 feet. The piston rod extended up through the vessel's three decks. There, atop the hurricane deck, the piston drove a large, parallelogram-shaped device called a walking beam, which transmitted power back down to the interior of the vessel. Inside the vessel, a crankshaft turned a pair of paddlewheels, one on each side of the hull. The walking beam was so named because its slow and steady up-and-down motion seemed to mimic the pace of someone out for a brisk stroll.

It was primitive, it was simple, and it worked. To be sure, paddlewheel propulsion had given way to screw propellers in many maritime applications by 1880, but for some specialized purposes—and passenger service up and down the Hudson River was one of them—sidewheels had many advantages. Paddlewheel boats were thus retained as a matter of choice by naval architects well into the twentieth century. In later years, the older vertical-beam engine would give way to multicylinder inclined engines for propelling sidewheel-equipped vessels, thus rendering the walking beam obsolete.

Albany was followed by a sister ship, the *New York,* in 1887, and for the rest of the nineteenth century the pair were the mainstays of the Hudson River Day Line's service. One typically handled an "up" trip from New York to Albany, while the other handled a "down" trip in the opposite direction. Then, after an overnight layover at either end of the line, the pattern was repeated the next day in the opposite direction.

Albany and *New York* each had three coal-fired boilers, and because they were positioned side-by-side down below, it was both efficient and convenient to have three funnels also arranged side-by-side. In the 1890s, both *Albany* and *New York* were cut in half and lengthened; *Albany*'s original stem-to-stern measurement of 284 feet was increased to 315, and the vessel was outfitted with a newer and more efficient kind of paddlewheel. Day Line's business was on the upswing year after year, and enlarging the vessels was seen as a quick fix for increasing the company's passenger-carrying capacity.

By the early years of the twentieth century, quick fixes were no longer sufficient, so newer and larger Day Line steamers were designed and built. *Hendrick Hudson* came out in 1906, a four-deck sidewheeler that featured the company's first inclined compound engine. She would have been quickly followed by a similar or even larger running mate had not a tragic fire in 1908 destroyed *New York*. To replace the vessel as quickly as possible, the company salvaged *New York*'s vertical-beam engine and designed a compromise vessel around it that was larger than *New York*, but smaller than *Hendrick Hudson*. This was the *Robert Fulton* of 1909, a vessel that survived to become in 1954 the last active vertical-

APPENDIX D

beam steamboat on the East Coast. As discussed in chapter 8, in 1951 B. B. Wills almost changed the ultimate fate of *Robert Fulton*.

Washington Irving of 1913 was the largest Day Liner of all, 400 feet long and with a massive capacity of 6,000 passengers. By contrast, the maximum carrying capacity of *Albany* was 2,500. *Washington Irving*, though, was lost in a collision with an oil barge in New York Harbor in 1926. *Alexander Hamilton*, built in 1924, was the company's final sidewheeler, although she set new records in neither size nor passenger capacity. She was more of a throwback to a *Robert Fulton*–sized boat than an advance on *Hendrick Hudson* or *Washington Irving*.

By the mid-twenties, the nature of Day Line service was also changing. Single-day round-trip excursions out of New York to parks and picnic grounds along the lower river were becoming more popular with the public than leisurely daylong trips up and down the Hudson between New York and Albany. More modest vessels were appropriate for such service, the company felt.

Alexander Hamilton, Day Line's last sidewheeler, shown at North River Pier 81 in New York. (Photograph by the author.)

It was also in the 1920s when the Day Line began to add propeller boats to its fleet. *Dewitt Clinton,* a former oceangoing steamship, was purchased in 1921; *Chauncey M. Depew* joined the ranks in 1925 after earlier service for the Maine Central Railroad and was a much smaller vessel that the company used for charter and special-purpose assignments. *Peter Stuyvesant* was built new in 1927.

Albany continued in service until 1930, when a general downturn in business brought on by the Great Depression caused Day Line to scale back its operations. As the oldest unit in the fleet, she was the obvious vessel to lay up. Then, in January 1933, the company was forced into receivership. Alfred V. S. Olcott, the line's president and general manager, was appointed by the court to serve as trustee. In 1934, *Albany* was sold to B. B. Wills.

The Hudson River Day Line remained in business through the excursion season of 1948, when the original company passed from the scene. In its stead, a successor Day Line was organized and maintained a modicum of service with some of the old company's vessels, but only on the lower Hudson River. The company's traditional signature serv-

Robert Fulton, the last active beam engine sidewheeler on the East Coast shown at Bear Mountain on August 30, 1954. (Photograph by the author.)

APPENDIX D

ice, daylong cruises in each direction between Albany and New York, was not revived by the new Day Line.

Day Line's last active steamboat, *Alexander Hamilton*, made her final trip in 1971 and was replaced the following season by a newly designed diesel-powered vessel called, simply enough, *Dayliner*. By the mid-1980s, however, *Dayliner* was also withdrawn and the Hudson River Day Line became a thing of the past.

Although the Hudson River Day Line was in operation for many years before *Albany* came on the scene in 1880, she was the first of a distinctive kind of day passenger vessel that would typify, and identify, this important American steamboat company for almost seventy-five years.

For a thorough history of the Hudson River Day Line, see Donald C. Ringwald, *Hudson River Day Line* (New York: Fordham University Press, 1990).

APPENDIX E

B. B. Wills's Perennial Competition: The Wilson Line

From the very beginning, the Wilson Line played an important role in the story of the excursion boat empire of B. B. Wills. His ventures and the Wilson Line met head to head in many excursion markets on the east coast and, later, even in Texas. Everywhere Wills turned, it seemed that he was facing competition with the Wilson Line. The two firms' search for similar markets in their expansion into all the major seaports along the east coast made their competition nearly constant. At times, however, the two companies cooperated in business ventures. Ironically, almost in unison, Wills and the Wilson Line first curtailed and then abandoned their various services, as the American excursion boat became a virtually extinct species of domestic transportation. The following table depicts the Wilson Line fleet at a key moment in its history, the excursion season of 1955—just after the line had been taken over by the City Investing Company of New York, and the fleet was given a new color scheme featuring a yellow and white superstructure topped off by a red and white funnel. The end was not far off, though.

For a history of the Wilson Line, see Richard V. Elliott, *Last of the Steamboats* (Cambridge, Md.: Tidewater Publishers, 1970).

APPENDIX E

The Wilson Line Fleet, 1955

Vessel	Type	Place built (year)	Assignment	Notes
(2) *Bay Belle* (1) *City of Wilmington* (3) *The Duchess*	st.s.	Wilmington, Del. (1910)	Baltimore– Betterton	—
(2) *Boston Belle* (1) *PC 1258* (USN) (3) *Ciudad de Rosario* (Argentina)	ol.s.	Stamford, Conn. (1945)	Boston– Provincetown	1
(2) *Hudson Belle* (1) *Delaware Belle* (3) *George Washington* (4) *Rella Mae*	ol.s.	Perryville, Md. (1946)	Charter work at New York	—
(2) *Liberty Belle* (1) *PCE(R) 854* (USN) (3) *Isla del Tesoro* (Cuba)	ol.s.	Chicago (1943)	New York– Rockaway Beach	1
(2) *Mount Vernon* (1) *City Of Camden* (3) *Charles S. Zimmerman*	st.s.	Wilmington, Del. (1916)	Washington– Marshall Hall– Mount Vernon	—
(3) *Pilgrim Belle* (1) *Brandywine* (2) *Dixie*	st.s.	Wilmington, Del. (1885)	Out of service at Wilmington, Del.	2
(3) *Pilgrim Belle* (II) (1) *City Of Chester* (2) *City Of Washington*	st.s.	Wilmington, Del. (1888)	Boston–Nantasket	3
(2) *Sea Belle* (1) *PC 1207* (USN)	ol.s.	New York City (1943)	Houston Ship Canal	1, 4

1. Converted U.S. Navy submarine chaser; see text.
2. Vessel never operated again.
3. Final year of operation.
4. Inaugurated Houston service in late 1955; returned to Boston–Nantasket route in 1956.

Abbreviations. st.s. = steam powered, propelled by screw propeller(s); ol.s. = diesel powered, propelled by screw propeller(s).

Note: The numbers preceding the vessel names signify the order in which the names progressed; the first name in the entry is the name of the vessel in 1955.

Boston Belle, the converted submarine chaser that competed with Wills's *Holiday* between Boston and Provincetown in 1950. (Photograph by the author.)

Wilson Line vessels in winter quarters at Wilmington, Delaware. The vessel to the right is *Bay Belle*. *Hudson Belle* (outside) and *State of Pennsylvania* (inside) are facing her. (Photograph by the author.)

Bay Belle, a vessel that competed with B. B. Wills for many years in Baltimore. (Photograph by the author.)

Notes

CHAPTER ONE
1. St. Thomas Manor, a residence for Catholic priests that adjoins St. Ignatius Church, was established in the 1640s after the Second Lord Baltimore gave the Jesuits over 4,000 acres of land in the area. The priests who lived there did missionary work among local Indian tribes, and Mass was celebrated in the residence for many years. St. Ignatius Church was built after the Revolution in 1798. For further details, see Jean B. Lee, *The Price of Nationhood: The American Revolution in Charles County* (New York: W. W. Norton, 1994), pp. 74–81, 194–95.
2. Roberta J. Wearmooth, ed., *Abstracts from the Port Tobacco Times and Charles County Register* (Bowie, Md.: Heritage Books, 1990) 1: 151–52.
3. Information on earlier generations of the Wills family is largely taken from a privately published biography of B. B. Wills's brother (*Francis Reed Wills* [Allentown, Pa.: GAC Corporation, 1971]).
4. B. B. Wills to Philip Reed Wills, September 30, 1916, Wills Papers, collected by Professor Jeffrey Wills of the University of Wisconsin (hereafter cited as Wills Papers).
5. B. B. Wills, *B.B. Wills: Progress in Making Money* (manuscript in Wills Papers) (hereafter cited as BBW, *Making Money*) p. 2.
6. BBW to W. A. Coombe, December 8, 1925, copy in Wills Papers.
7. Contract of Sale, Corporation of Roman Catholic Clergymen and BBW, June 13, 1926, copy in Wills Papers.
8. "Where Summer Is Glorious: Chapel Point on the Potomac," 1929 brochure in Wills Papers.
9. The miniature railway was purchased second-hand in 1931 from Pleasure Beach Park outside Bridgeport, Connecticut, an amusement park that was also once served by an excursion boat. The last vessel to operate between New York and Pleasure Beach was the 1911-built steamboat *Mayflower*, originally named *Moosehead*, and then *Porpoise*. *Mayflower* was purchased

by the U.S. government in 1943 for war-related duties and never returned to passenger service afterward. A sister ship of *Mayflower*, *Chauncey M. Depew*, will be discussed later.
10. *George Law* was built in New York in 1852, *Samuel J. Pentz*, originally named *Long Island*, was built in Baltimore in 1866. *John W. Thompson*, originally called *Harry Randall*, was built in Camden in 1875.
11. For a full account of the Wilson Line, see Richard V. Elliott, *Last of the Steamboats* (Cambridge, Md.: Tidewater Publishers, 1970).
12. Wilson Line, Inc., and BBW, agreement (undated and unsigned draft), Wills Papers. All specifics cited in the text were taken from this draft; the possibility of minor changes between this unsigned draft and the final signed version must be acknowledged.
13. George W. Lukens to BBW, March 8, 1929, Wills Papers; and Lukens Dredging and Contracting Corporation and BBW, contract, March 22, 1930, Wills Papers.
14. Quoted in Elliott, *Last of the Steamboats*, p. 69.
15. *Washington Post*, July 3, 1932.
16. BBW, *Making Money*, p. 4.
17. Rev. Francis A. Breen, S.J., to BBW, January 26, 1932, Wills Papers.
18. George W. Lukens to BBW, July 15, 1931; July 27, 931; July 17, 1933; August 7, 1933, Wills Papers.
19. BBW to Rev. James A. McGivney, S.J., August 29, 1931, copy in Wills Papers.
20. BBW to Rev. Francis A. Breen, S.J., June 21, 1932, copy in Wills Papers.
21. BBW to Rev. Francis A. Breen, S.J., July 12, 1932, copy in Wills Papers.
22. BBW, "Commercial Possibilities of Chapel Point" (undated single-page memorandum), Wills Papers.
23. Ibid.
24. Peninsula Transit Corporation and BBW, June 30, 1931, agreement, Wills Papers. The town of T.B., Maryland, derives its name from a boundary stone that one separated land owned by William Townsend—T—from that of Thomas Brooke—B.
25. BBW, *Making Money*, p. 5.
26. See, for example, David C. Holly, *Steamboat on the Chesapeake: Emma Giles and the Tolchester Line* (Centreville, Md.: Tidewater Publishers, 1987), p. 290.
27. BBW to Alfred V. S. Olcott, May 30, 1933, copy in Wills Papers.
28. Frank P. Gravatt (Atlantic City Steamship Company) to BBW, May 2, 1933, Wills Papers.
29. BBW to Alfred V. S. Olcott, May 30, 1933, copy in Wills Papers.

CHAPTER TWO

1. "Hudson Day Line in Receivership," *New York Times*, January 12, 1933. For the complete history of the Hudson River Day Line, see Donald C. Ringwald, *Hudson River Day Line* (New York: Fordham University Press, 1990).
2. See Raymond J. Mulligan (Marshall of the United States for the Southern District of New York) and BBW, April 17, 1934, United States Marshall's Bill of Sale of Vessel, Wills Papers; and BBW and Alfred V. S. Olcott, April 18, 1934, Preferred Mortgage on Steamship *Albany* of New York, N.Y., Wills Papers.
3. Frank B. Hall and Company, Inc., to BBW, April 18, 1934, Memorandum of Premiums Due.
4. Thomas E. Morton and N. H. Dunn (U.S. Department of Commerce, Bureau of Navigation and Steamboat Inspection) to BBW, March 29, 1934, Wills Papers.
5. Ernest H. Dendel (Tietjen and Lang Dry Dock Company) to BBW, April 14, 1934, Wills Papers.
6. Tietjen and Lang Dry Dock Company to Str. *Albany*, April 18, 1934, statement in Wills Papers.
7. BBW, *Making Money*, p. 5.
8. Steamship Agents Willard H. Collins and David B. Edwards to Str. *Albany*, April 20, 1934, statement in Wills Papers.
9. Ernest H. Dendel (Tietjen and Lang Dry Dock Company) to Str. *Albany*, April 30, 1934, Wills Papers.
10. Tietjen and Lang Dry Dock Company to Potomac River Line, Cox Station, Maryland, May 3, 1934, statement in Wills Papers.
11. "Payroll for *Albany* during Conversion to Oil at Chapel Point" (through July 1, 1934), Wills Papers.
12. In a marvelous article about *Potomac*, Harry Jones suggested that the vessel entered revenue service on May 30, 1934. See Harry Jones, "A Centennial Salute to *Albany*," *Steamboat Bill* 152 (Winter 1979): 215–26. Insurance documents among the Wills Papers support the contention that the vessel's first visit to Washington was not until June 8, 1934. Jones enjoys such an excellent reputation for accuracy, however, that the May 30 possibility must remain open.
13. The Red Sox rookie southpaw Fritz Ostermueller who beat the Washington Senators on the day that *Potomac* first steamed into Washington harbor pitched in the major leagues for fifteen consecutive seasons, 1934 through 1948, before retiring. B. B. Wills's newly acquired excursion boat operated on the Potomac River for the very same fifteen consecutive seasons, 1934 through 1948, before she too retired.
14. *Washington Post*, June 3, 1934, and June 22, 1934.

CHAPTER THREE

1. Author's interview with B.B. Wills's son J. Eugene Wills, December 29, 1995.
2. By-Laws of the Potomac River Line, March 21, 1934, p. 1, Certificate of Incorporation, Wills Papers.
3. Ibid., pp. 6–7.
4. BBW to various persons, 1934, form letter in Wills Papers.
5. BBW, *Making Money*, p. 6.
6. General Statement, Chapel Point Park, 1935, Wills Papers.
7. The Corporation of Roman Catholic Clergymen *v.* Benjamin B. Wills and Gertrude G. Wills. Circuit Court for Charles County (1936) W.M.A. No. 3 Folio 412; No. 787.
8. See, for example, BBW to Rev. James A. McGivney, S.J., September 15, 1931, copy in Wills Papers.
9. Corporation of Roman Catholic Clergymen to BBW, August 27, 1936, Release of Mortgage, Wills Papers.
10. Summary financial statement in what appears to be BBW's handwriting (undated), Wills Papers. The same document also states, "Property was definitely abandoned in 1936 by giving release to holder of mortgage of all rights herein by written agreement."
11. Kathleen Wills to J. Eugene Wills, March 19, 1990, Wills Papers.
12. Potomac River Line, 1936, brochure, Wills Papers.
13. Bertie L. Thompson, John R. Thompson, and Gertrude G. Wills, May 17, 1935, agreement, Wills Papers.
14. BBW, *Making Money*, pp. 6–7.
15. See, for example, Irving Feld (Music Corporation of America) and Wynn Lassner per Buddy Rich, May 26, 1952, contract for engagement aboard Potomac River Line, Wills Papers.
16. R.H. Lalevee (Manager, Potomac River Line) to L.C. Turner (Office of Defense Transportation), April 25, 1944, copy in Wills Papers.
17. R.H. Lalevee (Manager, Potomac River Line) to E.R. Holzborn (Office of Defense Transportation), April 20, 1944, copy in Wills Papers.
18. See, for example, Jones, *op. cit.*, p. 221.
19. See Potomac River Line, *Application for Fuel Oil, Diesel Oil, and Kerosene Ration for Industrial, Commercial and Governmental Uses* (April 21, 1943, and April 25, 1944), Wills Papers. The only documentation among the Wills Papers of governmental action in response to these applications involves an approval for a portion of the 1944 excursion season. See L.C. Turner (Office of Defense Transportation) to R.H. Lalevee (Potomac River Line), August 10, 1944, Wills Papers.
20. "Bolles Unrepresented at Blackout Hearing," *Washington News*, July 7, 1942.
21. Jones, *op. cit.*, p. 221.

22. John A. Meseck to BBW, July 24, 1942, Wills Papers.
23. BBW to Edward L. Maier, September 22, 1948, copy in Wills Papers.
24. BBW, *Making Money*, p. 7.
25. Twenty-fifth Infantry Association and Potomac River Line, April 25, 1951, contract, Wills Papers.
26. *Moody's Manual of Investments; Railroad Securities* (New York and London: Moody's Investors Service, 1930), pp. 720–21.
27. See, for example, Special Meeting of Directors of Robert E. Lee Steamboat Corporation, December 15, 1942, minutes, Wills Papers.
28. Walter B. Guy (Guy and Brookes) to BBW, July 27, 1942, Wills Papers.
29. Pilot House Log Book of *Robert E. Lee*, May 26, 1948, to August 20, 1950, Wills Papers.
30. "Helena Haley et al. *v.* Wilson Line Operating Company," *Interstate Commerce Commission Reports* (Washington, D.C.: Government Printing Office, 1952) 283 (30769): 362–64.
31. Special Meeting of the Board of Directors of the Robert E. Lee Steamboat Corporation, August 15, 1955, minutes, Wills Papers.

CHAPTER FOUR

1. For a thorough history of the Tolchester Line in the years prior to Wills's takeover, see David C. Holly, *Steamboat on the Chesapeake:* Emma Giles *and the Tolchester Line* (Centreville, Md.: Tidewater Publishers, 1987). For further information on Chesapeake Bay steamboats in general, including operations to Tolchester, see Robert H. Burgess and H. Graham Wood, *Steamboats Out of Baltimore* (Cambridge, Md.: Tidewater Publishers, 1968).
2. Holly, *Steamboats*, pp. 281 ff.
3. *Richard A. Lewis et al. v. Janon Fisher et al.,* Court of Appeals of Maryland (Jan. 1937), no 55; *Daily Record* [Baltimore], April 15, 1937; and Agreement to Purchase Property of Tolchester Beach Improvement Company, November 14, 1936, Wills Papers.
4. "Plans of the present management of Tolchester Lines, Inc.," January 12, 1938, p. 3, 2nd draft of typed manuscript in Wills Papers (hereafter cited as "Management Plan").
5. Ibid.
6. Ibid., p. 8. *Express* was built in Baltimore in 1888 as *Robert Garrett* for service in New York Harbor between St. George, Staten Island, and the foot of Whitehall Street, Manhattan. Her owner was the Staten Island Rapid Transit Company, a subsidiary of the Baltimore and Ohio Railroad. See Brian J. Cudahy, *Over and Back* (New York: Fordham University Press, 1990), pp. 124–27.
7. For a brief account of this vessel, see: J. W. Somerville, "The End of a Famous Side-Wheeler," *Nautical Gazette* (February 1942) 132: 27, 35.

NOTES TO PAGES 52–63   219

8. *Emma Giles,* perhaps the most beloved of the many steamboats that operated out of Baltimore over the years, was retired from service by the old Tolchester company around 1934; in 1938 she was sold and her hull converted into an unpowered barge. While Holly, *Steamboats,* p. 312, contends that *Emma Giles* was conveyed to the bondholder's protective committee in 1936, Wills never identifies her as an asset of Tolchester Lines and government records show her as being owned by the Tolchester Beach Improvement Company, not Tolchester Lines, through 1938.
9. "Management Plan," p. 26.
10. Ibid., p. 15.
11. For an account of *Chester W. Chapin's* career as a Chesapeake Bay overnight packet steamer, see Harry Jones and Timothy Jones, *Night Boat on the Potomac* (Providence, R.I.: Steamship Historical Society of America, 1996), pp. 82–85.
12. Edwin L. Dunbaugh, letter to author, December 16, 1996.
13. Cape Cod Steamship to BBW, May 1, 1942, telegram, Wills Papers.
14. "Tolchester Service Allowed to Operate," *Baltimore Sun,* June 30, 1937.
15. "Bills Passed at Session of Assembly," *Baltimore Sun,* April 5, 1939.
16. For a brief account of *Howard W. Jackson* and her service in Baltimore Harbor, see Robert H. Burgess, "The End of the Locust Point Ferry," *Baltimore Sun Magazine,* October 29, 1950, p. 2. See also Charles U. Freund (Norfolk County Ferries) to BBW, June 2, 1942, Wills Papers.
17. A 1937 photograph in Elliott, *Last of the Steamboats,* p. 97, depicts *Susquehanna* with Wilson Line's *State of Delaware,* at Rye Beach, New York. The Wilson boat had moved to New York after being replaced by her fleetmate *Dixie.*
18. Sound Steamship Lines, Inc. to Boat Sales, Inc., September 20, 1940, bill of sale, Wills Papers.
19. See, for example, Holly, *Steamboats,* p. 295.
20. "Referring to the chartering of our Str. *Mohawk* to the Tolchester Steamboat Company, will say that was mentioned by you, but was not favored by my partners and myself, as they were set on retiring from the steamboat business and did not want to charter" (Charles Efford to BBW, February 19, 1942, Wills Papers.) For further information on *Mohawk* during her earlier years running for the Weems Line as *Anne Arundel,* see David C. Holly, *Tidewater by Steamboat* (Baltimore: Johns Hopkins University Press, 1991).
21. "Urges War-Time Use of Inside Waterway," *Washington News,* April 4, 1942.
22. U.S. Coast Guard, "Merchant Ship Identification," April 13, 1943, Wills Papers.

23. Various documentary films about Lindbergh's achievement often include footage of his triumphant arrival in New York Harbor, with *Bear Mountain* clearly visible off the Battery as the young aviator steps ashore from a police boat. Lindbergh returned from France first to Washington, D.C., aboard the cruiser USS *Memphis* (CL-13), but then quickly headed north to New York.
24. "Investigation Begun into Ship Damage," *Baltimore Sun*, June 25, 1946.
25. Edward Mitchell to BBW, May 12, 1949, Wills Papers.
26. George W. Lukens to BBW, July 17, 1933, and August 7, 1933, Wills Papers.
27. "Of course you realize that we have not obtained the authority of the Court for the postponement of $2500. of the Note due August 15, 1935. It will be necessary in our annual report to make mention of the fact that this balance has not been paid" (Alfred V. S. Olcott [Receiver, Hudson River Day Line] to BBW, August 17, 1935).
28. Potomac River Line, May 5, 1945, Articles of Revival, Wills Papers.
29. Marine Midland Bank to BBW, April 25, 1954, Wills Papers.
30. See, for example, BBW to Senators Harry F. Byrd, Millard F. Tydings, and David I. Walsh, July 11, 1946, copy in Wills papers. The author recognizes that not all dealings with public officials are necessarily documented in the Wills Papers.
31. See, for example, BBW to Governor Herbert R. O'Connor (Maryland), October 26, 1946, copy of a letter enclosing a contribution of two hundred dollars, Wills Papers. See also William Preston Lane, Jr. to BBW, November 2, 1946, acknowledgement of a contribution received, Wills Papers.
32. A. Gwynn Bowie to BBW, May 7, 1942, Wills Papers.
33. BBW to A. Gwynn Bowie, May 13, 1942, copy in Wills Papers.
34. To give an example from a different era, decades later Wills was attempting to get a vessel certified by the Coast Guard for possible use in Massachusetts waters. In 1964, he exchanged correspondence with Senator Edward M. Kennedy, of Massachusetts, who assured him that he would contact the Coast Guard and ask them to expedite their review of Wills's petition. Senator Edward M. Kennedy to BBW, April 15, 1964, Wills Papers.
35. BBW to National Car Rental System, July 27, 1964, copy in Wills Papers.

CHAPTER FIVE

1. For a treatment of steamboat service between Nantasket and Boston, see R. Loren Graham, "Later Years on the Nantasket Beach Steamboat Company," *Steamboat Bill* 74 (summer 1960): 41–44, 46.
2. A similar phenomenon developed in the Baltimore area and contributed to the downfall of Tolchester Beach. The growing popularity of automo-

biles there, plus the construction of the Chesapeake Bay Bridge in 1952, put resorts like Rehoboth Beach, Delaware, and Ocean City, Maryland, within a one-day round-trip drive from Baltimore.
3. "Court Approves Nantasket Ship Line Reorganization Plan," *Boston Herald*, March 7, 1941.
4. "Nantasket Boat Service Seen," *Boston Herald*, April 15, 1942.
5. BBW to Philip R. White, March 14, 1942, copy in Wills Papers.
6. "Paragon Park Manager Acquires Nantasket Boats," *Boston Globe*, April 16, 1942. For the instrument that formalized the termination of their earlier agreement, see Nantasket–Boston Steamboat Company and BBW, release, April 17, 1942, Wills Papers.
7. BBW to Moran Towing, September 7, 1942, copy in Wills Papers.
8. Joseph H. Moran II to BBW, September 10, 1942, Wills Papers.
9. J. A. Barnes (Combustion Engineering Company) to BBW, March 18, 1942, Wills Papers.
10. I have written elsewhere of *Empire State*'s service between New York and Coney Island. See Brian J. Cudahy, *Around Manhattan Island and Other Tales of Maritime New York* (New York: Fordham University Press, 1997), pp. 147–51.
11. BBW to David Feinburg Company, December 10, 1942, copy in Wills Papers.
12. William B. Taylor, "SS *Town of Hull*," *Steamboat Bill* 21 (December 1946): 418–19.
13. See, for example, *Bill of Sale of Enrolled Vessel (Mayflower):* Nantasket–Boston Steamboat Company, Inc., to Maryland Boat Corp., November 24, 1944.
14. Meeting of the Incorporators of the Nantasket Boat Line, June 9, 1945, minutes, p. 1, Wills Papers.
15. BBW to Captain John H. Newton, Jr., January 16, 1946, copy in Wills Papers. Captain Newton had in mind running *Mayflower* between Beaufort, South Carolina, and Savannah, Georgia.
16. Capt. L. H. Bottum, "*Mayflower* Revisited," *Steamboat Bill* 154 (summer 1980): 87–92.
17. Nantasket Boat Line, April 30, 1946, balance sheet, Wills Papers.
18. Frank Manwell, "Florida–Georgia Focus," *Steamboat Bill* 133 (spring 1975): 52.
19. "Lightning Hits 12 Homes, 2 Churches," *Boston Globe*, July 29, 1947.
20. Joseph L. Tully (Commonwealth of Massachusetts; Board of Conciliation and Arbitration), June 3, 1949, recommendation, Wills Papers.
21. Steamer *Nantasket*, March 17, 1950, Statement of General and Particular Average, copy in Wills Papers. See also *Boston Globe*, July 15, 1949.
22. *Boston Post*, August 18, 1949.

23. "Rescue 827 on Grounded Ship, *Boston Globe*, August 18, 1949.

    CHAPTER SIX
1. For a historical treatment of ferry service to the Statue of Liberty, see Peter T. Eisele, "Fifty Years of Service to Miss Liberty," *Steamboat Bill* 130 (summer 1974): 77–85.
2. BBW to C. O. Donahue (Hawkins, Delafield and Longfellow), September 2, 1942, copy in Wills Papers.
3. BBW, *Making Money*, p. 8; Spedden Shipbuilding Company and BBW, September 16, 1946, agreement of sale, Wills Papers.
4. BBW to Curtis Towboat Company, February 2, 1946, copy in Wills Papers.
5. Ibid.
6. I have written elsewhere of the Circle Line. See Brian J. Cudahy, *Around Manhattan Island and Other Maritime Tales of New York* (New York: Fordham University Press, 1997), pp. 1–47, 225–40.
7. Donald C. Ringwald, *Hudson River Day Line* (New York: Fordham University Press, 1990), pp. 203-9.
8. Three individuals, I. James Brody, James V. Auditore, and Albert Gross, were indicted on matters having nothing to do with Sanders, Circle Line, or sightseeing service. See "Three Are Indicted in Pier Lease Case," *New York Times,* May 30, 1947.
9. "Mr. O'Driscoll appeared at the District Attorney's office yesterday with Francis Barry, second vice president of Sightseeing Yachts, Inc. [Circle Line], in connection with allegations that Commissioner Sanders had sought a 50 per cent interest in the company in return for assistance in getting it pier space." *New York Times,* May 27, 1947.
10. "Witness on Piers Released on Bail," *New York Times,* May 28, 1947.
11. Ibid.
12. "Jurors Act Today in the Pier Inquiry," *New York Times,* May 29, 1947.
13. George Sanders to BBW, July 16, 1946, Wills Papers.
14. BBW to Commissioner of Marine and Aviation, March 5, 1946, copy in Wills Papers.
15. C. R. Haffenden to BBW, March 8, 1946, Wills Papers.
16. Waterways Sightseeing, Inc., November 30, 1946, balance sheet, Wills Papers.
17. Jeremiah T. Driscoll, *Crime Circles Manhattan* (New York: by the author, 1980).
18. "We have made a tentative deal to lease on a time boat charter the motor vessel *Saltaire* to 'Sight Seeing Around New York Waterways, Inc.' Therefore, will you kindly include them in present and future endorsements of

the P and I policy until advised to the contrary." BBW to Towles and Company, July 20, 1946, copy in Wills Papers.
19. See, for example, BBW to Eads Johnson, May 11, 1946, copy of letter; Eads Johnson to BBW, May 16, 1946; and BBW to U.S. Coast Guard, New York, N.Y., May 18, 1946, copy of letter. All in Wills Papers.
20. "New Vessel Will Run to Statue of Liberty," *New York Times*, July 23, 1953.
21. Francis J. Barry to BBW, August 3, 1946, Wills Papers.
22. "Statue of Liberty Reopened by Pact," *New York Times*, June 30, 1953.

CHAPTER SEVEN
1. For background on this vessel, see Donald C. Ringwald, *Hudson River Day Line* (New York: Fordham University Press, 1990), pp. 158–61; see also U.S. Maritime Commission and BBW, April 14, 1947, bill of sale, Wills Papers.
2. Wills Lines, Inc., and Interstate Navigation Co., June 10, 1948, bareboat charter agreement, Wills Papers.
3. Wills Lines, Inc., and S. S. Sandy Hook, Inc., March 15, 1949, bareboat charter agreement, Wills Papers.
4. C. O. Donahue (Hawkins, Delafield and Wood) to BBW, August 9, 1950; and Monroe Fink (Hawkins, Delafield and Wood) to BBW, September 1, 1950, both in Wills Papers. A short note to BBW on the same law firm's letterhead dated September 20, 1950, and signed merely "Mike" makes this point: "The matter is pretty messed up and if we are going to win it we will have to get our heads together."
5. BBW and James Hamilton Parker, March 20, 1950, agreement, Wills Papers.
6. BBW and Wills Lines, Inc., March 18, 1950, application to U.S. Maritime Commission; and Wills Lines, Inc., and the Bermuda government, May 23, 1950, bill of sale of enrolled vessel. Both in Wills Papers.
7. For details about the final years of *Chauncey M. Depew,* see Jack Shaum, "Odyssey of the *Chauncey M.,*" *Steamboat Bill* 130 (summer 1974): 87–91.
8. On the "Honeymoon Convoy," see Jack Shaum, "Convoy RB-1: The Honeymoon Fleet," *Sea Classics* 10 (September 1977): 18–33; Roger Williams McAdam, *The Old Fall River Line*, rev. ed. (New York: Stephen Daye Press, 1955), pp. 254–59.
9. Richard V. Elliott, *Last of the Steamboats* (Cambridge, Md.: Tidewater Publishers, 1970), pp. 122–26.
10. BBW to Edward J. Maier, January 26, 1946, copy in Wills Papers.
11. Ibid.
12. "WHEREAS, by Power of Attorney dated February 12, I, Walter M. Drake . . . have authorized B. B. Wills, of Washington, District of Columbia, to

act as our agent and attorney in obtaining from the United States Government the return of the Steamer *Belle Island* . . ." Walter M. Drake and BBW, March 7, 1947, agreement of sale, Wills Papers.
13. Frank B. Hall and Co. to BBW, April 14, 1947, Wills Papers.
14. Comdr. C. C. G. Sharp (Royal Navy), letter to author, April 28, 1997.
15. Frank B. Hall and Company to BBW and/or Wills Export Line, SA, December 16 and 19, 1947, "Premium Due" notice, Wills Papers.
16. *The Port of Spain Gazette*, April 16, 1948. There are other clippings from Port of Spain newspapers among the Wills Papers telling of *Virginia Lee*'s stay there, but this is the only one I was able to identify by date.
17. BBW, *Making Money*, p. 9.
18. BBW to Gerald E. Bruen, August 9, 1947, copy in Wills Papers.
19. BBW to Edward J. Maier, January 26, 1946, copy in Wills Papers.
20. Lynn-Marie Richard (Maritime Museum of the Atlantic, Halifax) letter to author, April 22, 1997.
21. BBW to P. J. Saunders (Peninsular and Occidental Steamship Company), November 13, 1945, copy in Wills Papers.
22. Britain's Peninsula and Occidental Line still operates ocean liners, although as cruise ships, not basic transport links. Peninsula and Occidental is also the parent company of Princess Cruises, whose "Love Boats" proudly fly to P&O house flag.
23. "Option to Purchase Ferry *Howard W. Jackson*," to Norfolk County Ferries (Portsmouth), April 20, 1942; and Charles U. Freund (Norfolk County Ferries) to BBW, June 2, 1942, both in Wills Papers.
24. Gerald E. Bruen to BBW, October 17, 1945, Wills Papers.
25. Subsidiary Companies of Bethlehem Steel Corporation and Boat Sales, Inc., December 13, 1950, purchase order, Wills Papers.
26. The title of this section is also a marvelous two-part article about this wonderful steamboat written at the time of her retirement from revenue service. See Thomas A. Larremore, "Muffled Drums for *Albany-Potomac*," *Steamboat Bill* 30 (June 1949 and December 1949): 25–28, 82–85.
27. Norman Brewington (Acting Mayor, Town of Colonial Beach) to BBW, December 14, 1945, Wills Papers.
28. BBW to Norman Brewington, January 5, 1946, copy in Wills Papers.
29. *Potomac* Pilothouse Logbook, 1948, Wills Papers. While the finale was identified as trip no. 161, *Potomac* only made 157 trips during 1948. Four numbered trips were canceled during the season because of bad weather.
30. BBW to C. A. Hansen, October 29, 1954, copy in Wills Papers.
31. Gertrude G. Wills to J. Eugene Wills and Benjamin Wills, January 13, 1952, Wills Papers.

CHAPTER EIGHT
1. BBW, *Making Money*, p. 11.
2. BBW to Edward J. Maier, January 26, 1946, copy in Wills Papers.
3. BBW to Union Trust Company, January 7, 1964, Wills Papers.
4. Ibid.
5. Wills Lines, Inc., April 2, 1947, certificate of incorporation, Wills Papers. Eight vessels were registered in Baltimore: *Potomac, Robert E. Lee, Bear Mountain, Allerton, Nantasket, Madisonville, Virginia Lee,* and *Chauncey M. Depew*. The ninth, *Mayfair*, showed New York as its home port. See Wills Lines, Inc., February 2, 1948, Minutes, Special Meeting of the Board of Directors, pp. 1–4, Wills Papers.
6. Elliot, *Last of the Steamboats,* pp. 127–47.
7. *Decorations, Medals, Ribbons and Badges of the United States Navy, Marine Corps and Coast Guard* (Washington, D.C.: Navy Department, 1950), p. 107. For further information on navy submarine chasers, see Lloyd M. Stadum and Frank A. Clapp, "PCE Boats to Norway," *Steamboat Bill* 165 (spring 1983); pp. 22–26.
8. "Most of my equipment is old and it is not fair to expect it to compete with new modern equipment. Therefore, I am faced with two alternatives: either to surrender and sell out and get out of the boat business or start fighting to finance and build new and modern boats." BBW to National Metropolitan Bank of Washington, November 7, 1946, copy in Wills Papers.
9. *The Boston Herald,* March 8, 1951.
10. Ibid.
11. Ferdinand T. Kelley (Holy Cross Club of Boston) to "Fellow Alumnus," undated form letter in Wills Papers. See also "A Summary of the Proponents Case in Regard to House Bill #230 Amended Seeking to Regulate Vessels Which Are Common Carriers of Passengers by Water," mimeographed three-page summary in Wills Papers.
12. Wills Lines, Inc., January 1951, Minutes, Meeting of the Board of Directors, Wills Papers.
13. BBW to Kenneth Stevens (Fulton P. & I. Underwriting Insurance Co.), January 23, 1951, copy in Wills Papers.
14. "Disabled Cruiser Is Towed to Port," *Washington Times-Herald,* February 6, 1951.
15. MV *Holiday,* May 25, 1953, Statement of Particular Average, p. 2, copy in Wills Papers.
16. Ibid., p. 50.
17. At the same time and in the same James River shipyard, the superliner SS *United States* was being built.

18. Gertrude G. Wills to J. Eugene Wills, undated, envelope postmarked May 21, 1951, Wills Papers. The letter concludes with this admonition: "Destroy this letter as it is not good business to air things when others may get it."
19. "Ship Firms Sue for $3,750,000," *Baltimore Sun*, April 14, 1952; "Boat Owners Ask $3,750,000 in Suit against Wilson Line," *Boston Herald*, April 14, 1952.
20. BBW, *Making Money*, p. 9.
21. "Fog Here Causes Four Harbor Mishaps," *New York Times*, January 16, 1953.
22. U.S. Supreme Court (October term 1957), "Petition for Writ of Certiorari to the United States Court of Appeals for the Second Circuit 19"; Wills Lines, Inc. (petitioner) and Tankport Terminals, Inc. (respondent).
23. Ibid., p. 7.
24. *Wills Lines, Inc., v. Tankport Terminals, Inc.*, Supreme Court Reporter 78 (1959), 356 U.S. 939, p. 782. When *Mayfair* was sold by Wills himself to Wills Lines over the winter of 1947–48, the actual sale price was $25,000. Wills Lines, Inc., December 11, 1947, Minutes, Special Meeting of the Board of Directors, Wills Papers.

CHAPTER NINE

1. Madisonville had been purchased for government service during the war and was approved for return to the civilian sector in 1947. W. C. Banister (U.S. Maritime Commission) to BBW, May 16, 1947, telegram, Wills Papers.
2. *Madisonville*, pilothouse log, December 13, 1951, through December 12, 1952, Wills Papers.
3. See, for example, Henry W. Sweet (The Georgia Ports Authority) to BBW, October 3, 1952; and BBW to Henry W. Sweet, November 27, 1952. Both in Wills Papers.
4. See, for example, H. S. Benfield (Frank B. Hall and Company) to John W. Tobin, April 18, 1955, copy in Wills Papers; and John W. Tobin to BBW, April 12, 1955, Wills Papers.
5. Marvin Hurley (Houston Chamber of Commerce) to BBW, July 1, 1953, Wills Papers.
6. I have written of Circle Line and its former LCI(L)s elsewhere. See Brian J. Cudahy, *Around Manhattan Island and Other Maritime Tales of New York* (New York: Fordham University Press, 1997), pp. 1–47, 225–40.
7. Ibid., p. 232.
8. Circle Line–Sightseeing Yachts, Inc., to BBW, December 18, 1951, bill of sale of enrolled vessel, Wills Papers.
9. Newspaper accounts in Houston announcing the inauguration of the new service there spoke of the vessel as previously having operated in Jackson-

ville, Florida. The sole document among the Wills Papers to suggest such an assignment is a "deviation card" calibrating the vessel's compass issued in Jacksonville on April 4, 1954, prior to her departure for Houston.
10. "Excursion Cruiser to Ply in Channel," *Houston Chronicle*, March 28, 1954.
11. U.S. Customs Service, *Mortgage of Vessel*, Wills Lines, Inc., and Harrisburg National Bank of Houston, Texas, October 26, 1954.
12. J. Eugene Wills, interview with author, December 29, 1995.
13. *Houston Chronicle*, May 24, 1954.
14. The former *City of Washington* added a touch of drama to an otherwise routine season in Boston, by sinking! On a trip from Boston to Nantasket on June 22, 1955, the vessel's iron hull sprung a leak. Capt. James Goodwin beached his vessel on Spectacle Island, where water quickly reached the second deck. She was patched, refloated, and returned to service in a matter of days. For the announcement of Wilson Line's decision to inaugurate a Houston service, see *Houston Chronicle*, April 17, 1955.
15. The small mortgage to raise working capital was quickly discharged. Harrisburg National Bank of Houston and Wills Lines, Inc., July 5, 1956, satisfaction of mortgage; and M. P. Longley (Harrisburg National Bank of Houston) to BBW, June 30, 1956. Both in Wills Papers.
16. Harry Schroeder and Wills Lines, Inc., October 29, 1954, bill of sale of enrolled vessel, Wills Papers.
17. Wills Lines, Inc., and Jeremiah Driscoll and James O'Driscoll, June 15, 1956, unsigned draft contract. For further details about this transaction, see BBW and Frank Barry (Cambell and Gardiner), July 9, 1956; and Barry to BBW, July 16, 1956. All in Wills Papers.
18. Maryland Boat Corporation and Captain Bill, Inc., July 16, 1964, agreement of sale, Wills Papers.

CHAPTER TEN
1. There does not appear to be a copy of the March 1, 1957, contract between Wilson Line and Tolchester Lines among the Wills Papers. Several letters between the principals, however, cite various aspects of the contract. See, for example, Samuel R. Walker (City Excursion Corporation) to BBW, March 11, 1957, plus others cited in n. 2 below. City *Excursion* Corporation owned all the outstanding capital stock of Wilson Excursion Lines, and City *Investing* Company, in turn, owned all the outstanding capital stock of City Excursion.
2. BBW to James B. Hutchinson, (City Investing Company), March 20, 1957, copy in Wills Papers; and Allan E. MacNicol (Wilson Excursion Lines, Inc.), to BBW, April 3, 1957, Wills Papers.
3. BBW, *Making Money*, p. 7.
4. BBW to Wilson Shipyard, July 6, 1965, copy in Wills Papers.

5. See, for example, "If Ghosts Like Amusement, There's Tolchester Beach," *Baltimore Sun*, July 29, 1968.
6. BBW to John W. Tobin, March 6, 1958, copy in Wills Papers; Walter A. O'Brien to BBW, April 23, 1958, Wills Papers.
7. *Steamboat Bill* 63 (September 1957): 73.
8. "Bleak Seasons Believed Ahead for River Casinos," *Washington Evening Star*, March 7, 1958 and "Potomac 'Gambling Ship' Opposed on Both Shores," *Washington Post*, June 1, 1957.
9. "The First Preferred Mortgage, on the vessel S.S. *Potomac*," April 7, 1961, p. 6., Wills Papers.
10. An unsigned draft contract among the Wills Papers that called for Wills to receive ten thousand shares of common stock in the new Potomac River Line, with any dividends declared and paid during the term of the ship's mortgage credited against the outstanding balance. Whether such a contract was ever executed remains uncertain.
11. Potomac River Line, Inc., and ABC Vending Corp., Wills Homes, Inc., and Wills Development, Inc., May 1, 1961, unsigned draft of agreement in Wills Papers. Casey spelled out the details in a letter: "In view of the financial position and the lack of capital on the part of the Potomac River Line, Inc., we have told you that if you will put up sufficient cash to take the boat to Boston and try to establish it on the Boston–Nantasket run as well as trying to get moonlite parties, we agree that any cash you put up is to have preference over any other obligations of the Potomac River Line, Inc." Timothy J. Casey to BBW, May 31, 1961, Wills Papers.
12. BBW to Commander (5th Coast Guard District), July 26, 1963, copy in Wills Papers.
13. BBW to John W. Wronowski (Interstate Navigation), October 2, 1964, copy in Wills Papers.
14. BBW to Robert Rodriguez (J. Henry Holland Corp.), July 20, 1963, copy in Wills Papers.
15. The Wills Papers do not contain whatever agreement was executed for 1961. There is an agreement covering 1962, 1963, and 1964, however. See Town of Provincetown and Tolchester Lines, Inc., June 30, 1962, lease. Although *Martha's Vineyard* was originally steam powered, by 1960 Captain Gelinas had replaced her steam engine with a diesel.
16. Officer in Charge (U.S. Coast Guard Marine Inspection, Baltimore) to Maryland Boat Line, October 15, 1963, Wills Papers.
17. Maryland Boat Line, Inc., and Chesapeake Bay Line, Inc., December 18, 1964, agreement; and Maryland Boat Line, Inc., and Chesapeake Bay Line, Inc., January 8, 1965, memorandum of settlement. Both in Wills Papers.
18. BBW to Chesapeake Bay Line, Inc., January 3, 1965; and BBW to Charles C. Hoffberger, II, January 14, 1965. Copies of both letters in Wills Papers.

19. December 18, 1964, agreement, paragraph 5, p. 5, Wills Papers.
20. BBW to Massachusetts Port Authority, June 17, 1965, copy in Wills Papers.
21. BBW to "To Whom It May Concern," February 2, 1965, copy in Wills Papers.
22. John H. Shaum, Jr., "Steamer *District of Columbia*," *Steamboat Bill* 126 (summer 1973): 67–75.
23. For a short treatment of the Chesapeake Bay Ferry Commission, see Robert H. Burgess, *Chesapeake Circle* (Cambridge, Md.: Cornell Maritime Press, 1965), pp. 79–83.
24. *Steamboat Bill* 139 (fall 1976): 171.
25. BBW to W. E. LaBrack (Schine Ten Eyck Hotel), October 25, 1963, copy in Wills Papers.
26. Robert M. Young (Greater Albany Chamber of Commerce) to BBW, November 11, 1963; and W. E. LaBrack (Schine Ten Eyck Hotel) to BBW, November 5, 1963. Both in Wills Papers.
27. "After all, the fact that the Hudson River Day Line gave up that operation some years ago does not give us much grounds for optimism for a 1964 attempt to revive the run." J. Frank Morris (Marine Midland Trust Company) to BBW, February 6, 1964, Wills Papers.
28. BBW, "*Accomac*," undated memorandum to file, Wills Papers.
29. "Fire Destroys Three Vessels," *Norfolk Ledger-Star*, May 28, 1964.
30. BBW to Harry Connolly (Mendes and Mount), September 7, 1964, copy in Wills Papers. Wills showed his determination in another letter: "George, don't think for one minute that one fire has knocked out B. B. Just put it in your notebook, that we will be bouncing back stronger than ever." BBW to George Roper II, October 8, 1964, copy in Wills Papers.
31. BBW to Charles Stillwell (Catalina Island Sightseeing Lines), October 2, 1964, copy in Wills Papers.
32. BBW, *Making Money*, p. 10.
33. For an interesting description of this graveyard of old ships, including an account of how the hulk of *Accomac* was positively identified, see Donald C. Shomette, *Ghost Fleet of Mallows Bay and Other Tales of the Lost Chesapeake* (Centreville, Md.: Tidewater Publishers, 1996), pp. 201–338.
34. BBW to Marine Midland Trust Company, October 13, 1964, copy in Wills Papers. For documentation of the lifting of the capacity reduction, see W. F. Rea III (Captain, USCG) to Master *(SS Potomac)*, August 19, 1964, Wills Papers.
35. Interstate Commerce Commission, Order on March 26, 1941, in Ex Parte No. 140, "Determination of the Limits of New York Harbor and Harbors Contiguous Thereto."

36. Interstate Commerce Commission, *Cornell Steamboat Company Contract Carrier Application*, 250 I.C.C. 301.
37. *New York Times*, June 19, 1943.
38. W. G. Roden (Commander, USCG) to Wills Excursion Lines, July 10, 1964, Wills Papers.
39. See, for example, John J. Bergen (Operation Sail 1964) to BBW, August 20, 1964, Wills Papers.
40. *SS Potomac*, pilothouse logbook, 1965, Wills Papers. To be precise, any after-midnight activity at the tail end of an assignment is not counted as a separate day.
41. Ibid.
42. Interstate Commerce Commission, *Applicant's Exceptions to Examiner's Report and Recommended Order*, Docket No. W-1029 (February 7, 1966).
43. Interstate Commerce Commission, *Applicant's Petition for Reconsideration*, Docket No. W-1019 (June 20, 1966).
44. *SS Potomac*, pilothouse logbook, 1966, Wills Papers.
45. Ibid.
46. John H. Shaum, Jr., letter to author, November 8, 1996.
47. "Cruise Ordeal for 239 Points to Probe," *Baltimore Sun*, August 19, 1967.
48. "City of Philadelphia—S.S. Potomac," *Steamboat Bill* 125 (spring 1973): 26.

EPILOGUE

1. Rita Heintz (Greene Line Steamers, Inc.) to BBW, August 21, 1970. Wrote Ms. Heintz: "The *Queen* could be operated as a day excursion boat and carry over 1,000 passengers. Of course, this would mean that the passenger cabins would have to be removed, the lounges refurbished to offer more open deck area. This would destroy some of the *Queen*'s uniqueness and tradition."
2. W. W. Carlson (Blount Marine Corp.) to BBW, March 30, 1972.
3. *Washington Post*, October 11, 1986.
4. Kathleen Wills to J. Eugene Wills, March 19, 1990.

Subject Index

advertising, advertising expenses, 32–3, 62, 81, 115, 116, 183
Albany, N.Y., 24, 172
Alexandria, Va., 3, 35, 40, 126, 185
Amazon River, Amazon Valley, 107
American Revolutionary War, 3, 86, 162
America's Cup yacht races, 183
Anchorage Transportation, 198
AN-class submarine net layers, 109–10
Annandale, Va., 132
Annapolis Bus Line, 159
Anzio, Anzio landings, 150
Aquia Creek, 3
Arnold, Thurman, 142
Arrowsmith, 12
Athens, N.Y., 24, 27, 30
Atlantic Avenue (Boston), 75
Atlantic City, N.J., 21
Atlantic City Steamship, 21
Atlantic Coast Line Railroad, 173
Atlantic Highlands, N.J., 113
Atlantic Ocean, 11, 64, 137–8
Australia, 183
automobiles, automobile registrations, 12, 25, 37, 57, 71
Avenue P (Houston), 153

Bahamas, Bahama Islands, 174
Baltimore, Md., 10, 14, 19, 26, 44, 48, 49, 52, 54, 56, 58–9, 61, 63, 65–6, 84, 92, 105, 109–10, 113, 116, 120, 126, 131–2, 134, 141, 147–8, 151, 159, 165–6, 173, 177, 181, 183–5
Baltimore and Potomac Railroad, 6
Baltimore and Virginia Steamboat, 43
Baltimore, Chesapeake and Atlantic Railway, 43
Baltimore County, Md., 13
Baltimore Orioles, 169
Baltimore Steam Packet. *See* Old Bay Line
Bancroft Sales Agency, 9
bareboat charters, 64–5, 103–4
Barnegat light vessel, 181
barnstorming, 45–6, 147–9
Barry, Francis J., 60, 99, 171
Bartholdi, Frederic Auguste, 86
Battery Park, 157, 178–9, 180–1
Battery Place (New York), 179
Bayonne, N.J., 148, 151
Bay Ridge Beach, 198
Bay Shore, Md., 56–9
Beach Channel Drive (New York), 148
Beacon Hill, 137
Bear Mountain, N.Y., 64, 176–82
Bedloe's Island, 86–7, 88, 91, 97, 143, 151, 161
Bel Alton, Md., 6, 9, 27
Belém, Brazil, 107–10, 113, 171
Belise, British Honduras, 130
Bermuda, Bermuda government, 104–5, 188
Betterton, Md., 116, 158
Biscayne Bay, 62
Bishop, Henry, xiii
blackouts, civil defense, 40
Block Island, R.I., 103
Blount Marine, 101, 189
Blue and Gray Motor Tours, 198
Boat Concessions, 198
Boat Sales, Inc., 93, 197
Booth, John Wilkes, 4
Bordentown, N.J., 141
Boston Harbor, 73–4

231

Boston, Mass., 67, 72–3, 79–80, 82, 92, 101, 103, 113, 117–8, 126, 141, 147, 155, 165, 166, 167
Boston-Provincetown Line, 117–8
Boston Red Sox, 28
Boston Street (Baltimore), 92, 186
Bouy No. 38A (Long Island Sound), 179
Bowers, C. C., 129
Bowie, A. Gwynn, 30, 70
Bowling family, 4
Bowling, Mary Louise, 5, 6
Brandywine, Md., 30
Brazil, 106–10
Brewington, Norman, 127
Brewster, Elisha H., 73
Broad Creek, 128
Broadway (Baltimore), 181
Broadway Limited, 106
Broadway (New York), 64
Brooklyn, N.Y., 120
Bruen, Gerald E., 78–9, 118
Bryantown, Md., 4, 6
Bunker C fuel oil, 40, 63, 177
Burch, James, 132
Butterfield, Billy, 38

Calumet Harbor, 133
Calvert Marine Museum, xi
Cambell and Gardner, 60, 99
Cambridge, Md., 183
Camden, N.J., 56, 187
Campbell, Lawrence C., 142
Canadian Navy. *See* Royal Navy
Canadian Pacific Railway, 122
C and D Canal. *See* Chesapeake and Delaware Canal
Cape Charles, Va., 106, 113
Cape Cod, Mass., 73, 85, 103
Cape Cod Steamship, 55, 117, 120
Cape Hatteras, N.C., 62, 137, 147
Cape Henry, Va., 137
Cape May, N.J., 64
Cape May jetty, Cape May jetty buoy, 181
Capetown, South Africa, 113
Caribbean Sea, the Caribbean, 110, 130
Casey, Timothy, 162, 164, 165, 185–6
Castra, S., 152
Castro, Fidel, Castro revolution, 159
Catalina Island, 174, 189

Chapel Point, Md., 4, 5, 10–21, 22, 25–6, 30, 32, 34–5, 37, 126, 155, 166, 185, 190
Chapel Point Park (1926–1936), 10–21, 34–5, 37, 52
Chapel Point Park (contemporary), 37
Charles County, Md., 3, 4, 5, 27, 36, 94
Charles County Agricultural Fair, 4
Charleston, S.C., 52, 148, 161
Charlotte Amalie, U.S.V.I., 166, 174
Charlton, Norman W., 152
charters, charter contracts, 42–7, 84–5, 171–2, 176
Chesapeake and Delaware Canal, 26, 64, 92, 147, 181, 183, 186
Chesapeake and Ohio Railway, 56
Chesapeake Bay, 3, 43–5, 49, 61, 63, 65, 92, 105, 114, 128, 134, 138, 159, 165, 170, 182
Chesapeake Bay Bridge, 57, 221
Chesapeake Bay Bridge/Tunnel, 140, 170–1
Chesapeake Bay Ferry District, 171
Chesapeake Bay Line, 169–70
Chesapeake Beach, Md., 52
Chesapeake Channel, 170
Chesapeake Steamship, 50
Chester, Pa., 116, 145
Chestertown, Md., 6
Chicago, Ill., 133
Christiana River, 16
Circle Line, Circle Line Sightseeing Yachts, 94–5, 97, 99, 100–1, 150–1, 157, 171
Circle Line-Statue of Liberty Ferry, 93, 99, 100
Circuit Court for Charles County, Md., 36
City Investing, 155
City of New York, 59, 62, 64, 86–101, 176–7
  Department of Commerce, 94
  Department of Docks, 93
  Department of Marine and Aviation, 95–6
Civil War, the U.S., 6
Cleveland, Grover, 86
Clow and Nicholson Transportation, 55
Coca-Cola, Coca-Cola distributors, 67
college memorabilia, sales of, 9
College of the Holy Cross, xiii, 6, 9, 10, 135, 140

SUBJECT INDEX

Colombia, Colombian registry, 120
Colonial Beach, Va., 16–8, 32, 35, 40, 52, 62, 126–7, 161
Colonial Line, 54
Columbia Steamship, 41–3, 45, 59, 108
Combuston Engineering, 77
Coney Island, N.Y., 52, 77, 157
contiguous harbor zone, 176–7
Coolidge, Calvin A., 12
Corleone, Michael (fictional character), 122
Corporation of Roman Catholic Clergymen, 10, 18, 36. *See also* Jesuits
Corry, Jack, xiii, 38–9
corvettes. *See* revised Flower-class Corvettes
C. Reeders and Sons, 59
Crime Circles Manhattan, 97
Crosson, William F., 181, 182
Cuba, 16, 122, 159
Currituck, N.C., Currituck buoy, 137
Curtis Bay, 170
Curtis Bay Towing, 92

dance floors aboard excursion boats, 27–8, 77
David Feinburg Co., 77
Day, Carlton E., 82
Daytona Beach, Fla.
Death of a Salesman, 9
Deepwater, N.J., 90
Delaware Bay, 147, 181
Delaware River, 13–4, 26, 56
Delaware Valley, 14, 187
Delmarva Peninsula, 49
Depew, Chauncey M., 102, 106
Depression, the. *See* Great Depression
Detroit-Port Huron Steamship, 56
diesel engines, diesel conversions, 92, 97–8, 113, 131
Disneyland, 11
District of Columbia, 68. *See also* Washington, D.C.
Dixie Boat, 149, 161
Dolphin Excursion, 150
Donohue, John B., 181
Donohue, Maurice, 136
Dorsey, Tommy, vii
Dougherty, T. G., 100
Drake, Walter M., 108
Driscoll, Jeremiah, 97, 157, 198

Dunbaugh, Edwin L., xiii, 54
dust bowl, the, 29

East Boston subway, 123
East China Sea, 134
East End Foundries, 111
Eckner, Hugo, 16
Efford, Charles, 61
Egan, Elmore E. (Mrs.), 169
Eiffel, Alexandre Gustave, 86
Eisenhower, Dwight D., Eisenhower administration, 98–9
Ellington, Duke, 38
Elliott, Richard V., 107, 210
Elliott, William T., 65
Erie Basin, 178–9, 182

Fairbanks-Morse diesel engines, 98
Fairfax County, Va., 132
Falkland Islands, 113
Fells Point, 58
Fenway Park, 28
Feraldis, Eugene, 109–10
ferryboats, 56–9, 123–4
fireboats, 125, 128–9, 170
Fire Island, Fire Island ferry, 97
fires
    Light Street Pier 16, 60
    MV *Accomac*, 173
    SS *Howard W. Jackson*, 59
    SS *Provincetown*, 170
Firth of Forth, 109
Fletcher-Harrison, 205
Florida real estate market, 9
Flushing Meadows, 179
Fort Hancock, 106
Fort Lauderdale, Fla., 129
Fort McHenry, 60
Fort McNair, 32
Fort Washington, 3, 64, 128
Fort Wood, 87
Francis, Robert, 66
Frank B. Hall, 24
Freeport, Bahamas, 174
Freestone Point, 160–4
Friedrichshafen, Germany, 16
fuel rationing, 40, 63, 177

Galveston, Tex., 151
gambling, gambling ships, vii, 160–1
Gelinas, Joseph, 166

SUBJECT INDEX

General Motors, 111
General Motors Acceptance Corp., 98
General Motors diesel engines, 200
Geneva, Switzerland, 28
Gillespie, Dizzy, 38
Glen Echo, 39
Glenwood Landing, N.Y., 178
Godfather, The, 122
Gosnell, Gertrude Clementine, 13. *See also* Wills, Gertrude
Governor's Island, 143
Graf Zeppelin, 16
Graham, R. Loren, xii
　photographs taken by, 31, 45, 58, 61, 80, 83, 84, 89, 112, 118
Granite, Md., 13
Gravesend Bay, 103
Gray Line Auto Rental, 198
Gray Line sightseeing buses, 145
Gray Marine, Gray Marine diesel engines, 98
Great Britain, 106
Great Depression, 19, 73, 85, 200, 208
Great Lakes, 55
Great Sound, 105
Greene Line, 189
Griffith Stadium, 15
Guajara, Bay of, 107
Gump, Forrest (fictional character), 129
Guy, Ernest C., 30

Haines Point, 128
Hamilton Harbor, Bermuda, 105
Harborplace, 117
Harbor Towing, 66
Harlan and Hollingsworth, 64, 114
Harlem River, 150
Harrisburg National Bank of Houston, 152
Havana, Cuba, 16, 122
Heintz, Rita, 189
Helwig, William, 152–3
Hempstead Harbor, 178
Herman, Woody, vii
Herold, David, 4
Hickey, Alexander, 27
high school boat rides, 171–2, 176, 178
Hitler, Adolph, 28
Hoboken, N.J., 24, 27, 176, 178
Hoffberger, Alan D., 169
Hoffberger, Charles C., 169–70

Hoffberger, Gerry, 169
Hogan, Frank, 95
Holly, David, 50
Hollyhead, Wales, 109
Holy Cross. *See* College of the Holy Cross
Holy Cross Club of Boston, 136
Honeymoon Fleet, 106, 107
Hong Kong, 122, 174
Hoover, Herbert C., 15–6
Hopewell, Va., 44, 46
Hotel Belleview, 13
Houston Chamber of Commerce, 149
Houston Ship Canal, 151–2
Houston, Tex., 149–57
Howard, J. C., 13
Howard, W. M., 13
Hudson River, 22, 28, 64, 75, 80, 90, 172, 176–7, 178, 181
Hudson River Day Line, 21, 22–3, 25, 30, 68, 94, 102, 105, 108, 127, 140, 171, 177, 180, 197, 208–9
Hudson River Day Line, Inc., 94, 208–9
Hull Gut, 73
Hull, Mass., 73, 85, 140–1
Huppmann, G. G., 65

identification codes, 63
inclined engines, inclined compound engines, 77
India Wharf (Boston), 75
Indian Lane (Washington), xi
Inner Harbor (Baltimore), 117
insurance, marine insurance, 24, 67–8, 109–10, 180
International Longshoremen's Association, 100
Intracoastal Waterway, 62
Interstate Navigation, 92–3, 103
Island Transportation, 188

Jackson Heights, N.Y., 88
Jacksonville, Fla., 52
James River, 46, 109
Jamestown, Va., 169
Jersey City, N.J., 176
Jesuits, Jesuit Fathers, 10, 13, 18, 68, 214
Johnson, Eads, 98
Jones, Harry, xiii
Jones Point, 128
Junkin, George B., 142

SUBJECT INDEX 235

Kabernagel, Alfred W., 66
Kahn, S. Harrison, 182
Keansburg Steamboat, 177
Kent County, Md., 49, 183
Key, Francis Scott, 60
keystone, keystone logo, 107
King, David, 84
Kiptopeke, Va., 138, 171
Knickerbocker Ice, 24
Krupa, Gene, vii, 38

Lackawanna Terminal (Hoboken, N.J.), 178
LaGuardia, Fiorello, LaGuardia administration, 94
Lake George Steamboat, 152
LaPlata, Md., 4, 6
LCI(L)-class landing craft, 149–50
LeBlanc, E. R., 179
Lee, "Light Horse" Harry, 3, 162
Lee, Robert E., 3, 162
Leesylvania State Park, 162
L'Enfant, Pierre, 3
Lesser Antilles, 110
Lewes, Del., 25
Lewis, Harry, 84
Lewis, Sinclair, 12
Leyte Gulf, 134
Liberty Island, 87, 100–1
Light Street (Baltimore), 116
Light Street piers, 56, 63, 119
Lincoln, Abraham, 4, 16
Lindbergh, Charles A., 11, 64
Lingayen Gulf, 134
Little Creek, Va., 138, 171
Liverpool Point, Md., 37–8, 126, 175
Locust Point, 56, 58
Logan Airport, 123
Loman, Willy, 9
Londonderry, Northern Ireland, 122
Long Bridge, 41
Long Island Railroad, 77
Long Island Sound, 176, 178
Lower New York Bay, 106
Lukens Dredging and Contracting, 14–5, 17, 19, 37, 68
Luna Park, 11

McAllister, Daniel, 88, 99
McAllister Navigation, 88
McAllister Steamboat, 64, 88

McKay, Douglas, 99
McKeon, Winfield H., 137
Madisonville, La., 92
Maier, Edward, 41, 108
Maine coast, Maine coast steamboats, 41, 102
Mallows Bay, 175
Mandalay Line, 64
Manhattan Island, 52, 87, 97, 105–6, 113, 150
Manwell, Frank, xiii, 82
Marine Basin (shipyard), 103, 120
marine insurance. *See* insurance
Marine Midland Trust Co., 172
Mariners' Museum, 128
Marshall Hall, 18, 32, 47, 128
Martha's Vineyard, Mass., 166
Maryland, Maryland state government, 68
   Public Service Commission, 56, 57
   state legislature, 58, 70
Maryland Boat Corp., 79, 93, 175, 198
Maryland Boat Lines, 175
Maryland Dry Dock, 60, 114
Maryland Steel, 44
Maryland Tercentennial celebration, 29
Mason-Dixon Line, 9
Massachusetts, Massachusetts state government
   Department of Labor and Industries, 82
   legislature, 135–7
Massachusetts Bay, 85, 117, 167
Meadowlands. *See* New Jersey Meadowlands
Medford, Mass., 77
Merchant Vessels of the United States, 77, 150, 152, 164
Meseck Excursion Line, 107, 177
Meseck, John A., 41
Miami, Fla., 9, 62, 129, 131, 147, 169
Miami Beach, Fla., 62
midnight cruises, 38, 128
Miller, Arthur, 9
miniature railways, 11, 214
Mississippi River, 188
Mitchell, Edward F., 67, 169
Monmouth Park, 104–5
Moon, Guy, 147
moonlight cruises, 38, 62, 128, 145, 181
Moran, Joseph H., II, 77
Moran Towing and Transport, 76–7

Morehead City, N.C., 137–8, 147
Morton Engine and Dry Dock, 122
Mount Vernon, Va., 3, 18
Mudd, Samuel, M.D., Mudd family, 4
Mussolini, 28

Nantasket Beach, Mass., 72–6, 82, 84, 127, 141, 156, 159, 164
Nantasket Boat Line, ix, 78–85, 141–2
Nantasket-Boston Steamboat, 55, 72–8, 86
Nantucket, Mass., 167
Nasdor, Suzanne H., 169
National Bankruptcy Act, 50
National Car Rental System, 71
National Organization of Masters, Mates and Pilots, 82
Nearer My God to Thee, 66
New England Steamship, 54–5
Newfoundland, 106
New Jersey Meadowlands, 105
New Jersey Turnpike, 105
Newport News, Va., 56, 138
Newport News Shipbuilding and Dry Dock, 138, 139
Newport, R.I., 54, 103, 183
New York Bay. *See* Upper New York Bay, Lower New York Bay
New York Central and Hudson River Railroad, 205
New York Central Railroad, 102
New York City. *See* City of New York
New York Harbor, 64
New York Mets, 178–9
New York, N.Y., 86–101, 126, 147–8, 173
New York, Philadelphia and Norfolk Railroad, 106
New York Sun, 95
New York Times, 95, 100
New York World's Fair (1964–65), 172
night club converted from steamboat, 80, 196
Noble Street (Brooklyn), 178
Noel, Fabian P., 43, 45, 54, 109
Norfolk, Va., 19, 21, 44, 106, 129, 147, 165, 169
Norfolk and Washington Steamboat, 166
Norfolk County Ferries, 123
Normandy, Normandy invasion, 106
North American Smelting, 141
North Atlantic. *See* Atlantic Ocean

Ober, Beverly, 50
O'Brien, Walter A., 148, 161
O'Connell, Rev. Edward P., S.J., xiii
O'Driscoll, James, 179
O'Dwyer, William, O'Dwyer administration, 94–5
Ohio River, 188
oil fuel, oil fuel conversion, 26–7
Olcott, Alfred V. S., 21
Old Bay Line, 125, 165–7
Old North Church (Boston), 141
Operation Sail, 1964, 177
Ossining, N.Y., 181
Ostermueller, Fritz, 28

Palm Beach, Fla., 174
Panama, 120
Panama Canal, 134
Panamanian flag, 109, 120, 122
P. and O. Lines. *See* Peninsula and Oriental Steam Navigation Co. and Peninsula and Occidental Steamship Co.
Paoli local, 106
Para (state, Brazil), 107
Para River, 107
Paragon Park, 72, 75, 78, 101
Parker, James Hamilton, 105
Parrillo, Ben S., 179
Patapsco Scrap Corp., 123
Patuxent River, 157
PC- and PCE(R)-class submarine chasers, 133–5
Peat, Marwick and Mitchell, 79
Peddocks Island, 77, 82, 84
Peninsula and Occidental Steamship, 122
Peninsula and Oriental Steam Navigation, 122
Peninsula Transit, 19
Pennsylvania Avenue (Washington), 12
Pennsylvania Railroad, 6, 19, 27, 43–4, 65, 138
Philadelphia and Wilmington Steamboat, 13
Philadelphia, Pa., 56, 107
Phnom-Pehn, Cambodia, 122
Pier 3 (Pratt Street, Baltimore), 120, 170, 183
Pier 16 (Light Street, Baltimore), 60, 66, 117, 120, 121
Pier 46 (Erie Basin, Brooklyn), 179, 181

SUBJECT INDEX

Pier 80 (North River, New York), 178
Pier 81 (North River, New York), 25, 181
Pier A (North River, New York), 147
Pinners Point (Portsmouth, Va.), 173
Pittsburgh, Pa., 150–1
Playland. See Rye Beach, N.Y.
Plymouth, Mass., 103, 136
Point Lookout, Md., 3, 16
Popes Creek Branch, Popes Creek Secondary Track, 6, 19
Port Deposit, Md., 59
Port Everglades, Fla., 169
Port of Spain, Trinidad, 110–3
port risk, 24, 68
port rules (wartime), 73, 75
Portsmouth, Va., 173
Port Tobacco, Md., 3, 6
Port Tobacco River, 3, 16, 19, 190
Potomac Excavating, 48
Potomac River, 3, 10, 11, 13, 22, 52, 64, 66, 160–1, 190
Potomac River Line (1934–52), ix, 30–41, 46, 49, 64, 68, 84, 127, 129, 144, 164
Potomac River Line (ca. 1961), 164, 184
Pravda, 28
Preference, 4, 6
Pride of the Potomac, 10, 35
Prince George's County, Md., 19, 30, 70
Provincetown, Mass., 113, 117–8, 131, 135–6, 141, 164, 166–7, 183
Providence, R.I., 103, 183
Public Garden (Boston), 141
public service commission. See under individual states
Pullman-Standard, 133
Purdy, Elmer, 84
Puzo, Mario, 122

Quincy, Mass., 107

racial segregation aboard excursion boats, 41–3, 45, 46–7
rationing. See fuel rationing
Rau, William, xiii
Reading Company (railroad), 56, 57–8
Reagan, Ronald W., 87
real estate interests, 9, 132, 197–8, 200
refrigeration aboard fishing boats, 129–30
Requa, Charles, 27
revised Flower-class Corvettes (Royal Navy), 122, 124

Richard, Lynn-Marie, xiii
Richmond, Va., 44, 46, 147
Ringwald, Donald C., 209
Rio de Janiero, Brazil, 16
Robert E. Lee Steamboat, ix, 43–8, 54, 126, 197
Rockaway Beach, N.Y., 52, 148, 178, 182
Rock Creek Development, 61
Roosevelt, Franklin D., Roosevelt Administration, 28, 86
Roosevelt Roads, 174
Rowes Wharf (Boston), 75, 82
Royal Navy, Royal Navy (Canada), 106, 109, 122
Russel, Frank, 177
Ryan, Edward, xiii
Rye Beach, N.Y., 176–9, 182

Sacred Heart R.C. Church, 13
Saigon, VietNam, 122
Saint George's, Bermuda, 104
Saint Ignatius R.C. Church, 4, 10, 37, 190
Saint John's, Newfoundland, 106
Saint Louis Browns, 29
Saint Mary's City, Md., 29
Saint Mary's R.C. Church, 4, 6
Saint Paul, Minn., 157
Saint Vincent Jetty (Port of Spain), 110
Sanders, George, 88, 90, 94–8, 140
San Diego, Calif., 134
Sandy Hook Line, 103–5
Sandy Hook, N.J., 64
San Francisco, Calif., 174
San Jacinto Boat Line, 152
San Juan, P.R., 112
San Pedro Harbor, 189
Savannah, Ga., Savannah Harbor, 79–80, 148
Seaside Park, Md., 52–3
Seventh Street Wharf (Washington), 16, 33
Seventy-fifth Street (Houston), 153
Sharp, Commander C. C. G., RN, xiii
Shaum, John H., Jr., 183
Shea Stadium, 178
Shelter Island, N.Y., 77
ship brokering, 59, 120–5
Shipowners Limitation of Liability Act, 143–4
shrimp boats, xi, 129–30
Sightseeing Around New York Waterways, 95–7

sightseeing buses, xi, 145
Slye, Henry E., Jr., 128
Solomons, Solomons Island, Md., xi, 157
Sound Steamship Lines, 55, 59
South America, 107–9
Southern Maryland National Bank, 6
South Station (Boston), 75
Sparrows Point, Md., 44
Spedden Yard, 92
Springfield, Mass., 74
S.S. Sandy Hook, Inc., 103
Statue of Liberty, 25, 65, 86–8, 143
Statue of Liberty Boat Line, 93, 198
Statue of Liberty ferry, 86–93, 142–3, 151
Statue of Liberty Line, 93, 198
Steamboat Bill, 82, 161
steam engines (marine). *See* vertical beam engines, triple-expansion engines, inclined engines
Steamer Belle Island Co., 108
Steeplechase Amusement Co., 76
Stepping Stones, 179
Stone, David, 75
Stone family, 75, 78, 164
Stone, Joseph, 75
Stoney Point, 179
submarines, Nazi submarines, 62, 107
submarine chasers, 123, 125, 133–5
submarine net layers, 109, 125
Suffolk County Superior Court, 140
Sullivan, John V., 141
Sun Shipbuilding, 145
Susquehanna River, 59
Sutton, Charles, 88, 147
Sutton Line, 55, 62, 88–9, 90, 94, 147, 177
Sweeney, George C., 74–5

Tammany Hall, 94
Tampa Bay, 137
Tampa, Fla., 137
Tankport Terminals, 143
Tan-Pa, 122
Tappan Zee Bridge, 179
T.B., Md., 19
T.B. Bus Terminal, 19, 30
Thimble Shoal Channel, 171
Tietjen and Lang Dry Dock, 24–7
Times Square, 65
Tobin, J. W., 148–9, 161
Todd Shipbuilding, 98

Tolchester Beach Improvement Co., 50, 59
Tolchester Beach, Md., 49–50, 53, 56–9, 60, 62–5, 70, 73, 77, 88, 105, 113, 116, 147–8, 160, 173
Tolchester Lines, ix, 50, 52, 56, 59, 62, 64, 115–6, 158, 175, 183
triple-expansion steam engines, 116
Trojan Steamship, 55
trolley cars, vii, 32, 33, 56, 63
Truman, Harry S, Truman administration, 43
Turkey Point, 183
Twenty-fifth Infantry Assoc., 43
Twain, Mark, 160
Twin Rocks Passage, 105

unions, labor unions. *See* names of individual organizations
United States, United States Government
  Army, Dept. of the Army, 43, 64, 75
  Adjutant General's School, 64
  Bureau of Navigation and Steamboat Inspection, 24
  Coast Guard, 25, 28, 63, 65–6, 69–70, 73, 82, 98, 123, 137–8, 147, 165, 169–70, 172, 174–5, 177
  Congress, 28, 69, 189
  Court of Appeals, Second Circuit, 144
  Department of the Interior, 98–9
  Federal Mediation and Conciliation Service, 100
  Internal Revenue Service, 79
  Interstate Commerce Commission, 47, 70, 176–7, 181–2
  Maritime Commission, 105–6, 113, 174
  national anthem, 60
  National Park Service, 87, 98–9
  Navy, Navy Dept., 92, 114, 123, 150
  Office of Defense Transportation, 40
  Office of Price Administration, 177
  Reconstruction Finance Corp., 132
  Senate, senators, 15, 220
  Steamboat Inspection Service, 24, 70
  Supreme Court, 142–3
  War Department, 87, 98
University of Maryland, 4
University of Wisconsin, xi
Upper Marlboro, Md., 30
Upper New York Bay, 25, 86, 94

SUBJECT INDEX 239

VanMetre, Alfred, 132
Venezuela, 110
Verazzano-Narrows Bridge, 181
vertical beam engines, 52, 205
Virginia Ferry, 138
Virgin Islands, xi, 174, 188
VJ Day, 41

W. and A. Fletcher Company, 205
War of 1812, 3
Warren, R.I., 101
Washington College, 6
Washington, D.C., 3, 12, 13–4, 21, 22, 40–1, 49, 60–2, 101, 120, 126, 147, 157, 184
Washington Excursion Line, 183
Washington, George, 3
Washington harbor, 28, 32
Washington Senators (baseball team), 15, 28
Washington, Virginia and Maryland Coach, 12
Waterman Steamship, 174
Water Street (Washington), 32
Waterways Sightseeing, 97
Watson, Jack, 75–6
Weber, Frank, 142
Weems Line, 61
West 125 Street (New York) 178–9
West 155 Street (New York), 64
White, Philip, 74
Whitestone Point, N.Y., 178
Wide Water, Va., 3
Wiesand, Vernon H., 142
Williamsburg, Va., Colonial Williamsburg, 169
Wills, the Wills family, 4
Wills, Benjamin Bowling, viii, 6–10, 190, 197–204, passim
  (highlights)
  birth, 6
  Chapel Point, 10–21
  children, 13, 48
  chronology, 201–4
  companies founded or established, 30, 49, 78, 88, 117, 149
  death, 190
  early career path, 9
  education, 6, 9
  financial interests, 197–8
  first steamboat, 22
  grandparents, 4–5
  litigation, 50, 74–5, 140–4
  management style, 67–71
  marriage and spouse, 13, 38, 48, 79
  parents, 6–8
  photographs of, 6, 48, 156, 184
  real estate interests, 9, 132, 197–8, 200
  ship brokering, xi, 120–5, 166–7
  travels, 9, 108–9, 129–30
Wills, other family members
  Benjamin B., Jr., 13, 48, 130
  Catherine Lee "Polly," 6
  Francis Reed, M.D., 4–5
  Francis Reed, 214
  Gertrude, 38, 48, 79, 93, 130, 190, 197
  Jeffrey, xi, xiii, 33, 214
  Kathleen, 37
  Kemp B. B., xiii
  J. Eugene, xiii, 13, 48, 130, 140, 153
  Olivia (Kane), xiii
  Philip Reed, 5,6
  P. Reed II, 13, 48
Wills-Bowers, 129–30, 198
Wills Development Corp., 175
Wills Export Lines, SA, 120–1, 198
Wills Homes, 175
Wills Lines, 132, 142
Wills Papers, xi, 97, 105, 142, 171, 179, 189
Wills-Spedden, 92, 198
Wills-VanMetre, 132
Wil-Mar, 198
Wilmington, Del., 14, 64, 114, 141
Wilson, J. Shields, 13–4
Wilson Excursion Line, 14. *See also* Wilson Line
Wilson Line, 13–21, 33, 46–7, 53, 63, 90, 102, 107, 114, 116, 133–6, 140–1, 142, 144–5, 155–6, 158, 166, 197, 210–3
Wilson-Tolchester Steamship, 159, 175
Worcester, Mass., 6, 9, 10,
world's fair. *See* New York World's Fair
World War II, 13, 62, 64, 70, 73, 78, 82, 90, 94, 102, 106, 113, 120, 128
writs of certiorari, 143–4

Yonkers, N.Y., 178, 180
zeppelins, 16

Vessel Index

Accomac, 138–40, 171–4, 194, 200
Albany, 21, 22–3, 191, 205–8
Alexander Hamilton, 140, 171, 207, 209
Allerton, 75, 77–9, 80, 83, 85, 126, 140–1, 193
Alura, 194
Ambrose (lightship), 148
Americana, 177
American Veteran, 143
AN-76 (USN), 109, 113, 124
AN-77 (USN), 109–10, 113, 121, 124
Anne Arundel, 61, 192
Asbury Park, 113, 195

Bay Belle, 63, 114, 116, 159–60, 175, 182, 211
Bear Mountain, 64–7, 126, 129, 141, 144, 184, 192
Belle Island, 107–8
Bengo, 123
Benjamin Bros. II, 124
Blanche T. Rogers, 66
Boston Belle, 133, 135, 138, 140, 159, 211–2
Brandywine, 53, 211

Camarones, 130
Campuchea, 122
Carib Star, 189–90
CG-85009 (USCG), 65
Chauncey M. Depew, 102–6, 113, 118, 194, 208
Chelsea, 56–58
Cherokee (USCG), 137
Chesapeake. *See* District of Columbia
Chester W. Chapin, 54–5, 108

City of Camden, 211
City of Chester, 14, 211
City of Keansburg, 182–3
City of Norfolk, 125, 166–7
City of Philadelphia, 114, 133, 187, 195, 211
City of Richmond, 125, 166–7
City of Washington, 14–8, 32, 52, 145–6, 155, 211
City of Wilmington, 116, 211
Claremont, 90, 177

Dame Pattie, 183
Delta Queen, 188–9
Deepwater, 89, 92–3, 192, 198
Delaware Belle, 133, 211
District of Columbia, 166–7, 186, 196
Dixie, 53, 63, 211
Dixie Queen, 148, 161, 195
Dolphin, 150–1, 196
Dorchester, 43–4, 191
Dreamland, 52
Dusky, 130

Earl E., 153
Emma Giles, 52
Empire State, 76–7
Ethel B., 152
Express, 57

Francis Scott Key, x, 60–4, 80, 84, 91–3, 104, 126–7, 140–1, 147, 192, 198
Freestone, 160, 162, 195

General, 156–7, 186, 196, 198
George Law, 13

VESSEL INDEX

Gold Star Mother, 143

Harry Randall, 13
Hendrick Hudson, 127, 206–7
HMCS Hawkesbury (K-415), 122–4
HMCS Whitby (K-346), 122–4
HMS Preventer, 109
Holiday, 113, 117–20, 125–26, 132–3, 135, 137–40, 147, 171, 184, 186, 194
Howard W. Jackson, 58–59, 121, 123–4
Hudson Belle, 211
Hustler, 66

Intrepid, 183
Isere, 86
Islander, 188

JayBee, 130
J. Harold Grady, 170

LCU 1518 (USN), 125
Liberty, 92–3, 101, 126, 132, 148, 192
Liberty Belle, 133, 135, 159, 211
Liberty Belle (ex-City of Philadelphia), 114, 133, 195, 211
Louise, 52
LST 306 (USN), 125

Madisonville, 90, 92–93, 101, 147–8, 161, 195
Mako, 130
Marion (USCG), 137
Martha's Vineyard, 166, 183
Mayfair, viii, 90, 92–3, 101, 126, 141–5, 148, 186, 195, 198
Mayflower, 75, 77–9, 126, 193
Mayflower (ex-Moosehead), 214–5
Meteor, 54
Miami, 21, 118
Milbon, 123, 125
Miss Liberty, 101
Mohawk, 61, 80–2, 85, 93, 126, 192
Montauk, 55, 92
Mount Vernon, 145, 146, 211

Nantasket, 75, 77–80, 82, 84–5, 126–7, 140–1, 193
Natchez, 44
Naugatuck, 55
Nelseco II, 92, 93

Nicholaus, 152
Northampton, 171

Old Point Comfort, 171

Palmetto (WAGL-265) (USCG) 123, 125
Pansy, 195
PC 1207 (USN), 133, 211
PC 1258 (USN), 133, 211
PCE (R) 848 (USN), 124, 134
PCE (R) 853 (USN), 134
PCE (R) 854 (USN), 133
Peter Stuyvesant, 140, 208
Philadelphia, 65
Pilgrim Belle, 135, 211
Pilgrim Belle (ex-City of Washington), 155
Port Welcome, 175
Potomac, xiii, 30–41, 62, 68, 102, 126–9, 144, 161, 167, 186, 190
Provincetown, 167–70
P.W. Wilkinson, 170

Queen Elizabeth, RMS, 181

Rangeley, 102
Rensselaer, 55
Robert E. Lee, 44
Robert E. Lee (ex-Dorchester), 44, 126, 147, 191
Robert Fulton, 140, 206–8

Sachem, 130
St. George, 110
Saltaire, 97, 101, 193
Samuel J. Pentz, 13
Sandy Hook, 103
San Jacinto, 151–7, 196
Sea Belle, 133, 155–6, 159, 211
Shinnecock, 77
Sightseer, 96–7, 145, 161–2, 173, 194
Southport, 41–3, 57–8, 60, 191
SS Potomac, 164–5, 167, 173, 173–87, 188–9, 195, 198
State of Delaware, 52–3, 107, 133
State of Pennsylvania, 159, 211
Steel Pier, 21, 25, 55, 108, 118, 135
Susan, 130
Susquehanna, 59–60, 192

Ticonderoga, 151, 152
Tolchester, 51–2, 54–6, 60–1, 65, 75–7, 107, 186, 191
Tolchester (II), 113–7, 119, 126, 129, 133, 158–9, 160, 163, 183, 186, 195
Town of Hull, 55, 75, 76

United States, 225
USS Iowa (BB-61), 87
USS Memphis (CL-13), 220

Virginia Lee, 106–13, 120, 122, 132, 138, 194
Ware River, 128
Washington Irving, 207
Wauketa, 55, 62, 88
Westchester, 107
William G. Payne, 64, 192
William T. Belt, 125, 128–9

Yankee, 169, 183